THE GIFT OF PROPHECY

The Gift
of Prophecy
IN THE NEW TESTAMENT
AND TODAY

Wayne A. Grudem

CROSSWAY BOOKS • WESTCHESTER, ILLINOIS
A DIVISION OF GOOD NEWS PUBLISHERS

To Elliot, Oliver and Alexander,
who bring joy to my life every day

"Sons are a heritage from the Lord" (Ps 127:3)

Contents

Preface

This book started out to be a popular version of my doctoral thesis (*The Gift of Prophecy in 1 Corinthians* [University Press of America 1982]). But it has ended up as more than that, because it includes discussions of many more practical questions, and interaction with quite a few other popular books on prophecy from both charismatic and non-charismatic perspectives. Moreover, though my understanding of New Testament prophecy remains the same as it was when I completed my doctoral dissertation, I have found that subsequent interaction with students and colleagues has led me to refine or modify several points of detail. I hope that the overall result, though here expressed in popular form without all the footnotes and trappings of a doctoral thesis, is a statement that is somewhat more mature and more clearly stated.

It should perhaps be noted that since I finished writing my doctoral thesis in 1977 two very significant scholarly books on New Testament prophecy have appeared, by David Hill and David Aune. Because of their more academic nature, neither book has received detailed discussion in this volume, but I have reviewed both of them elsewhere. My review of David Hill, *New Testament Prophecy*, New Foundations Theological Library (Marshall, Morgan and Scott, and John Knox Press 1979) is in *Themelios* 7:2 (Jan 1982), pp. 25–26, and my review of David Aune, *Prophecy in Early Christianity and the Ancient Mediterranean World* (Eerdmans 1983) is in *Evangelical Quarterly*

59:4 (Oct, 1987), pp. 351–355.

Many people have, in the providence of God, influenced my thinking in this area. Both my more 'charismatic' friends (I think especially of Bob Slosser and Harald Bredesen) and my more 'non-charismatic' (or even 'anti-charismatic') friends (especially John Frame, Edmund Clowney, Richard Gaffin, and O. Palmer Robertson), as well as friends who are really in neither camp (especially Vern Poythress, Kim Batteau, Randy Hekman, and my doctoral supervisor C.F.D. Moule) have, in conversation and writing, caused me to think through these questions again and again, and have helped my understanding.

I wish to thank Mary Morris, Marie Birkinshaw and Jane Preston, who graciously and accurately typed various sections of the manuscript, and Don Rothwell, who compiled the indices.

I am thankful for my parents, Arden and Jean Grudem, who have helped in many ways in making it possible for me to write this book and the previous thesis on which it is based. And without the polite but persistent encouragement of Christopher Catherwood, Editor at Kingsway Publications, I do not think I would have undertaken this book. But once I had agreed to do it, it was the wise and gentle (but also persistent) reminders from my wife Margaret that kept me from undue involvement with other projects and resulted in the completion of the manuscript nearly on time.

Finally, my sons Elliot, Oliver, and Alexander have been a great source of joy and encouragement throughout the work. I dedicate this book to them, in the hope that they may grow up to find stronger churches and a stronger evangelical movement, no longer divided over gifts of the Holy Spirit, but united in using those gifts in the 'power and love and self-control' (2 Tim 1:7) which the Holy Spirit gives to those who love Jesus Christ and obey his word.

Wayne Grudem
September 1987

INTRODUCTION

The Problem of Prophecy Today

What is the gift of prophecy? Should we use it in our churches? There is wide disagreement among Christians on those questions today.

Many charismatic and Pentecostal Christians answer that prophecy is 'a word from the Lord' which brings God's guidance to specific details of our lives, gives much personal edification, and brings to our times of worship an intense awareness of God's presence.

But many reformed and dispensational Christians say that such a view threatens the unique authority of the Bible as God's completed word to us, and leads people to pay too little attention to Scripture and too much attention to unreliable forms of 'subjective' guidance. They would say that the gift of prophecy is the ability to speak (or write) God's very words such as we have in the Bible—and that this gift ended when the New Testament was completed. Their view is often called a 'cessationist' view, because they hold that prophecy and some other miraculous gifts 'ceased' once the New Testament was written.

Then there are many Christians who are neither 'charismatic' nor 'cessationist' and are simply unsure about what to think of the gift of prophecy (and other more unusual gifts). They do not see prophecy presently functioning in their own churches, and they are a bit suspicious of some of the excesses they have seen in the charismatic movement, but, on the other hand, they do not have any settled convictions opposing the use of such gifts.

Can a fresh examination of the New Testament give us a resolution of these views? Does the text of Scripture itself indicate a 'middle ground' or a 'third position' which preserves what is really important to both sides and yet is faithful to the teaching of the New Testament? I think the answer to these questions is yes.

In this book I am suggesting an understanding of the gift of prophecy which would require a bit of modification in the views of each of these three groups. I am asking that charismatics go on using the gift of prophecy, but that they stop calling it 'a word from the Lord'—simply because that label makes it sound exactly like the Bible in authority, and leads to much misunderstanding. On the practical level, I have quoted at length from several responsible leaders in the charismatic movement, asking churches that use this gift to heed the wise counsel of these leaders on evaluating prophecies and preventing abuses.

On the other side, I am asking those in the cessationist camp to give serious thought to the possibility that prophecy in ordinary New Testament churches was not equal to Scripture in authority, but was simply a very human—and sometimes partially mistaken—report of something the Holy Spirit brought to someone's mind. And I am asking that they think again about those arguments for the cessation of certain gifts, arguments which I have examined afresh at some length in chapter 12.

Finally, for all other Christians who have no strong convictions one way or the other on these matters, I am asking that they give some consideration to the New Testament teachings on the gift of prophecy—and to the possibility that, in certain settings, and following scriptural safeguards, this gift may bring much personal edification and new spiritual vitality to worship.

I should make it very clear at the beginning that I am not saying that the charismatic and cessationist views are mostly wrong. Rather, I think they are both mostly right (in the things they count essential), and I think that an adjustment in how they understand the nature of prophecy (especially its authority) has the potential for bringing about a resolution of this issue which would safeguard items that both sides see as crucial. On the cessationist side, this view of prophecy would still include a strong affirmation of the closing of the New Testament canon (so that no new words of equal authority are given today), of the sufficiency of Scripture, and of the supremacy and unique authority of the Bible in guidance. On the charismatic side, this view of prophecy would still preserve the continuing use of prophecy as the spontaneous, powerful working of the Holy Spirit, bringing things to mind when the church is gathered for worship, giving 'edification, encouragement, and comfort' which speaks directly to the needs of the moment and causes people to realize that 'truly God is among you' (1 Cor 14:25). Moreover, with respect to matters which all Christians count important, I hope that this view of New Testament prophecy may contribute to greater unity among God's people over gifts of the Holy Spirit and a better understanding of how these gifts may rightly be used today.

The book deals with several practical questions as well. On the personal level, is it right to seek the gift of prophecy? How can I know if I have received it? When and how should I use this gift? Can the gift be strengthened, or can it be lost? And for churches which allow, or may consider allowing this gift, what teaching should be given about it? What are appropriate settings for it? What safeguards should be taken to prevent abuses such as disorder, false teaching, or excessive reliance on subjective guidance? How can we guard against false prophecies? Should everyone in the church be allowed to prophesy? Can this matter be handled in a way that will avoid divisions in the church?

This book is not a collection of personal experiences, valuable as those are in encouraging people to rejoice in what God is doing or warning people to avoid the tragic abuses that others have encountered. Anyone who reads current literature on the gift of prophecy soon discovers that many good and bad testimonies can be collected on both sides of this question, and in the end they are inconclusive. Ultimately this whole question must be decided on the basis of what the Bible itself says. So this book is almost entirely a careful examination of the teachings of Scripture. I have included a more detailed than usual Table of Contents for those who wish to see where the whole argument is going. I encourage Christians to read this book with a Bible in hand, and to ask themselves whether what I am here suggesting is in fact what the New Testament teaches about the gift of prophecy, a gift which Paul says Christians should 'earnestly desire' (1 Cor 14:39, RSV).

1

Old Testament Prophets:
Speaking God's Very Words

Before we begin a study of the gift of prophecy in the New Testament we need to look briefly at the Old Testament prophets —men like Moses and Samuel, or Nathan, or Isaiah, Jeremiah, and Daniel.

What was their purpose? How much authority did they have? What happened if someone dared to disobey them? Did they ever make mistakes?

We are making no assumptions at this point about whether these Old Testament prophets were the same as prophets in the New Testament. (In fact, I shall argue in chapter 3 that there were some very important differences.) For now, we simply intend to survey the evidence in the text of the Old Testament and draw some conclusions, especially about the kind of authority these Old Testament prophets had.

The prophets are messengers of God

The main function of Old Testament prophets was to be *messengers from God*, sent to speak to men and women with words from God.

So we read of Haggai the prophet, 'Then Haggai, the messenger of the Lord, spoke to the people with the Lord's message' (Hag. 1:13, RSV; cf. Obad 1:1). Similarly, the Lord 'sent a message by Nathan the prophet' to King David (2 Sam 12:25, RSV), and the Lord gave Isaiah the prophet a message to deliver to King Hezekiah (2 Kings 20:4–6).

In fact, a true prophet is one whom 'the Lord has truly sent' (Jer 28:9, RSV). But false prophets who prophesy lies are ones of whom the Lord says, 'I did not send them' (Jer 29:9, RSV; cf. Ezek 13:6).

Quite often the prophet is a special kind of messenger. He is a 'messenger of the covenant'—sent to remind Israel of the terms of her covenant with the Lord, calling the disobedient to repentance and warning that the penalties of disobedience will soon be applied (see, for example, Jer 7:25; 2 Chron 24:19; Neh 9:26, 30; Mal 4:4–6).

Why is this important? It is because official messengers do not just carry their own authority. They speak with the authority of the one who sent them.

Think of the ambassador to a foreign country who carries a message from his President or Prime Minister. He does not think of the message as his own, nor does it come merely with his own personal authority. The message he delivers comes with the authority of the leader who sent him.

So it was with the Old Testament prophets. They knew they were not speaking for themselves but for God who had sent them, and they spoke with his authority.

The prophet's words are words of God

The authority of God's messengers, the prophets, was not limited to the general content or just the main ideas of their messages. Rather, they claimed repeatedly that *their very words* were words which God had given them to deliver.

We see this in the fact that the characteristic which distinguished a true prophet was this: he did not speak his own words or 'words of his own heart', but words which God had sent him to deliver.

The fact that the prophets speak the very words which God has given them to deliver is emphasized frequently in the Old Testament:

'I will be with your mouth and teach you what you shall speak' (Ex 4:12, RSV; cf. 24:3).

'I will put my words in his mouth' (Deut 18:18, RSV; cf. vv. 21-22).

'I have put my words in your mouth' (Jer 1:9, RSV).

'The word that God puts in my mouth, that must I speak' (Num 22:38, RSV; cf. 23:5, 16).

'And you shall speak my words to them' (Ezek 2:7, RSV; cf. 3:17).

It is not surprising then that we find the Old Testament prophets very frequently speaking for God in the first person, saying things like, 'I will do this,' or, 'I have done that,' when they were speaking for the Lord, obviously not for themselves (2 Sam 7:4–16; 1 Kings 20:13, 42; 2 Kings 17:13; 19:25–28, 34; 21:12–15; 22:16–20, 2 Chron 12:5; and hundreds of times in the latter prophets).

This complete identification of the prophet's words with the words of the Lord is seen when the prophet says things like, 'You shall know that I am the Lord' (1 Kings 20:13, RSV), or, 'I am the Lord, and there is no other, besides me there is no God' (Is 45:5, RSV). Clearly no Israelite would have thought that the prophet was claiming to speak his own words in such cases; he was simply thought to be repeating the words of the one who had sent him.

One final indication of a belief in the divine origin of prophetic words is seen in the frequency with which God is referred to as the speaker of something a prophet said. In 1 Kings 13:26 (RSV), 'the word which the Lord spoke to him' is the word which the *prophet* spoke in verse 21. Similarly, *Elijah's* words in 1 Kings 21:19 are quoted in 2 Kings 9:25f. as a burden which the Lord put on Ahab, and Elijah is not even referred to (cf. Hag 1:12; 1 Sam 15:3, 18). It is common to read of 'the word of the Lord, which he spoke by his servant the prophet' (1 Kings 14:18; 16:12; 2 Kings 9:36; 14:25, 17:23; 24:2; 2 Chron 29:25; Ezra 9:10–11; Neh 9:30; Jer 37:2; Zech 7:7, 12; etc).

The absolute divine authority of prophetic words

To disbelieve or disobey a prophet's words is to disbelieve or disobey God

There was a practical consequence to this idea of the prophet speaking God's very words—it made a lot of difference to how people listened to him! In fact, once the people who listen to a prophet are convinced that the prophet's very words have absolute divine authority, they will not risk disobeying or disbelieving even the slightest part of the message for fear of being punished by God himself for disobedience or disbelief (note Deut 18:19; 1 Sam 8:7; 15:3, with vv. 18 and 23; 1 Kings 20:36; 2 Chron 25:16; Is 30:12–14; Jer 6:10–11, 16–19; etc).

Other passages could be given, but the pattern should be clear: To disbelieve or disobey anything a prophet says in God's name is no minor matter—it is to disbelieve or disobey God.

The words of a true prophet are beyond challenge or question

There was another consequence of the fact that true prophets were thought to be speaking the very words of God. If these were God's words, then they were true and good and pure by definition, because they came from God himself.

Therefore we do not find in the Old Testament any instance where the prophecy of someone who is acknowledged to be a true prophet is 'evaluated' or 'sifted' so that the good might be sorted from the bad, the true from the false. Rather, when Samuel was established as a prophet, 'the Lord was with him and let none of his words fall to the ground' (1 Sam 3:19, RSV). Because Samuel was a man of God (that is, a prophet), Saul's servant could say, 'All that he says comes true' (1 Sam 9:6, RSV).

This meant that when a prophet spoke in the name of the Lord, if *even one prophecy* did not come true, he was a false prophet (Deut 18:22). The authority attached to the prophetic office was so great, and thus the effect on the people resulting from the emergence of a false prophet was so disastrous, that the penalty for false prophecy was death (Deut 18:20; 13:5).

So what we find in the Old Testament is that every *prophet* is judged or evaluated, but not the various parts of every *prophecy*. The people ask, 'Is this a true prophet or not? Is he speaking God's words or not?' They never ask, 'Which parts of this prophecy are true and which are false? Which parts are good and which are bad?' For one bit of falsehood would disqualify the whole prophecy and would show the prophet to be a false prophet. A true prophet who claimed a divine authority of actual words could never speak in his prophecy some of his own words and some of God's—they were all to be God's words, or he was a false prophet.

Thus, when it was plain that the Lord was with Samuel and let none of his words fall to the ground (1 Sam 3:19), then 'all Israel ... knew that Samuel was established as a prophet of the Lord' (v. 20, RSV). Then it was seen that to disobey Samuel or to second-guess even seemingly arbitrary commands was wrong and would lead to punishment from God (1 Sam 13:13 with 10:18; 15:23 with v. 3).

Similarly, Micaiah was willing to stake his entire reputation as a prophet on the fulfilment of one prophecy (1 Kings 22:28). Because God was thought to be the speaker of all that a prophet spoke in his name, it was unthinkable that a true prophet should deliver some oracle which was a mixture of good and bad or true and false elements. Whatever a true prophet received from the Lord, he spoke. What the Lord thus spoke through the prophet had absolute divine authority, extending even to the very words the prophet used.

Of course, this does not mean that a true prophet would never apostatize (1 Kings 13:18). The distinction I am trying to make here concerns the type of evaluation which the people were expected to perform.

If the people of Israel usually thought that a prophet was just speaking his own words and not those of the Lord, then every sentence he spoke would be subject to evaluation and question. The hearers would ask of each statement, 'Is this true or not? Is this right or not?' This sort of word from a prophet would be a word of men among other words of men, and would possess no more authority than any other word. Critical discernment would be necessary in hearing all the prophet's words, even if he claimed that the general contents of his message were from God, for minor mistakes might occur at any point.

But if the prophet claims to be speaking God's very words, another sort of evaluation takes place. There are only two possibilities, and there is no middle ground. The question becomes, 'Are these God's words, or not? If so, I must obey. If not, the prophet is misrepresenting God and must be put to death' (Deut 18:20). Once his words are accepted (by whatever means) as God's words, they have a different status and are beyond challenge or question.

Application for today

Although our study has not yet dealt with the question of New Testament prophecy, it still has some useful application for contemporary Christians. This is because many of the words of God spoken by Old Testament prophets have not been lost, but have been preserved for us in the pages of the Old Testament. In fact, there is some indication that all of the Old Testament was thought to have been written by those who were functioning as 'prophets', for we read in Luke's gospel: 'And beginning with Moses and *all the prophets* he interpreted to them in *all the scriptures* the things concerning himself' (Lk 24:27, RSV).

But whether we think of much or all of the written Old Testament as having come from those who were writing as 'prophets', it can certainly be shown that Scripture claims for all of the Old Testament this same kind of authority: the authority of the very words of God.[1]

There is a practical consequence in this for modern readers. We should fully trust the words of the Old Testament scriptures, and (whenever its commands apply to us today) we should fully obey its commands, for they are commands from God.

And if the Old Testament has this kind of authority, we must never disregard it or think it to contain falsehood or elements unworthy of our trust. We must rather treasure it and continually return to it to hear in it the voice of our Creator speaking to us, giving guidance for our lives and spiritual nourishment to our souls. What the Old Testament says, God says, and to disbelieve or disobey it is to disbelieve or disobey God himself.

2

New Testament Apostles:

Speaking God's Very Words

If we search the New Testament, will we find any counterparts to the Old Testament prophets?

At first we might expect that New Testament prophets would be like the Old Testament prophets. But when we look through the New Testament itself this does not seem to be the case. There is little if any evidence for a group of *prophets* in the New Testament churches who could speak with God's very words (with 'absolute divine authority' that could not be questioned) and who had the authority to write books of scripture for inclusion in the New Testament.

On the other hand, there is a very prominent group of people in the New Testament who *do* speak with absolute divine authority and who *did* write most of the books of the New Testament. These men are called not 'prophets', however, but 'apostles'. In many ways they are similar to the Old Testament prophets.

New Testament apostles are messengers of Christ

One marked parallel between the Old Testament prophet and the New Testament apostle is that an apostle was commissioned by Christ, 'sent' by him on a specific apostolic mission, just as Old Testament prophets were 'sent' by God as his messengers.

To the disciples (who were to become the 'apostles' after Pentecost) Jesus said, 'As the Father has sent me, even so I send you' (Jn 20:21, RSV). In a similar way he told the eleven disciples,

25

'Go therefore and make disciples of all nations' (Mt 28:19, RSV).

And on the Damascus Road Christ said to Paul, 'I will send you far away to the Gentiles' (Acts 22:21, RSV; cf. Acts 26:17; 1 Cor 1:17; Gal 2:7–8). In fact, just as the Old Testament prophets were *covenant* messengers, so in 2 Corinthians 3:6 Paul calls himself a minister of the New Covenant, and Paul often referred to the fact that Christ had entrusted him with a specific commission as an apostle (note 1 Cor 9:17; 2 Cor 1:1; 5:20; Gal 1:1; Eph 1:1; Col 1:1, 25; 1 Tim 1:1; etc).

New Testament apostles are connected with Old Testament prophets

It is not surprising, then, that when we read the New Testament we find that there are several times when the *apostles* are connected with the Old Testament prophets, but New Testament prophets, by contrast, are never connected with Old Testament prophets in the same way.

First, this is true of Jesus when the term 'apostle' is applied to him. Hebrews 1 begins, 'In many and various ways God spoke of old to our fathers by the *prophets*; but in these last days he has spoken to us by a Son' (Heb 1:1–2a, RSV). And then in Hebrews 3:1, (RSV), instead of calling Jesus a 'prophet' on the basis of such speaking, the author says, 'Therefore ... consider Jesus, the *apostle* and high priest of our confession,' and goes on to contrast him with Moses, the archetypal Old Testament prophet according to Jewish tradition.

According to the author of Hebrews, then, God spoke through *prophets* in the Old Testament and through Jesus the *apostle* in the New Testament. But this usage is unusual—it is the only time Jesus is called an 'apostle'. Far more common is the use of the word 'apostle' to refer to Christ's authoritative messengers. Here also there is a connection with Old Testament prophets.

For example, in 2 Peter 3:2, the readers are urged to remember 'the words spoken beforehand by the holy *prophets* and the commandment of the Lord and Saviour through your *apostles'*. And in Luke 11:49 (RSV) we read, 'I will send them prophets and apostles,' a statement which in context must use 'prophets' to refer to Old Testament prophets.

In the early church also, the apostles are connected with Old Testament prophets, but I am aware of no instance where New Testament prophets are associated with Old Testament prophets.

Ignatius, Bishop of Antioch (died about A.D. 107) wrote that Christ is the door 'through which enter Abraham and Isaac and Jacob and the Prophets and the Apostles and the Church.... For the beloved Prophets had a message pointing to Him' (Ignatius, *To the Philadelphians* 9:1–2).

Polycarp, Bishop of Smyrna (died A.D. 155), encouraged the church at Philippi:

> So then 'Let us serve Him with fear and all reverence,' as He Himself commanded us, and as did the Apostles who brought us the Gospel, and the Prophets who foretold the coming of our Lord (*To the Philippians* 6.3). (Compare Hermas, *The Shepherd: Similitudes* 9.15.4; Justin Martyr, *Dialogue with Trypho*, 75.)

The apostles' words are words of God

The most significant parallel between Old Testament prophets and New Testament apostles, however, is the ability to write words of Scripture, words which have absolute divine authority.

The apostles are primary recipients of the gospel of Christ

This ability begins with the fact that the message of the apostles came directly from Christ. The Apostle Paul, for example, adamantly insists that his message has not come from men, but from Jesus Christ himself: 'The gospel which was preached by me is not man's gospel. For I did not receive it from man, nor was I taught it, but it came through a revelation of Jesus Christ' (Gal 1:11–12, RSV).

Such an insistence on the divine origin of his message is clearly in the tradition of the Old Testament prophets (Deut 18:20; Jer 23:16ff.; Ezek 13:1ff.; 1 Kings 22:14, 28).

The New Testament also claims for the other apostles a unique access to totally accurate information about the life and work of Christ. It is primarily the apostles who are given the ability from the Holy Spirit to recall accurately the words and deeds of Jesus and to interpret them rightly for subsequent generations.

Jesus promised this empowering to his disciples (who were called apostles after the resurrection) in John 14:26 (RSV): 'But the Counsellor, the Holy Spirit, whom the Father will send in my name, he will teach you all things, and bring to your remembrance all that I have said to you.'

Similarly, Jesus promised further revelation of truth from the Holy Spirit when he told his disciples:

> When the Spirit of truth comes, he will guide you into all the truth; for he will not speak on his own authority, but whatever he hears he will speak, and he will declare to you the things that are to come. He will glorify me, for he will take what is mine and declare it to you (Jn 16:13–14, RSV).

Thus, the disciples are promised amazing gifts to enable them to write Scripture: the Holy Spirit would teach them 'all things', would cause them to remember *all* that Jesus had said, and would guide them into 'all the truth'.

The apostles speak and write the very words of God

But even more explicit parallels with the Old Testament apostles are seen in the actual claims the apostles make to be speaking not just a message which is generally from the Lord, but to be speaking the very words of God—a claim to be equal in authority to the Old Testament prophets.

Peter encourages his readers to remember 'the commandment of the Lord and Saviour through your *apostles*' (2 Pet 3:2, RSV). (And he apparently claims that to lie to the apostles [Acts 5:2] is equivalent to lying to the Holy Spirit [Acts 5:3] and lying to God [Acts 5:4].)

This claim to be able to speak words which were the words of

God himself is especially frequent in the writings of the Apostle Paul. He claims not only that the Holy Spirit has revealed to him 'what no eye has seen, nor ear heard, nor the heart of man conceived' (1 Cor 2:9, RSV), but also that when he declares this revelation, he speaks it 'in *words* not taught by human wisdom but *taught by the Spirit*, interpreting spiritual things in spiritual words' (1 Cor 2:13).

Later, in defending his apostolic office, Paul says that he will give the Corinthians 'proof that Christ is speaking in me' (2 Cor 13:3, RSV). He claims that 'my gospel' (Rom 2:16, RSV) is the message which predicts the final judgement of all men. He says that if any other person or even an angel from heaven proclaims a gospel different from the one he preaches, that person is to be 'anathema'—eternally cursed by God (Gal 1:8–9).

Moreover, he commends the Thessalonians for accepting 'the word of God which you heard from us' and for receiving it 'not as the word of men but as what it really is, the word of God' (1 Thess 2:13, RSV). And, lest they misunderstand, he warns them concerning his instructions for moral conduct, 'Therefore whoever disregards this, disregards not man but God' (1 Thess 4:8, RSV). So he can solemnly charge them before the Lord to have his letter read to 'all the brethren' (1 Thess 5:27, RSV)—it is not merely a piece of human correspondence, but something which the Lord himself requires to be read to all the church.

Paul could therefore give commands and make detailed predictions about the end of the age and the Lord's return, all with the absolute authority of the Lord Jesus Christ himself: 'This we declare to you in a word of the Lord...' (1 Thess 4:15). 'Now we command you, brethren, in the name of our Lord Jesus Christ (2 Thess 3:6, RSV).

Therefore, if someone disobeyed Paul's instructions, he was to be excluded for a time from the fellowship of the Christian community: 'If any one refuses to obey what we say in this letter, note that man, and have nothing to do with him, that he may be ashamed' (2 Thess 3:14, RSV).

It is not surprising, then, that Peter can classify Paul's writings as 'Scripture', thus ranking them on a level of authority equal to all the Old Testament scriptures:

> So also our beloved brother Paul wrote to you according to the wisdom given him, speaking of this as he does in all his letters. There are some things in them hard to understand, which the ignorant and unstable twist to their own destruction, as they do *the other scriptures* (2 Pet 3:15-16, RSV).

When Peter mentions 'the other scriptures', he must be speaking of the Old Testament scriptures, for that is what this word 'scripture' (Greek *graphē*) means all fifty of the other times it is used in the New Testament. It always refers to the words of the Bible which were accepted as the very words of God. But this means that the writings of Paul the apostle are given a status equal to the words of the Old Testament prophets—they are the very words of God.

For the purposes of this study one of the most significant passages on this topic is 1 Corinthians 14:37–38, because here Paul is writing to a community where several prophets were active, and he still asserts his authority over the entire community, even over the prophets. Paul writes, 'If any one thinks that he is a prophet, or spiritual, he should acknowledge that what I am writing to you is a command of the Lord. If anyone does not recognize this, he is not recognized' (RSV).

The word translated 'what' in this verse is a plural pronoun in Greek *(ha)* and more literally could be translated '*the things that I am writing to you*'. Thus, Paul claims that his directives to the church at Corinth are not merely his own but a command of the Lord.

But how much of the preceding material is Paul referring to by saying 'the things I am writing to you'? We probably cannot be certain, but we can note that it comes exactly at the end of the discussion of spiritual gifts (chapters 12—14) and would seem most naturally to apply at least to these three chapters.

Of course, someone might argue that this statement refers only to the preceding sentence, or to the directive about women (vv. 33–35). However, the statement is so general ('the things I am writing to you'), and is made so indefinite by the use of the plural (Greek *ha*), that such a restriction to a small section would seem quite artificial. Paul's purpose is to conclude the discussion and at the same time to bar the way for any prophet at Corinth to propound new rules which would contradict those which he has written. Certainly this concern would apply at least to the whole range of directives for worship, reaching back to chapters 12 and 13, and perhaps even to chapter 11.

But this means that we have in 1 Corinthians 14:37 a very strong statement of Paul's authority. Paul has here instituted a number of new rules for church worship at Corinth and has claimed for them the status of 'a command of the Lord'. Furthermore, the penalty is severe: the man who refuses to acknowledge Paul's divine authority will himself not be known or recognized by the Lord (or, on some interpretations, by the congregation). Thomas Edwards summarizes 1 Corinthians 14:38: 'He that refuses to hear Christ's apostles refuses to hear Christ himself and incurs his displeasure.'[2]

So we have here a very close parallel to Old Testament prophetic authority. Anyone who disobeyed Paul's instructions would be disobeying a 'command of the Lord'. On the other hand, nothing even approaching this kind of claim is made for New Testament prophets. Indeed, even the prophets at Corinth were expected to be subject to Paul's apostolic authority. G.W.H. Lampe notes that Paul 'was driven flatly to refuse to admit the possibility that a prophet might be right and he himself be wrong (1 Cor 14:37–38).'[3]

The apostles, then, have authority to write words which are God's own words, equal in truth status and authority to the words of the Old Testament. They do this in order to write in Scripture the central events of redemptive history—to record and apply to the lives of believers the facts and the meaning of the life, death, and resurrection of Christ. To disbelieve or disobey an apostle's authoritative words is to disbelieve or disobey

God. The apostles are the New Testament counterpart of the divinely authoritative Old Testament prophets.

Why the name 'apostle' instead of the name 'prophet'?

But if the New Testament apostles are so similar to the Old Testament prophets, why did Jesus not call them 'prophets'? Why did he use a new name, 'apostles'? There seem to be three reasons.

Joel's prediction of prophecy for all God's people

First, Joel had predicted the outpouring of God's Spirit on all flesh, resulting in prophecy not just for a few people (such as those who had the authority to write the very words of Scripture), but for all God's people:

> And it shall come to pass afterward, that I will pour out my spirit on all flesh; your sons and your daughters *shall prophesy*, your old men shall dream dreams, and your young men shall see visions. Even upon the menservants and maidservants in those days, I will pour out my spirit (Joel 2:28–29, RSV).

Similarly, Moses had looked forward to a time when there would be widespread prophesying: 'Would that all the Lord's people were prophets', (Num 11:29, RSV). And there is a well-known Rabbinic statement in the *Midrash Rabbah on Numbers* 15.25: 'In the world to come all Israel will be made prophets.'

So 'prophet' would have been too broad a term to apply to a special, limited group of men such as the apostles, who had the unique authority to write God's words in Scripture. The New Covenant age was expected to be an age when *all* God's people would be able to prophesy.

The meaning of the word 'prophet'

(a) *Its meaning in secular Greek usage.* Yet there was a second reason why Jesus did not call his uniquely-commissioned messengers 'prophets'. That reason had to do with the meaning of the word 'prophet' in ordinary speech at the time of the New Testament.

By the time of the New Testament the term 'prophet' (Greek *prophētēs*) in everyday use often simply meant 'one who has supernatural knowledge' or 'one who predicts the future'—or even just 'spokesman' (without any connotations of divine authority).

Several examples near the time of the New Testament are given by Helmut Krämer (TDNT 6, p. 794; also in LSJ, p. 1540):

> a philosopher is called 'a *prophet* of immortal nature' (Dio Chrysostom, A.D. 40–120)
>
> a teacher (Diogenes) wants to be 'a *prophet* of truth and candour' (Lucian of Samosata, A.D. 120–180)
>
> those who advocate Epicurean philosophy are called '*prophets* of Epicurus' (Plutarch, A.D. 50–120)
>
> written history is called 'the *prophetess* of truth' (Diodorus Siculus, wrote ca. 60-30 B.C.)
>
> a 'specialist' in botany is called a '*prophet*' (Dioscurides of Cilicia, 1st century A.D.)
>
> a 'quack' in medicine is called a '*prophet*' (Galen of Pergamum, A.D. 129-199)

Krämer concludes that the Greek word for 'prophet' (*prophētēs*) 'simply expresses the formal function of declaring, proclaiming, making known'. Yet, because 'every prophet declares something which is not his own', the Greek word for 'herald' *(kērux)* 'is the closest synonym' (*TDNT* 6, p. 795).

The use of the Greek word for 'prophet' in the ancient world has also received extensive treatment in Erich Fascher's book, *PROPHĒTĒS*.[4] After an extensive survey, Fascher concludes (pp. 51-54) that *prophētēs* itself is a 'frame-word' without a narrowly-defined meaning of its own. Rather, it is used in the widest number of circumstances and takes its meaning from the context. One general definition which fits almost every case, however, is 'proclaimer' or 'announcer'. Fascher says that *prophētēs* ('prophet') alone almost never has the sense of 'predictor, foreteller', but must receive this meaning from other qualifying words in the context. Similarly with the verb *prophēteuō*: it never means 'to predict, foretell, divine', but can mean 'to speak in the name of a god', or 'to reveal something hidden', or 'to hold the office of a prophet'.

Because of this wide range of meanings, one thing is clear. The word 'prophet' would not automatically suggest 'one who speaks with absolute divine authority' or 'one who speaks the very words of God'. That was not the sense of the word in its everyday use in the Greek-speaking world.

This means that if Jesus and the New Testament authors had wanted a word which, in the first-century world, would mean 'one who speaks the very words of God', the Greek word 'prophet' was not well suited to the task. It was too watered down in meaning—it just meant 'spokesman' in a general way, and did not imply the possession of the full authority of the one for whom the prophet was speaking.

But is this information from 'secular' Greek writers at all relevant for Jesus and the writers of the New Testament? Are these quotations from secular Greek writers significant for our study of the New Testament? Or is the New Testament written in a different language than this secular use of Greek?

These quotations are significant in this way. They show the wide range of meanings the word 'prophet' (Greek *prophētēs*) had for ordinary speakers of Greek around the time of the New Testament. The word 'prophet' could, of course, mean 'one who spoke for a god', just as in the Greek translation of the Old Testament it meant 'one who spoke for God'. But it could also just mean 'spokesman, proclaimer'.

Now the early Christians spoke ordinary Greek as it was used throughout the Roman Empire. They could have easily read and understood the writings of any of the 'secular' Greek writers quoted above. They could have carried on a personal conversation with any of these writers as well, if they had met them. (For example, Paul readily conversed with pagan Greek philosophers on Mars Hill in Athens.) This was because they used the same language—they had a common understanding of the meanings of thousands and thousands of words.[5]

Moreover, any of these secular writers could have read and understood the New Testament writings—indeed, the gospels were written so that unbelievers who spoke the ordinary Greek language of the day could read them and come to faith in Christ. (If there was any failure to understand, it was not due to a different language being used, but due to sin blinding their hearts: 1 Corinthians 2:14; 2 Corinthians 4:4.)

Therefore, it is useful for us to understand the meanings of Greek words as they were used in ordinary conversation and writing in the Roman Empire in the first century AD.

This does not mean that the New Testament always has to use words in exactly the same way, of course. Some very important words (for example, the Greek words for 'God', 'heaven', 'salvation', 'church', etc.) received greatly-altered meanings from their use by the early Christians. And this *might* have been the same with the word 'prophet'—Jesus and the New Testament authors could have retained the word if they wished and used it instead of the word 'apostle' to apply to Jesus' authoritative representatives who led the early church and wrote Scripture for it. The twelve disciples *could* have been called 'prophets' after Pentecost, for example, and Peter, James, John, and the others could have then made it clear that they shouldn't be thought of as 'prophets' in the way the word 'prophet' was ordinarily understood, but rather in a specialized way, similar to the way in which the writing prophets of the Old Testament were called 'prophets'. That could have happened, we must admit. But it didn't.

Instead, a new term was chosen, 'apostle'. What we are trying to do here is show why that choice of a new term was an entirely appropriate one: it prevented much misunderstanding which would have come, not just from secular uses of the word, but even from current Jewish uses and even from the Old Testament itself.

(b) *Its meaning in first-century Jewish usage.* But someone may object that the word 'prophet' would have had a far stronger meaning to first-century Jews who knew the Old Testament background of the word 'prophet' to refer to God's messengers who spoke his very words. Wouldn't they use the word 'prophet' in a different way, similar to the way the Old Testament used it to refer to the prophets who wrote Scripture?

Surprisingly, this was not necessarily the case. Although Jewish people in the first century certainly did use 'prophet' to refer to the Old Testament prophets, there were other, much broader, uses as well. The evidence shows that both the Hebrew and the Greek words for 'prophet' had a wide range of meanings in Jewish literature.

For example, in the rabbinic literature the words for 'prophet', 'prophecy', and 'to prophesy' (Hebrew *nabi'* and cognates) are sometimes used of a person who simply has knowledge of things beyond sense perception. The words can refer, for example, to people who predicted the future but who were never thought to speak God's very words or to have God's authority attached to the very words they spoke.

Some examples from the Babylonian Talmud are in stories about Rebekah (b. Sot. 13a refers to 'her prophecy' and the context shows that the idea of prediction, not that of authority, is what motivated the choice of this word), Miriam (b. Meg. 14a calls her a 'prophetess' simply because of something she predicted), and Hannah (a prediction is said to justify the application of the term 'prophetess' to her in b. Meg. 14a).

There also seems to be an emphasis on prophecy in the sense of revealed knowledge in b. Ber. 55b and 57b: Rabbi Johann said, 'If one rises early and a Scriptural verse comes to his mind, this is a small prophecy.'

Similarly, Rabbi Hanina b. Isaac said, 'The incomplete form of prophecy is the dream' (*Midrash Rabbah on Genesis*, 17.5; again in 44.7).

That the term 'prophecy' can be applied to such phenomena is not due to the fact that the recipient would authoritatively deliver the message to someone else, or would claim a divine authority of actual words, but rather to the suggestion in each case of some kind of special impartation of knowledge to the prophet from without. The examples indicate that a broad range of meanings is attached to the word 'prophet' and related terms.

In the Apocrypha we note Wisd. 7.27 (late 1st c. B.C.): speaking of wisdom, it says, 'In every generation she passes into holy souls and makes them friends of God, and prophets.'

Josephus (A.D. 37/38 — ca. A.D. 100) quite clearly designates John Hyrcanus (who died in 105 B.C.) as a prophet: he 'was accounted by God worthy of the greatest privileges, the rule of the nation, the office of high priest, and the gift of prophecy, for the Deity was with him and enabled him to foresee and foretell the future; so, for example, he foretold of his two elder sons that they would not remain masters of the state' (*Antiquities* 13.299–300; parallel account in *Jewish Wars*. 1. 68–69).

The passage is significant because in it Josephus makes explicit what it was that qualified John for the title 'prophet': not the ability to speak with a divine authority attaching to his actual words, but simply the ability to predict the future. Since this ability was thought to come from God, his predictions might have been thought generally to come from God, but an absolute divine authority attaching to his actual words (like the Old Testament prophets) is never claimed or even implied.

In Philo (ca. 30 B.C. — A.D. 45) we read that the mind in dreams *prophesies* future events (*Spec. Leg.* 1.219). Then Philo also uses 'prophet' to mean simply 'spokesman', in a sense more often found in secular Greek literature. In *Quod Deus* 138 reason is said to be the 'prophet' of God. And speech is said to act as 'prophet' for our understanding in *Det*. 40 and *Mig*. 169.

So there are various strands of Jewish tradition showing that first-century Jews, like their pagan Greek contemporaries, could use the word 'prophet' and related terms to refer to a wide range of persons and activities *without* any sense of absolute divine authority attaching to the very words the prophet spoke.

(c) *Influence on New Testament usage of the word 'prophet'*.
When we turn to the New Testament we must take into account
this large diversity in usage. New Testament Christians had
their understanding of the meanings of words influenced by the
Old Testament, by contemporary Jewish usage, and by the
everyday Greek usage of the culture in which they lived. When
these influences combined, it meant that the word 'prophet'
and its related terms had a range of meanings much broader
than simply 'a messenger for God who speaks with a divine
authority of actual words'.

Of course, when the New Testament writers have occasion to
use the words 'prophet', 'prophecy' and 'to prophesy', it will
most often be in contexts dealing with the great writing
prophets of the Old Testament, whose writings they saw
fulfilled in Christ. In these contexts, 'prophet' and related
terms will generally refer to men in the Old Testament who
spoke God's very words. But that does not tell us what
'prophet' will mean when it is applied to people other than
these Old Testament prophets. It may take any one of the various meanings current in Greek at that time.

In fact, this is what happens. In Titus 1:12 we find 'prophet'
(Greek *prophētēs*) in the general sense of 'proclaimer,
announcer, spokesman' Referring to Epimenides (Cretan
religious teacher ca. 6th c. B.C.), the verse reads: 'One of themselves, a prophet of their own, said, "Cretans are always liars,
evil beasts, lazy gluttons."' (RSV). Certainly Epimenides was
not someone who spoke the very words of God! But Paul
nonetheless calls him a 'prophet' (Greek *prophētēs*).

Then in Luke 22:64 the high priest's assistants who had
blindfolded Jesus demand, 'Prophesy! Who is it that struck
you?' (RSV). In this case their meaning is not, 'Speak words with
absolute divine authority,' but rather a mocking challenge,
'Show that you have knowledge by supernatural means—tell
us who hit you even though you cannot see us.'

In the narrative about the woman at the well, as soon as Jesus
tells the woman the secrets of her past life, she says, 'Sir, I per-

ceive that you are a prophet' (Jn 4:19, RSV). Now Jesus had not yet convinced her that he could speak with a divine authority in his actual words; he had just demonstrated that he had knowledge which had not come by ordinary means (he knew about her five previous husbands).

These last two examples are especially interesting because they give us a glimpse of the sense attached to the words 'prophet' and 'prophesy' by ordinary people of first-century Palestine, who had nevertheless had some contact with the Old Testament through their religious background.

Similar indications come from Christian writings outside the New Testament. In *Testament of Solomon* 15.8 (a composition with Christian influence from around A.D.100) there is a story about a demon who *prophesies* (Greek *prophēteuō*) to Solomon that his kingdom will be broken. In *Martyrdom of Polycarp* 12.3 (about A.D. 154–160) we read that Polycarp had said prophetically (Greek *prophētikōs*), 'I must be burnt alive.' In both cases prediction as a result of some supernatural knowledge, not speaking the very words of God, is in view.

A new term for Christ's representatives showed the newness of the New Covenant church

There may have been yet a third factor making a word other than 'prophet' appropriate. Although there was much continuity between the Old Covenant and the New Covenant, there was also much difference. In order to emphasize the newness of the New Covenant which Christ established, he may have deemed it appropriate to have a new name to designate the first leaders of the New Covenant community, the church. So the earthly leaders of the church are not called 'prophets of Jesus Christ'. Rather, the distinctive change from the Old Covenant is signalled in part by a new name, 'apostles of Jesus Christ'.

Conclusion: 'prophet' does not necessarily imply absolute divine authority

The result of this study, then, is the realization that when the

New Testament writers apply the word 'prophet' and cognate words to someone other than an Old Testament prophet, it is impossible to decide in advance what sense the term will have. The precise meaning will have to be determined from the context. Certainly one cannot say that the word always must mean 'one who speaks God's very words' after the pattern of the Old Testament prophets.

The suitability of the word 'apostle'

At this point two factors mentioned above must be kept in mind: the prediction of prophetic ability being given to all God's people, and the frequent use of the 'prophet' word group in Hebrew and Greek to refer to speech which did not have God's absolute authority attaching to the words. Because of these two factors, a different term from 'prophet' (Greek *prophētēs*) would be appropriate for those who had the task of writing the very words of God in New Testament Scripture.

To meet this need, the word 'apostle' (Greek *apostolos*) was well suited to the task.

Firstly, as we noted in chapter 1, one thing which distinguished those who spoke with divine authority in the Old Testament from those who did not was the status of 'messenger'. An Old Testament prophet who was sent by God to speak to the people was the only kind of prophet who spoke God's words. Now the Greek word *apostolos* meant 'someone or something that is sent', or simply 'messenger'. The related verb *apostellō* meant 'to send'. So this word, while not the same as the word 'prophet', still gave some sense of connection with the Old Testament prophets.

And it could serve as a more restricted term than 'prophet' for one specific aspect of the broad range of meaning possessed by the 'prophet' word group. It could refer to men who were the New Testament counterpart of the messengers of God in the Old Testament, and who spoke with divine authority.

Secondly, since *apostolos* in this sense was a new term, it could be used of a limited group of men without seeming to conflict with any Old Testament or rabbinic expectations of a wide distribution of prophetic abilities.

Thirdly, the word *apostle* (Greek *apostolos*) was a rather uncommon word before the time of the New Testament. It occurs only once in the Greek Old Testament (the Septuagint), once in Josephus, and not at all in Philo. Secular Greek used the word only occasionally to refer to military expeditions or naval vessels which had been 'sent' somewhere, but it was not the common Greek term for 'messenger'.

So the word 'apostle' was apparently chosen by Jesus as a word meaning 'one who is sent'—yet it was a term largely free from misleading implications from either Old Testament or secular Greek usage. It was a term suitable to be given much fuller meaning in the title, 'apostle of Jesus Christ'. This new title was then used throughout the New Testament of those men whom Christ sent with his authority to found and govern the church, and to write for the church the words of the New Testament Scriptures.

Are the apostles ever called 'prophets'?

After the previous discussion, it may be clear why the apostles are not usually called by the title 'prophet' in the New Testament. 'Apostle' was a far more suitable term.

But are the apostles *ever* referred to as 'prophets'? Might there be cases where they are said to 'prophesy'?

In fact there are such cases. But before looking at them, it is good to put this question in a larger perspective: Are there cases where *other* titles or designations of function are used of the apostles? Here also the answer is yes.

Other functional titles given to apostles

For example, in 1 Timothy 2:7 Paul calls himself 'a *preacher* and *apostle*' and 'a *teacher* of the Gentiles in faith and truth' (RSV). Three terms, 'preacher', 'apostle' and 'teacher', are all applied to him. Similarly, in 2 Timothy 1:11 he says, 'For this gospel I was appointed a *preacher* and *apostle* and *teacher*' (RSV).

Then Peter calls himself a 'fellow elder' in 1 Peter 5:1 (RSV).

Now these examples do not prove that *all* New Testament 'teachers' had the same authority as Paul the apostle, or that everyone in the New Testament who was a 'preacher' was able to speak 'commands of the Lord' as Paul was. Nor does 1 Peter 5:1 prove that *all* New Testament 'elders' had the same authority as the Apostle Peter.

These examples just show that words describing certain *functions* could be applied to the apostles when they were emphasizing that function—Paul could call himself a 'teacher' when he wanted to highlight his teaching role, for example.

Now the same thing happens with respect to the words 'prophet' and 'to prophesy'. They also can be used to refer to the apostles.

For example, Paul could talk about himself prophesying when he came to Corinth: 'Now, brethren, if I come to you speaking in tongues, how shall I benefit you unless I bring you some revelation or knowledge or prophecy or teaching?' (1 Cor 14:6, RSV). Similarly, he seems to include himself in 1 Corinthians 13:9, 'We prophesy in part.'

As I shall argue in chapters 5 and 6, the distinctive characteristic about New Testament prophecy was that a person received a 'revelation' (or something God brought to mind), and reported it in the church. So if an apostle wished to emphasize his role of receiving and reporting revelations from God, it would be possible for him to refer to himself as a 'prophet'.

Yet it is significant that Paul never appeals to a gift of prophecy to establish his authority—something which would have been very natural and very easy if New Testament prophets had been commonly thought to speak words with absolute divine authority. Rather, when Paul wants to establish his authority, he appeals to his status as an 'apostle'. This is a further indication that for New Testament authors the title which signified authority similar to that of the Old Testament prophets was not 'prophet' but 'apostle'.

And certainly there were 'prophets' in the church at Corinth who were not apostles like Paul—for Paul gives many instructions about how they were to function. At a later point our concern will be to look closely at those instructions and define the gift of prophecy more precisely. But first we must look at two other New Testament passages where the word 'prophet' is apparently used to refer to the apostles.

The book of Revelation

The largest example in the New Testament of a 'prophecy' given by an *apostle* is the book of Revelation.

The entire book claims to be a prophecy: 'Blessed is he who reads aloud the words of the *prophecy*, and blessed are those who hear' (Rev 1:3, RSV).

Then at the end of the book we read, 'Blessed is he who keeps of the *prophecy* of this book.... Do not seal up the words of the *prophecy* of this book, for the time is near' (22:7, 10, RSV; cf. 22:19).

And finally, John is told, 'You must again *prophesy* about many peoples and nations and tongues and kings' (Rev. 10:11, RSV).

So the entire book is viewed as a prophecy, and John, in recording the book, is acting as a prophet.

If we accept the view that the author 'John' (Rev 1:1, 4, 9) was in fact the apostle John—and this is the view that has been most common since the earliest history of the book's acceptance in the church—then, again, we have in this book an example of a New Testament apostle functioning as a prophet and writing for the church an extended prophecy. And indeed we can see why it is appropriate to call this book a 'prophecy'. The content of the book is similar to that of the great prophetic predictions of the future found in the writing prophets of the Old Testament. But here there are predictions which look beyond the church age into God's plan for the final great events of redemptive history.

And the authority which John claims is an absolute divine authority, like that claimed by the other apostles in the New Testament. His words are beyond challenge or question (Rev 22:18–19), and obeying them brings great blessings (Rev 1:3; 22:7), while altering them at all brings direct punishment from God (Rev 22:18–19).

Like the Old Testament prophets and the other New Testament apostles, John is commissioned as a messenger by Jesus Christ who appears to him and commands, 'Write what you see in a book and send it to the seven churches' (Rev 1:11, RSV). Repeatedly, John is commanded, 'Write what you see' (Rev 1:19, RSV) or simply, 'Write' (Rev 2:1, 8, 12, 18; 3:1, 7, 14; 14:13; 19:9; 21:5).

Since there are some things which are revealed to John but which he has no authority to write (cf. Rev 10:4), the implication is that he has written no more and no less than that for which he had a divine commission, and it is this commission which gives authority to his words. Thus the author 'claims for himself an authority which can be compared only with that of apostles' (G. Friedrich, *TDNT* 6, p.849).

But should we look at the book of Revelation as evidence of what the gift of prophecy was like in ordinary New Testament churches? No, it would not be appropriate to do so. This is not a prophecy given by some ordinary Christian, but rather a very prominent apostle of Jesus Christ. Moreover, this was not a prophecy given in the worship service of some local group of Christians, but given to John in exile on the island of Patmos for the benefit of seven churches in Asia Minor (Rev 1:4), and ultimately for the benefit of the entire Christian church. And this was not a brief prophetic word given to meet the need of the moment in some local church, but was a unique glimpse of God's final plans for history given once-for-all in an extensive discourse (over 9,800 words) for inclusion in the New Testament canon.

It is safe to say that in authority, in content, and in scope, no other prophecy like this has ever been given to the New Testament church.

In conclusion, the book of Revelation shows that an apostle could function as a prophet and record a prophecy for the New Testament church. But because its author was an apostle, and because it is unique, it does not provide information which is directly relevant to the gift of prophecy as it functioned among ordinary Christians in first century churches.[6]

Note to readers: The following section is rather long and detailed. Many readers may wish to skip to the conclusion at the top of page 62.

Ephesians 2:20 and 3:5

There is one other place where the word 'prophet' occurs with a mention of the apostles: Ephesians 2:20 and 3:5.

The first of these two verses, addressed to Gentile Christians in the church at Ephesus, reads:

> Therefore you are no longer strangers and aliens, but you are fellow citizens with the saints and members of the household of God, having been built up on the foundation of *the apostles and prophets*, Christ Jesus Himself being the chief cornerstone (Eph 2:19–20).

Then a few verses later Paul tells his Gentile readers:

> When you read this you can perceive my insight into the mystery of Christ, which was not made known to the sons of men in other generations as it has now been revealed to *his holy apostles and prophets* by the Spirit; that is, how the Gentiles are fellow heirs, members of the same body, and partakers of the promise in Christ Jesus through the Gospel (Eph 3:4–6, RSV).

Now some people have argued that Ephesians 2:20 shows what *all* New Testament prophets were like, and, furthermore, that the unique 'foundational' role of the prophets in Ephesians 2:20 means that they could speak with authority equal to the apostles and equal to Scripture. For example, Richard Gaffin a careful New Testament scholar at Westminster Seminary in Philadelphia, says, 'Ephesians 2:20 makes a generalization that covers all the other New Testament statements on prophecy.'[7]

This is an important question, because if everyone with the gift of prophecy in the New Testament church *did* have this kind of absolute divine authority, then we would expect this gift to die out as soon as the writings of the New Testament were completed and given to the churches. Most Christians today would certainly agree that the New Testament is complete and that no one today can speak or write words with the same authority as the words of the Bible.[8]

But is this position a persuasive one? Is this really the implication of Ephesians 2:20 and 3:5?

The central question is whether these verses refer to all the Christians who had the gift of prophecy in first-century churches. Are the prophets mentioned here those with the gift of prophecy at Corinth, at Thessalonica, at Ephesus, etc?

If so—if these verses are referring to all the prophets in all the local congregations in first century churches—then it would seem that they are portrayed in a unique 'foundational' role in the New Testament church, and we have to agree with Dr Gaffin—we would clearly expect this gift to cease once the New Testament was complete.

But personally I will say at the outset that I do not find this 'all church prophets' position persuasive. I shall argue for another position, namely, that Ephesians 2:20 and 3:5 is talking not about two groups of people, apostles *and* prophets, but about one group, 'apostle-prophets'. But before reaching that point, it is appropriate to give an overview of the most common views of these verses.

The four most common interpretations of Ephesians 2:20 and 3:5 may be summarized as follows:

'The foundation of the apostles and prophets' means:

1. The apostles and the *Old Testament prophets*.

2. The *teaching* of the apostles and *New Testament prophets*.

3. The apostles and *New Testament prophets* themselves.

4. The *apostle-prophets* themselves.

We shall consider these possible views in order.

(a) *View 1: the foundation = the apostles and the Old Testament prophets*. In favour of the idea that 'the foundation of the apostles and prophets' means the apostles and the Old Testament prophets is the fact that the New Testament apostles are indeed like the Old Testament prophets and are elsewhere connected with them (as we saw in the section above).

But this position has hardly been persuasive to any careful readers, primarily because in Ephesians 3:5, where Paul is still talking about the same subject (the inclusion of Gentiles in the church), and where the grammatical construction is so similar, the Old Testament prophets cannot be in view. This is because the mystery that Gentiles should be included in the church, according to Paul, 'has *now* been revealed to his holy apostles and prophets' in a way that 'it was not made known to the sons of men in other generations'. This more full revelation of the Gentile inclusion in the church came after Pentecost, and Paul explicitly says that it had not been made known in other generations, thus ruling out Old Testament prophets from consideration here.

Furthermore, the word order would not ordinarily give this meaning. If Paul had meant to talk about Old Testament apostles and New Testament prophets, it would have been very natural to say 'the prophets and apostles', (cf. Lk 11:49; 2 Pet 3:2), but here he says instead 'the apostles and prophets'.

(b) *View 2: The foundation = the teaching of the apostles and prophets*. This second position would say that the teaching of the New Testament apostles and prophets, or perhaps their authoritative preaching of the gospel, or their work of founding the church, is what Paul means by the 'foundation of the apostles and prophets' here. The important part about this interpretation is that it understands the 'foundation' to be not the apostles and prophets themselves, but some aspect of their work.

In favour of this interpretation is the fact that Paul elsewhere speaks of apostolic work as a 'foundation', especially in 1 Corinthians 3:10–15 where he says, 'Like a skilled master builder I laid a foundation, and another man is building upon it. Let each man take care how he builds upon it' (1 Cor 3:10, RSV; note a similar metaphor in Rom 15:20).

In addition to this parallel in 1 Corinthians, another argument in favour of this view would be the fact that preaching and teaching about Christ are foundational in starting any church, and this would make the metaphor seem appropriate.

But there are several arguments against this position.

(1) In 1 Corinthians 3:10–15 the subject is entirely different and the metaphor serves a different purpose. There the question is one of work done in building up the church. But in Ephesians 2:20 the context is one of inclusion of Jews and Gentiles together in the church. In Ephesians 2:20 *the people themselves*, both Jews and Gentiles, are being added to the church, 'built up' on its foundation. But in 1 Corinthians the people are themselves doing the work, they are building onto the church.

(2) In Ephesians 2:20 the other parts of the building are persons, and this almost requires that the 'foundation' be persons as well, to make the metaphor understandable.

For example, the cornerstone of the building in Ephesians 2:20 is 'Christ Jesus *himself*' not just some teaching about him, and then the 'superstructure' of the building, the part that is being built up on the foundation, consists of all other Christians, Jews and Gentiles together who are becoming 'fellow citizens' in God's house.

But if the cornerstone is a person (Christ) and the rest of the building is made of persons (all other Jew and Gentile Christians), then the foundation must be understood to be persons also, namely, the 'apostles and prophets' themselves.

(3) Unlike 1 Corinthians 3, this context has no mention of the work or teaching of the apostles. God's work in joining Jews and Gentiles together in the church is in view, not the work of those believers but they themselves as joined together by God.

(c) *View 3: the foundation = the apostles and the New Testament prophets.* This is the position taken by Dr Gaffin in the argument mentioned above, where he suggests that the gift of prophecy was so 'foundational' to the church that it does not continue today. And others who may not hold Dr Gaffin's position on the early cessation of the gift of prophecy still would see this verse as referring to two groups: (1) the apostles, and (2) the New Testament prophets.

In favour of the position that Paul is here talking about two different groups is the fact that the word 'prophet' in the New Testament is often used to refer to a different group than the apostles. (In fact, most of the rest of this book will focus on those other instances where 'prophets' are viewed as a group separate from the apostles.)

Moreover, in Ephesians 4:11, a passage just a bit further on in this same epistle, prophets are clearly distinguished from apostles. There, Paul says, 'And he gave some *apostles*, some *prophets*, some evangelists, some pastor-teachers....'

One could argue that the use of the word 'prophet' in Ephesians 4:11 should indicate for us how the same word should be used in Ephesians 2:20 and 3:5. In all three cases, one could argue, the word should refer to a group distinct from the apostles. This is the position taken by Dr Gaffin, for instance, in his argument that the gift of prophecy has ceased and is no longer valid for use today.[9]

However, there are some significant arguments against this position as well:

(1) The grammar does not require that two groups are intended here. The same grammatical construction used here is often used in the New Testament to speak of one person or one group with two different names.

This Greek construction takes the form *the* [noun] *and* [noun]. If the New Testament authors want to make it clear that they are talking about two different items or two different groups, they add the word 'the' before the second noun, giving this construction: *the* [noun] *and the* [noun]. If Paul had given this kind of construction, it would have been clear that he meant two different groups, the apostles and the prophets. But when he omitted the word 'the' before the second noun ('prophets'), he used a construction which let the readers know that he was somehow bracketing 'apostles and prophets' as a unit.

A nearby example of this is found in Ephesians 4:11, where Paul speaks about 'some pastor-teachers'. Although the grammar does not require it, it is fair to say that it would be more likely to understand this as 'pastor-teachers' than as two groups, 'pastors and teachers', and many interpreters understand it that way today.

I have listed here several other examples from the New Testament where one person or group of persons is meant, but the same construction as in Ephesians 2:20 and 3:5 is used:

Romans 16:17 (RSV): 'Greet Andronicus and Junias, my kinsmen and my fellow prisoners' (Paul is not talking about two groups, 'kinsmen', and 'fellow prisoners', but one group, 'kinsmen who are also fellow prisoners'). Yet this is the same Greek construction as is found in Ephesians 2:20 and 3:5—as are all of the following examples:

Galatians 1:7: 'The ones troubling you and wanting to pervert the gospel of Christ' (one group).

Ephesians 6:21 (RSV): 'Tychicus the beloved brother and faithful minister' (one person).

Philippians 2:25 (RSV): 'Epaphroditus my brother and fellow worker and fellow soldier' (one person).

Colossians 1:2 (RSV): 'To the saints and faithful brethren in Christ at Colossae' (one group).

1 Thessalonians 5:12 (RSV): 'Those who labour among you and are over you in the Lord' (one group).

Titus 2:13 (RSV): 'The glory of our great God and Saviour Jesus Christ' (one person).

Philemon 1: 'To Philemon our loved one and fellow worker' (though the Greek construction is the same here, literally, 'the loved one and fellow worker of us,' it is so clear that only one person is meant that it is commonly translated 'our beloved fellow worker').

Hebrews 3:1 (RSV): 'Jesus, the apostle and high priest of our confession' (one person).

2 Peter 1:1 (RSV): 'Our God and Saviour Jesus Christ' (one person).

2 Peter 1:11 (RSV): 'Our Lord and Saviour Jesus Christ' (one person).

More examples could be given, but it should be clear that this construction which Paul used in Ephesians 2:20 and 3:5 does not have to be translated 'the apostles and prophets'. It is just as valid, and perhaps even more in keeping with New Testament usage, to translate it 'the apostle-prophets' or 'the apostles who are also prophets', showing that Paul is only referring to one group, not two. In that case, Ephesians 3:5 would be translated 'his holy apostle-prophets' or 'his holy apostles who are also prophets' (one group, not two).

I am not implying here that it is *necessary* to translate Ephesians 2:20 and 3:5 this way, for other examples can be found where this construction does refer to two separate persons or items[10] but it is certainly a legitimate translation, and, in the absence of contextual or other indications to the contrary, it may even be a preferable translation. I was not able to find in Paul's writings even one clear example where two distinct people or classes of people (as opposed to things) are joined in this kind of construction.

(2) A second reason against the view that this verse represents the New Testament apostles and the New Testament prophets is the fact that the prophets in the New Testament did not receive the revelation that Gentiles were to be included in the New Testament church on an equal standing with Jewish believers. This remarkable revelation of the Gentile inclusion is many times said to come to the apostles, but is never in the New Testament said to be given to any 'prophet' or groups of prophets who were not just apostles functioning in a prophetic role.

Here are some New Testament passages showing God's revelation concerning the inclusion of the Gentiles in the church:

Matthew 28:19 (RSV): 'Go therefore and make disciples of all nations' (spoken to the apostles).

Luke 24:46–47 (RSV): 'And (Jesus) said to them, "Thus it is written, that the Christ should suffer and on the third day rise from the dead, and that repentance and forgiveness of sins should be preached in his name to all nations, beginning from Jerusalem"' (spoken to the apostles).

Acts 1:8 (RSV): 'You shall be my witnesses in Jerusalem and in all Judea and Samaria and to the end of the earth' (spoken to the apostles).

Acts 10:15 (RSV): 'And the voice came to him again a second time, "What God has cleansed, you must not call common."' (spoken to Peter the apostle).

Acts 10:34–35 (RSV): 'And Peter opened his mouth and said: "Truly I perceive that God shows no partiality, but in every nation any one who fears him and does what is right is acceptable to him."' (Peter's statement after receiving the vision from heaven and visiting Cornelius' house).

Acts 10.46–48 (RSV): 'Then Peter declared, "Can any one forbid water for baptizing these people who have received the Holy Spirit just as we have?" And he commanded them to be baptized in the name of Jesus Christ' (Peter the apostle declares the acceptance of Gentiles into the church).

Acts 11:2–18: Peter's explanation to the Jerusalem church about how the Gentile inclusion had been revealed to him in a vision and in the coming of the Holy Spirit to the household of Cornelius.

Acts 15:6–29: At the Jerusalem council, crucial speeches are made by Peter and James, both apostles.[11]

Acts 22:21 (RSV): 'Depart; for I will send you far away to the Gentiles' (Christ speaking to Paul the apostle on the Damascus road).

Acts 26:17–18 (RSV): '... delivering you from the people and from the Gentiles—to whom I send you to open their eyes, that they may turn from darkness to light and from the power of Satan to God, that they may receive forgiveness of sins and a place among those who are sanctified by faith in me' (Christ speaking to Paul on the Damascus road).

Galatians 1:16 (RSV): '(God) was pleased to reveal his Son to me, in order that I might preach him among the Gentiles' (Paul the apostle).

Galatians 2:7–8 (RSV): 'They saw that I had been entrusted with the gospel to the uncircumcised, just as Peter had been entrusted with the gospel to the circumcised (for he who worked through Peter for the mission to the circumcised worked through me also for the Gentiles)', (Paul the apostle speaking of his commissioning by Christ to preach to the Gentiles).

Ephesians 2:11—3:21: Paul gives a lengthy explanation of his insight into the 'mystery' of the inclusion of Gentiles in the church. He says, 'When you read this you can perceive my insight into the mystery of Christ, which was not made known to the sons of men in other generations as it has now been revealed to his holy apostles and prophets by the Spirit; that is, *how the Gentiles are fellow heirs, members of the same body, and partakers of the promise in Christ Jesus through the gospel'* (Eph 3:4–6, RSV).

We can also note here the emphasis Paul places on his own role in proclaiming this inclusion of the Gentiles:

> To me, though I am the very least of all the saints, this grace was given, *to preach to the Gentiles the unsearchable riches of Christ*, and to make all men see what is the plan of the mystery hidden for ages in God who created all things (Eph 3:8–9, RSV).

The remarkable thing about all of these passages is that there is no suggestion anywhere that this revelation of something that was only hinted at in the Old Testament but made explicit in the preaching of the apostles, this revelation of the Gentile inclusion, was ever made to any 'prophets' in New Testament churches. The references are all on one side of the question, and they all point to this major item of revelation in the history of redemption as coming to the *apostles* and to others only through them.

(3) A third reason why Ephesians 2:20 and 3:5 do not seem to be referring to New Testament apostles and New Testament prophets (two groups) is that the metaphor of a *foundation* gives a picture of something that is complete, something that will not be added on to, after the rest of the building is begun. Now if this 'foundation' equals the New Testament apostles only, then the metaphor fits well: the apostles were a distinct, limited group who had seen the risen Lord Jesus and had been commissioned by him in the special role of 'Apostle of Jesus Christ'.

But if the foundation consists of apostles plus all those who had the gift of prophecy in all the New Testament churches in the entire Mediterranean world, then it would have to be a 'foundation' that is continually being changed and added on to. As Paul and others preached the gospel throughout the Roman world, more and more people were becoming Christians, and in every congregation there apparently were those with the gift of prophecy. Thus this 'foundation' would have more and more elements added to it as people became Christians and received spiritual gifts. Moreover, as people obeyed Paul's directions like the one in 1 Corinthians 14:1 (RSV), 'Earnestly desire the spiritual gifts, especially that you may prophesy,' people who were not part of the 'foundation' of the church would desire and pray for the gift of prophecy, and some would receive that gift. Then they would be added to the 'foundation' of the church. But all this is quite inconsistent with the metaphor of a 'foundation' which gives a picture of something that is completed before the rest of the building is begun.

(4) Related to the reason given above is another factor which suggests that the readers of Ephesians would not think of ordinary congregational prophets as part of this foundation. We note that Paul is speaking in Ephesians 2 and 3 not of one local

congregation, but of the church universal. It is that church in which all Gentile believers are 'no longer strangers and sojourners', but 'fellow citizens with the saints and members of the household of God' (Eph 2:19, RSV). It is that church in which Christ Jesus himself is the cornerstone, and in which the 'apostles and prophets' are the 'foundation'.

But the ordinary readers of Paul's epistle in the church at Ephesus, and in surrounding local churches which also read Ephesians, would not think of the men and women (and perhaps even children) who were their friends and neighbours and who had the gift of prophecy in their local churches, as part of the 'foundation' of the universal church, on a level of importance with Peter, Paul, and the other apostles.

(5) A fifth difficulty with this understanding of 'apostles and prophets' has to do with Paul's purpose in this section. His goal is to prove that Jews and Gentiles are equal members in Christ's church. To do this he shows that both Jewish and Gentile believers are part of this metaphorical 'building' which represents the church.

But if all New Testament prophets were part of the 'foundation' of the church, then there were certainly *Gentile* prophets in that foundation, for certainly many Gentile believers received the gift of prophecy in local churches. But if that was so, then it is hard to understand why Paul would not emphasize that fact to prove the equality of Jews and Gentiles in the church. He could well have said, 'Some of you are even part of the *foundation* of the church! And you are Gentiles!' This would have been a very strong argument for him, but he completely fails to use it—suggesting that he did not think of Gentile Christians with the gift of prophecy in local churches as part of this 'foundation'.

(6) There are other passages in the New Testament which explicitly talk about ordinary prophets in local congregations, passages such as 1 Corinthians 12—14, 1 Thessalonians 5:20–21 and several passages in Acts. These other passages describing the New Testament gift of prophecy give strong evidence

that ordinary congregational prophets did *not* carry out activities or possess authority which would give them such a 'foundational' role in the church. And while Ephesians 2:20 and 3:5 are certainly open to dispute about whether they refer to ordinary congregational prophets or not, many of these other passages are not at all ambiguous: they are clearly and explicitly talking about the gift of prophecy as it functioned in local congregations.

It would seem to be an appropriate method of investigation, then, to allow passages which clearly and explicitly discuss ordinary congregational prophecy (such as 1 Corinthians 12—14) to influence our understanding of whether or not a less explicit passage (such as Ephesians 2:20 or 3:5) is in fact describing ordinary congregational prophecy or not.

(7) A final objection to the view which understands Ephesians 2:20 and 3:5 to refer to New Testament apostles and New Testament prophets as two separate groups, is an unanswered question: Where are all these prophets? If there indeed was such an important group as this position suggests, a group of 'prophets' *who were not also apostles* but who spoke God's very words with absolute divine authority, and were part of the 'foundation' of the church universal, then would we not expect to find some record of them in the pages of the New Testament? But there is no such record.

To my knowledge, nowhere in the New Testament is there a record of a prophet who is not an apostle but who spoke with absolute divine authority attaching to his very words. And we have no books of the New Testament written by anyone who claims to be a 'prophet' but not an apostle as well. Moreover, in the first 150 years of the church, there is (to my knowledge) no record of any divinely authoritative word spoken by these prophets. We have no collections of 'words of the prophets at Corinth', or 'words of the prophets at Thessalonica', or 'words of the prophets at Ephesus', or at Tyre, or at Caesarea, etc. Yet if all these prophets were speaking the very words of God, is it not reasonable to suppose that many of these words would have been recorded and preserved for us as Scripture? If such words were indeed equal to Scripture in authority, then why were they not preserved by the early Christians? And why is there no indication that any churches *tried* to preserve them?

Thus, if we assume that there was a group of non-apostolic 'prophets' who nevertheless had authority equal to the Old Testament prophets, we encounter a major difficulty: We are put in a position of advocating the existence of a highly significant group which has left no record, no trace of itself in the pages of the New Testament or the writings of the first few generations of Christians. We begin to wonder if there ever was such a group at all, a group of New Testament prophets who were not apostles but who also spoke with the absolute divine authority of Old Testament prophets. And it makes us wonder if there isn't a better understanding of Ephesians 2:20 and 3:5 than to say it refers to two separate groups, New Testament apostles and New Testament prophets, both of whom were 'foundational' in the church.

(d) *View 4: the foundation = apostle-prophets (one group).* This fourth and final interpretation of Ephesians 2:20 and 3:5 suggests that there are not two groups in view (New Testament apostles and New Testament prophets), but only one group (New Testament apostle-prophets, or 'apostles who are also prophets').

There are several reasons why such an understanding of the passage seems persuasive.

(1) First, this interpretation is certainly possible in terms of Greek grammar (see discussion above). Moreover, it is consistent with Paul's grammatical usage in Ephesians 4:11 where he uses the same construction to speak of 'pastor-teachers'.

(2) This interpretation best fits the historical data mentioned above, data which showed that it was to the apostles only, not to any prophets also, that God revealed the truth of the Gentile inclusion in a new and full way in the New Covenant age. Thus Paul can rightly say:

When you read this you can perceive my insight into the mystery of

> Christ, which was not made known to the sons of men in other gen-
> erations as it has now been revealed to his holy *apostles who are
> also prophets* by the Spirit; that is, how the Gentiles are fellow
> heirs... (Eph 3:4–6, RSV).

(3) To understand the apostles alone as the 'foundation' of
the New Testament church is consistent with another New Testament picture of a 'foundation', a picture which clearly
emphasizes the unique foundational role of the apostles alone,
not of the apostles and some other group of prophets. That picture is found in the vision of the heavenly city which was given
to the Apostle John in Revelation 21:14 (RSV): 'And the wall of
the city had twelve foundations, and on them the twelve names
of the twelve apostles of the Lamb.'[12]

(4) Such a designation of the apostles as 'also prophets'
would be appropriate for Paul's argument here. He would be
showing that the fact of Gentile inclusion was not revealed
simply to some minor or insignificant Christians in some far off
province, but was revealed specifically to those who were *foundational* in the church, the apostles themselves. And it was in
their role as 'prophets', that is, as the recipients of revelation
from God, that this inclusion of the Gentiles was revealed to
them.

So the Gentiles can be certain of their equality in the church
because those who are 'the apostles', the divinely authoritative
proclaimers of the true gospel, are 'also prophets', or the recipients of new directions from the Holy Spirit and especially of
directions about the inclusion of the Gentiles. Thus, the full
inclusion of the Gentiles is not some weakly-based idea; rather,
it is a central concept which was first made known to and is now
endorsed by the principal members and leaders of the church.[13]

In response to this interpretation ('the apostles who are also
prophets'), Dr Gaffin says the following:

> This is possible grammatically and the apostles do exercise prophe-
> tic functions (e.g. Rom 11:25ff.; 1 Cor 15:51ff.; 1 Thess 4:15ff.; cf.
> 1 Cor 14:6). Probably there is nothing that absolutely excludes this

view. A combination of considerations, however, is decisively against it.[14]

He then lists four objections to this view:

(1) In Ephesians 4:11, apostles and prophets are clearly distinguished, and this is in the same larger context as Ephesians 2:20 and 3:5.

(2) Apostles and prophets are also distinguished in 1 Corinthians 12:28.

(3) Apostles as a group are never called 'prophets' or 'teachers' or by any other terms which distinguish ministries in the New Testament.

(4) Therefore this different sense of 'prophet' would have been lost on the readers without further indication in the context.[15]

We can now respond to these four objections in order.

(1) It must be admitted that Paul is using the word 'prophets' in Ephesians 4:11 to refer to those who had the gift of prophecy in local congregations. Thus he is using it to refer to different people then in 2:20 and 3:5.

But Paul makes this difference quite clear in the grammatical constructions he uses. In Ephesians 4:11 he puts the definite article 'the' before the word 'apostles', and then uses it again before the word 'prophets'. In doing this, he clearly shows that two different groups are in mind.

In fact, he makes it more explicit than that by two more Greek words that are often untranslated but that mean 'on the one hand ... on the other hand'. Quite literally we could translate Ephesians 4:11: 'And he gave *on the one hand the* apostles, *on the other hand the* prophets, *on the other hand the* evangelists, *on the other hand the* pastors and teachers....'

So here the apostles are placed in a separate group, and are clearly distinguished from the prophets, evangelists, and pastor-teachers.

A similar case is found in 1 Peter 5:1 (RSV), where Peter says: 'So I exhort the elders among you, as a fellow-elder and a witness of the sufferings of Christ....' Here Peter uses the word 'elders' to refer to church officers who are not apostles but merely members of local congregations. Then in the same sentence he uses the word 'fellow-elder' to refer to himself as an apostle, not to all elders generally. But the context makes this clear.[16]

Similarly, in 1 Timothy 2:7 Paul calls himself a 'teacher' but later in the epistle talks about teaching functions which are to be performed by elders (1 Tim 3:2; 5:17) and earlier had talked about people who desire to be teachers of the law (a compound word is used here). And in 2 Timothy 1:11 he calls himself a 'teacher' but later it talks about people accumulating for themselves 'teachers to suit their own likings' (2 Tim 4:3, RSV). In all these cases the context makes it clear that words like 'elder', 'teacher', and 'prophet' are used in different ways in different contexts, and the differences are made clear by the context and the exact wording used in each case.

(2) I of course agree that 1 Corinthians 12:28 distinguishes apostles from prophets—but that does not mean the words have to be used of different groups every time they are used in the New Testament. One example of the use of a word does not prove that it must have the same sense in other examples, and here the issue is the meaning of the word in Ephesians 2:20 and 3:5.

(3) The fact that apostles 'as a group' are not elsewhere called by a certain name is not decisive for the meaning of Ephesians 2:20 and 3:5, for there are many examples in the New Testament where a particular term is applied to people in the singular but not in the plural, or only once or twice in the plural. Paul was a 'preacher' of the gospel, and it would have been appropriate to call the apostles 'preachers' of the gospel, but the New Testament never happens to do so. Paul was a 'teacher' and the apostles appropriately could have been called 'teachers' but in fact are not. So the apostles had prophetic functions, but are only twice actually called by the plural term 'prophets' (or, more accurately, 'apostle-prophets') in the New Testament. Many things said in the New Testament are said only once or twice, and to require that they be said in a certain

way *more than twice* before we will accept it seems an unreasonable requirement.

(Note that elders are apparently called 'pastors' only once in the New Testament [Eph 4:11], but many people still think that Ephesians 4:11 is talking about elders. Moreover, the apostles are elsewhere called by the plural terms 'disciples' [frequently in the gospels] and 'witnesses' [Acts 2:32].)

Therefore, if the apostles performed prophetic functions (as Dr Gaffin agrees), and if Paul the apostle could talk about bringing a 'prophecy' to Corinth, and if the Apostle John calls his writing a 'prophecy' (Rev 1:3; 22:7), there is no inherent reason why the apostles could not be called 'prophets' twice in Ephesians 2:20 and 3:5, provided that the grammar and context favour this interpretation.

(4) Would the readers have understood this? I have given several reasons above why both the grammar and the subject matter give clear indications to the readers, signalling them that Paul was speaking about 'the apostle-prophets' in these verses.

At this point one further objection to view 4 remains. It is in addition to the ones brought up by Dr Gaffin, yet it is perhaps the most significant factor causing hesitation in modern readers' minds over this view. That objection, or perhaps obstacle, is the fact that our English translations generally read 'apostles and prophets', and in such a construction the English word 'and' seems so clearly to imply two separate groups, the apostles and the prophets. This is not really an objection based on the meaning of the Greek text, but it does highlight the difficulty that many English readers have in understanding the verse to mean 'the apostles who are also prophets' (one group of people).

The response to this objection is simply to notice how often Paul and other New Testament writers use this same construction to refer to one person or group of people. Grammatically there is really nothing which would require a first-century, Greek-speaking reader of Ephesians to think that Paul had two groups in mind.

So it seems best to conclude that Ephesians 2:20 means that the church is 'built upon the foundation of the apostles who are also prophets', and Ephesians 3:5 should be understood to mean that the mystery of the Gentile inclusion in the church 'was not made known to the sons of men in other generations as it has now been revealed to his holy apostles who are also prophets by the Spirit'.

(e) *What if someone nonetheless sees two groups in Ephesians 2:20 and 3:5?* Finally, one further point must be made. Even if someone were not persuaded by the argument above, and found view 3 more persuasive, namely, that these verses refer to two groups of people, 'New Testament apostles', and 'New Testament prophets,' it would not be necessary to conclude that these verses referred to *all* New Testament prophets. Indeed, it would be very difficult to argue that such a brief reference to 'prophets' as we have in these two verses described all those who have the gift of prophecy in every New Testament congregation, especially if many other New Testament passages indicated prophets functioning in a 'non-foundational' role in local churches.[17]

Therefore, even if a reader did prefer, for example, view 3, it should not significantly affect the argument of the rest of this book. That is because I would simply respond that, if Ephesians 2:20 and 3:5 talk about two distinct groups, apostles and prophets, then the 'prophets' mentioned here would be those who share authority similar to the apostles—and they would therefore be *unlike* the ordinary prophets scattered throughout many early Christian congregations who are described in much more detail in other parts of the New Testament. It must be said that Dr Gaffin gives much attention to Ephesians 2:20, and *says* that it describes *all* the prophets in all New Testament churches, but he gives very little analysis to the actual data in the rest of the New Testament in order to demonstrate that this is true—that prophecy in these other contexts is in fact fulfilling the same 'foundational' role. (He devotes only two pages [60–61], for example, to the question of the authority of prophecy in 1 Corinthians 14.)

For our purposes in this study, those ordinary Christian prophets who use the gift of prophecy in regular congregational meetings are much more relevant than this special group of 'prophets' (or 'apostle-prophets') in Ephesians 2:20 and 3:5 to whom the great fact of the Gentile inclusion was revealed. And it is to a study of these prophets in ordinary Christian congregations that we turn in the following chapter.

Are there then two kinds of prophecy?

If I argue, as I do in this book, that the apostles could 'prophesy' with absolute divine authority, but that ordinary congregational prophets did not have that kind of authority, am I then saying that there are two kinds of prophecy in the New Testament? Someone could make that distinction, and in fact I did speak that way in an earlier, more technical book on this subject, in keeping with terminology that had been used in previous scholarly discussions of prophecy.[18]

However, I have decided in this book not to speak of 'two kinds of prophecy' in the New Testament, because such language can be misunderstood to imply that the 'kinds' of prophecy were different in *many* ways, with large differences in the prophet's own experience, etc. But the New Testament does not support such differences (and I did not affirm them in the earlier book).

The distinction I attempted to make in the earlier book, and am attempting to make here as well, is only at one point: the type of authority which attaches to the words spoken in a prophecy. When the prophecy is spoken (or written) by an apostle, then the words have unique authority—absolute divine authority (as I argued earlier in this chapter). To disbelieve or disobey a prophecy spoken by an *apostle* is to disbelieve or disobey God. That is why the apostles' words can be written down and included in Scripture—they have the authority of Scripture. But such absolute authority simply does not apply to the words of ordinary prophets in local New Testament congre-

gations (as we shall see in the next chapters). Their prophesying is 'different' in this sense.

But this is not surprising. This is the same thing that happens,
for example, with 'teaching' and 'preaching'. The teaching and
preaching of the *apostles* has absolute divine authority, but we
do not ususaly say that there were 'two kinds of teaching' in the
New Testament, or 'two kinds of preaching'. If we want to say
that to emphasize the difference in authority between the apostles and everyone else, it would not be wrong. But usually such
language would be misleading because it would tend to
emphasize the differences and minimize the similarities
between apostolic preaching and teaching and all other preaching and teaching in the New Testament churches.

So in this book I have not used the terminology 'two kinds of
prophecy'. I have simply spoken about prophecy as it was carried out by the apostles, and then 'ordinary congregational
prophecy' as it occurred in many local Christian congregations.
Prophecy by the apostles was different not exactly in 'kind' (or
in many ways), but only in authority. Prophecy by all other
Christians in local churches was 'ordinary' and 'usual', and it is
the primary concern of this book.

Application for today

Once we realize that the New Testament apostles are the counterpart to the Old Testament prophets, then we ought to apply
that realization to our lives by giving close attention to the writings of those 'apostles of Jesus Christ'. Specifically, we should
read the writings of the New Testament as God's very words,
still living and powerful to speak to our hearts today with the
authority of God himself. No other words spoken today can
ever equal the words of Scripture itself in authority, in purity,
or in power.

In our daily lives, it is the words of Scripture alone that must
have first place in our hearts and our minds. We must read
them, believe them, memorize them, love them and cherish

them as the very words of our Creator speaking to us. All other gifts and teachings today are to be subject to the words of Scripture and are to be judged by them. No other gift or teaching or writing should be allowed to compete with them for absolute priority in our lives.

3

New Testament Prophets at Corinth:

Speaking Merely Human Words to Report Something God Brings to Mind

The structure of 1 Corinthians 12—14

Before we look in detail at Paul's discussion of the gift of prophecy in 1 Corinthians, it will be helpful to gain an overview of the teaching and the structure of 1 Corinthians 12—14.

Among the many problems Paul was forced to deal with at Corinth were the problems of pride on the part of those who had noticeable spiritual gifts (1 Cor 1:31; 4:7; 5:6; 8:1; 10:12; 11:21ff.; 13:4–5) and resultant jealousy or feelings of unimportance on the part of those who were less noticeably gifted (1 Cor 3:3; 10:10; 12:14–26; 13:4). Paul deals with both problems at once in 1 Corinthians 12:28 (RSV) when he says, 'And God has appointed in the church first apostles, second prophets, third teachers, then workers of miracles, then healers, helpers, administrators, speakers in various kinds of tongues.'

On the one hand, by pointing out that such ministries are *from God*, he reminds the Corinthians that they should not be proud but *humble* (note 1 Corinthians 4:7 (RSV): 'What have you that you did not receive? If then you received it, why do you boast as if it were not a gift?').

On the other hand, since God has *distributed* gifts as he thought best (note 1 Corinthians 12:11, 18, 28), the Corinthians should neither be jealous of one another nor grumble about God's decisions, but should be content. Furthermore, since *each* believer had been given some kind of gift (1 Corinthians 12:6, 7, 11), and since *every* gift is needed (1 Corinthians 12:7,

15, 17, 21, 23, 26), no one need feel unimportant.

Yet in solving these problems Paul might have created another one if he had stopped there. The Corinthians might have become fatalistic through an unbalanced emphasis on God's sovereignty in the distribution of gifts. They might have made no further progress towards attaining those gifts which would most help the church. So Paul adds a corrective command: *although* God has placed gifts in the church as he wanted (1 Cor 12. 28–30), you should *nevertheless continue to seek* the greater gifts (1 Cor 12:31).

However, even the greater gifts could be misused if the Corinthians had wrong attitudes. So Paul goes on to something even better than seeking the greater gifts ('a still more excellent way,' 1 Cor 12: 31b, RSV), namely, using the gifts they had or wanted in love (1 Cor 13:1–13).

And how does that work out in practice? In the use of gifts, following the way of love means this: speak in an intelligible and orderly way so that the church might be built up (1 Cor 14:1–35).

So the structure of these chapters in very brief summary is this:

1. It is good to use the different gifts God has given all of you (1 Cor 12:1–31).

2. It is even better to use the gifts you have or seek in love (1 Cor 13:1–13).

3. Using gifts in love means speaking in an intelligible and orderly way (1 Cor 14:1–40).

This structural understanding of 1 Corinthians 12—14 can help us understand what Paul means by 'greater' gifts in 1 Corinthians 12:31, and what he means by 'first ... second ... third ...' in 1 Corinthians 12:28.

In 1 Corinthians 12:28, the kind of ranking implied by Paul's 'first ... second ... third ... then ...' is certainly not chronological, for tongues are last here but came at the very beginning of the church (Acts 2:4).

Is it a ranking of 'dignity' or 'spiritual eminence'? This is unlikely, since Paul is trying to combat spiritual pride, and rather than claiming dignity for himself sees the apostles as exhibited 'last of all . . .a spectacle to the world, to angels, and to men' (1 Cor 4:9, RSV).

The correct answer is partly provided by 1 Corinthians 12:31a. Paul's readers would most naturally assume that the 'greater (Greek *meizōn*) gifts' are those which Paul has just finished ranking 'first, second, third'. Paul's thought is then made explicit in 1 Corinthians 14:5b (RSV), where in a probably intentional use of the same word, he says that 'he who prophesies is greater' (again, Greek *meizōn*) because through him the church is edified.

Thus, greatness in this context measures usefulness to the church. So in 1 Corinthians 12:28, apostles are first because they are most useful in building up the church. Prophets are second and teachers are third, because they also contribute greatly to the church's edification. This interpretation fits with Paul's overall purpose of encouraging gifts and attitudes which build up the church (note this emphasis at crucial summary points: 1 Corinthians 12:7, 25–26; 14:5b, 12, 26b).

Even though some of the details presuppose later conclusions from this study, it is helpful here to put in some of the transition statements and once again summarize all of 1 Corinthians 12—14:

Concerning spiritual gifts (12:1):

(1) you *all* have useful gifts (12:2–30), and it is *good* to seek the greater gifts (12:31a).

(2) But it is *even better* (12:31b) to use the gifts you have or want in love (13:1–13), that is, speaking intelligibly and worshipping in an orderly way so that the church may be built up (14:1–36).

(3) You must obey my words, for they are the Lord's command (14:37–38).

(4) Now to summarize: 'With regard to the specific matters of prophecy and tongues, desire prophecy, don't forbid tongues, but do all in order' (14:39–40).

So 1 Corinthians 14.29–33a is, on this understanding of chapters 12—14, part of a larger section of the epistle (1 Cor 14:1–36), in which Paul is giving instructions to the Corinthians on how to conduct themselves in a worship service. Verse 29 onwards expresses Paul's views about the proper use of the gift of prophecy in particular.

1 Corinthians 14:29: Prophecies which need to be sifted

Paul says, 'Let two or three prophets speak, and let the others weigh what is said' (1 Cor 14:29, RSV).

The first question to be decided is, who are 'the others' whom Paul commands to do this evaluation of what the prophet said?

Are 'the others' those with the gift of 'distinguishing between spirits' in 1 Corinthians 12:10?

Some, though not many, New Testament commentators claim that 'the others' mentioned here are those with the gift of 'distinguishing between spirits' in 1 Corinthians 12:10. The major reason in favour of this view is the similarity between the noun 'evaluation, discrimination, distinguishing' (Greek *diakrisis*) in 1 Corinthians 12:10 and the verb 'evaluate, weigh, discern' (Greek *diakrinō*) in 1 Corinthians 14:29.

But it must be noted that both the noun and the verb have a wide range of meaning. It is not at all unlikely that Paul would have used *diakrisis* in 1 Corinthians 12:10 to mean 'distinguishing' (among different kinds of spirits) while using *diakrinō* in 1 Corinthians 14:29 to mean something quite different, such as 'evaluate' or 'judge' (prophetic utterances). In fact, in 1 Corinthians alone Paul uses the verb *diakrinō* in several senses.[19]

In view of this wide range of Pauline meaning, it would be overly bold to assume that the noun in 1 Corinthians 12.10 must have the same sense as the verb in 14:29, *and* must refer to the same activity or gift.[20]

Moreover, it is not legitimate simply to suppose that 1

Corinthians 12:10 is restricted to the testing of prophets and prophecies. Bittlinger, for instance, suggests as examples of 'distinguishing between spirits' some of the exorcisms of Jesus where he knew there was a demon present, and the cases of Elymas (Acts 13:8ff.) and the soothsaying girl (Acts 16:16–18).[21] And Robertson and Plummer define the ability as, 'The gift of discerning in various cases (hence the plural) whether extraordinary spiritual manifestations were from above or not.'[22]

If we resist the temptation to read into the text a limitation to the specific testing of prophecies, then a more general definition, like the one just mentioned by Robertson and Plummer, is in order. Something like 'the ability to recognize the influence of the Holy Spirit or of demonic spirits in a person' is more appropriate.

This means that any situation in which first century Christians would have seen demonic influence was a potential opportunity for the use of the gift of distinguishing between spirits. Was some sickness the result of demonic influence (cf. Mt 12:22; Mt 9:32–34)? Then the person with this gift could recognize it and the demon could be cast out. Was an evil spirit causing someone to interrupt preaching or teaching or worship services (cf. Acts 16:16–18)? Then the person with this gift could recognize the source of the trouble. Was someone prophesying by the power of an evil spirit (1 Jn 4:1–6)? Then the person with this gift could call attention to it. Since Paul mentions that demons were involved in pagan worship in Corinth (cf. 1 Cor 10:20ff.), one can imagine a large number of cases where this gift would have been thought useful.

But if 1 Corinthians 12:10 is understood in this way, then 'the others' in 1 Corinthians 14:29 need not be restricted to those who possess the gift of distinguishing between spirits. For that gift would include a much broader range of activity than simply judging prophets.

Furthermore, if Paul had meant to restrict his instructions in 1 Corinthians 14:29 to those with this gift, he would not have used such a general term as 'the others' and left it without further specification. He would have had to say something like, 'those with the gift of distinguishing between spirits' if he had wanted to convey this meaning to his readers.

Are 'the others' in 1 Corinthians 14:29 the other prophets?

A more common view of 1 Corinthians 14:29 is that when Paul said, 'Let the others weigh what is said,' he meant, 'Let *the other prophets* weigh what is said.'

Those who hold this view also usually appeal to 1 Corinthians 12:10, where it is clear that only some, not all Christians, had the gift of distinguishing between spirits. But then those who hold this view make two unwarranted assumptions:

(a) that the limited group possessing the gift of 'distinguishing between spirits' includes mostly prophets; and

(b) that this gift of 'distinguishing between spirits' is used in the 'evaluation' of prophecies in 1 Corinthians 14:29.

The problem with this is that in 1 Corinthians 12:10, Paul makes a clear distinction between one who has the gift of prophecy and one who has the gift of distinguishing between spirits ('to another' 1 Corinthians 12:10). He certainly does not say that all prophets had the gift of distinguishing between spirits.

And several other considerations make it very unlikely that 'the others' in 1 Corinthians 14:29 means 'the other prophets':

(a) In other places where judging congregational speech is discussed, it seems that all the congregation is involved. 1 Corinthians 12:3 gives a test anyone could apply: is the speaker saying, 'Jesus be cursed'? Then he is not speaking by the Holy Spirit. Does the speaker make a credible confession of faith that Jesus is Lord? Then he is speaking by the Holy Spirit.

Similarly, 1 Thessalonians 5:20–21 (RSV) is addressed to a whole church: 'Do not despise prophesying, but test everything; hold fast what is good.' And similar evaluations by whole churches are implied in 1 John 4:1–6 and Acts 17:11.

Now this does not mean that all would play an equal role in

the public evaluation of what was said. We would expect the mature (cf. Heb 5:14), the wise (cf. 1 Cor 6:5), those perhaps with the gift of distinguishing between spirits (1 Cor 12:10) to speak more often and with more authority. But nowhere do we find judging limited to those with one particular office or gift.

(b) If Paul had meant to say, 'Let the rest of the prophets weigh what is said,' he would probably have used words other than 'the others'. Godet rightly points out that words meaning 'the rest of the prophets' (Greek *hoi loipoi*) would have been most appropriate if this had been Paul's meaning.[23]

(c) If we understand 'the others' to be restricted to a special group of prophets, we have much difficulty picturing what the rest of the congregation would do during the prophecy and the judging. Would they sit 'neutrally', waiting for the prophecy to end and be judged before knowing whether to believe any of it? This can hardly be true. They would sit and immediately evaluate in their own minds what was being said.

But this mental process of evaluation would be well described by Paul's expression 'weigh what is said'. Therefore it is difficult to exclude anyone from what Paul says in 1 Corinthians 14:29 about evaluating prophecies. Especially hard to believe is the idea that teachers, administrators and other church leaders who did *not* have special gifts of prophecy would sit passively awaiting the verdict of an elite group before they knew whether to accept a prophecy as genuine. Much to be preferred is the view which pictures such leaders as taking a prominent role in the judging of prophecies.

Conclusion: 'the others' refers to the entire congregation

The preceding arguments have shown several serious difficulties in attempting to make 'the others' refer to any special or limited group of Christians. These arguments give good reason for letting the phrase have reference to the whole church.[24]

As a prophet was speaking, each member of the congregation would listen carefully, evaluating the prophecy in the light of the Scripture and the authoritative teaching which he or she already knew to be true. Soon there would be an opportunity to speak in the response, with the wise and mature no doubt making the most contribution. But no member of the body would have needed to feel useless (cf. 1 Cor 12:22), for every member at least silently would weigh and evaluate what was said.

How is the prophecy judged?

The next major question to be decided in 1 Corinthians 14:29 (RSV) is: What kind of evaluation or judging does Paul imply when he says, 'Let two or three prophets speak, and let the others *weigh what is said*'?

An examination of this statement will show that Paul had in mind the kind of evaluation whereby each person would 'weigh what is said' in his own mind, accepting some of the prophecy as good and helpful and rejecting some of it as erroneous or misleading. This is evident both from the general context and from the sense which attaches to the Greek word Paul uses, the word *diakrinō*.

(a) *The argument from context.* At first one might suppose that 'let the others weigh what is said' meant that the others were to judge whether the speaker was a true or false prophet. This would fit the picture given in an early Christian writing (of unknown authorship) called the *Didache*, for instance, where criteria are given by which the congregation could decide whether a prophet who came was true or false (*Didache* 11:3–12). Similarly, Matthew has a warning about false prophets 'who come to you in sheep's clothing but inwardly are ravenous wolves': these will be known by their fruits (Mt 7:15–20, RSV; cf. Mt 24:11, 24). 1 John 4:1–6 also has a warning about false prophets and a test for distinguishing them.

Yet on closer inspection it turns out that 1 Corinthians 14:29 is unlike these other passages. The other passages give warnings of strangers coming to the church *from outside* (Mt 7:15; 1 Jn 4:1, 3; note also *Didache* 11:5, 6) and provide criteria by which they could be tested. But in 1 Corinthians 14, Paul is talking about a meeting of those who are already accepted in the fellowship of the church ('when you come together' v. 26, RSV; 'earnestly desire to prophesy' v. 39, RSV).

When Paul says, 'Let two or three prophets speak,' he certainly does not mean that at every worship service there would be two or three more prophets newly arrived at Corinth, waiting their turn to be tested and (so they hoped) approved by the congregation. Rather, the picture is one of several prophets who are known and accepted by the congregation, each speaking in turn. In such a case, it would be very unlikely that they would be 'judged' and declared 'true' prophets again and again, every time they spoke, month after month.

A better parallel to 1 Corinthians 14:29 than Matthew 7, 1 John 4 or *Didache* 11 could be found in another Pauline passage, 1 Thessalonians 5:19–21. There it is the *prophecies* (v. 20) that are evaluated or judged, not the prophets. This Pauline passage is much closer to 1 Corinthians 14:29 than the other non-Pauline passages, which may be speaking to situations which are quite dissimilar. In fact, in both 1 Thessalonians 5:19–21 and 1 Corinthians 14:29ff. there is an absence of any warning about false prophets, a lack of any criteria for judging them and an absence of any hint of strangers coming from outside and pretending to be prophets. While the other passages speak of tests to reveal false prophets, 1 Corinthians 14:29 and 1 Thessalonians 5:19–21 speak rather of a different sort of evaluation, the *evaluation of the actual prophecies* of those who are already accepted by the congregation.

Finally, the idea that the prophet would be judged 'true' or 'false' simply does not fit with the picture which Paul gives of a congregational meeting. The only way an entire congregation could pass judgement and make a declaration of 'true' or 'false' would be by some kind of vote, a complex process indeed. On such an important matter, no doubt several members would wish to express their opinions. In Matthew 7 and *Didache* 11 the judging would take several days of watching and evaluating a prophet, and perhaps longer. Yet Paul's 'and let the others weigh what is said' seems to indicate an activity which would take place during the meeting while the prophets are speaking, or just when they finish (cf. 1 Cor 14:27, on tongues and interpretation). In fact, the prophets can speak so closely in succession that one could interrupt another (1 Cor 14:30).

In conclusion, the *context* of 1 Corinthians 14:29 indicates that the members of the congregation would all listen to the prophet's *speech* and evaluate it in some way, but they would not judge the prophet *himself* to be 'true' or 'false'.

(b) *The meaning of the word diakrinō.* Paul's use of the Greek word *diakrinō* helps us to define more precisely the kind of evaluation which could be done. Although the word has quite a wide range of meanings, it very frequently carries a sense of separating, distinguishing, or making careful distinctions among related things or ideas.

This word can be used, for instance, of sifting wheat (Philo, *Mut.* 249, *Jos.* 113), of distinguishing clean from unclean animals (Josephus, *Ant.* 259), or of separating persons who were guilty of wrongdoing from the rest of the crowd (Josephus, *Wars* 4.118, 543). It is used of distinguishing good from evil (*Testament of Asher* 1.5; compare the cognate noun used in the same way in Hebrews 5:14), and of sorting true words from false (Philo, *Congr*, 18; cf. Job 12:11: 'for the ear tests words').

In the New Testament, *diakrinō* can be used of distinguishing between Jewish and Gentile believers (Acts 15:9; probably also Acts 11:12). Paul says in 1 Corinthians 4:7, 'Who *distinguishes* you?' (from other people and thereby regards you as more important). Then in 1 Corinthians 11:31 we read, 'If we (correctly) *evaluated* ourselves, we should not be judged.' The idea is one of conscientiously weighing one's own attitudes and actions, carefully sorting and evaluating them, and determining which are right and which are not.

This sense of 'making distinctions' or 'carefully evaluating' would make *diakrinō* an appropriate word in 1 Corinthians 14:29—appropriate, that is, *if* Paul had meant to speak of a process whereby every member of the congregation would listen carefully and evaluate each statement, distinguishing what he or she felt to be good from the less good, what was thought to be helpful from the unhelpful, what was perceived to be true from the false.[25]

Furthermore, if Paul had meant that the Corinthians were to judge whether each speaker was a true or false prophet, he probably would have used some other word, not *diakrinō* but probably *krinō*. This is the term the New Testament prefers when speaking of judgements where there are only two possibilities, such as 'guilty' or 'not guilty', 'right' or 'wrong', or 'true' or 'false' (cf. Mt 7:1; 19:28; Jn 7:51; 18:31; Acts 16:15; 25:10; Rom 2:1; 14:3; 4, 10, 13; 1 Cor 4:5; 5:3, 12; 6:1, 2, 3, 6; 10:15; 11:13; Col 2:16; Heb 10:30; 13:4; Jas 4:11; etc). In fact, in 1 Corinthians 6:2–6, Paul may consciously be distinguishing formal legal judgements outside the church (for which he uses *krinō*) from more informal decisions inside the church (for which he uses *diakrinō*). Within the church, it is less likely that one party will be declared 'guilty' or the other 'not guilty' and more likely that a careful evaluation will find some fault on both sides.

Whether this weighing and evaluating would be completely silent or whether some members of the congregation would respond orally cannot be determined from the term *diakrinō* alone. The emphasis of the verb is on the deliberative process itself, not on what results from that mental deliberation. However, spoken responses to prophecies by leaders in the congregation no doubt would have been appropriate, at least sometimes, and would certainly have contributed to the process of 'edification' which Paul sets as the goal (1 Cor 14:26) for congregational worship.

By what standards would such 'weighing' of the prophecies be made? Elsewhere in the New Testament, the criterion for evaluation of public speech in the churches seems always to have been conformity to Scripture or received teaching (Gal 1:8; 1 Cor 14:37–38; 1 Jn 4:2–3, 6; Acts 17:11), and we may expect that that would be the standard used here as well.

Before concluding this discussion about the evaluation of

prophecies, a word should be said about false prophets. While Paul is talking in 1 Corinthians 14:29 about the evaluation of true prophets (genuine Christian believers speaking under the influence of the Holy Spirit), nevertheless, the possibility of false prophets coming and speaking under the influence of some demonic spirit certainly existed (cf. 1 Jn 4:1, 3). Though Paul did not discuss such a possibility explicitly in 1 Corinthians, it is fair to conclude from what Paul does say that he no doubt expected that false prophets would have been detected by those with the ability to distinguish between spirits (1 Cor 12:10), and they would have betrayed themselves by their blatantly aberrant doctrine (1 Cor 12:3; 1 Jn 4:2–3).

(c) *Conclusion*. Taking into consideration both the context of 1 Corinthians 14:29 and the sense usually attached to the Greek term *diakrinō*, we can conclude that 1 Corinthians 14:29 indicates that the whole congregation would listen and evaluate what was said by the prophet, forming opinions about it, and some would perhaps discuss it publicly. Each prophecy might have both true and false elements in it, and those would be sifted and evaluated for what they were. The Revised Standard Version translation captures this process well: 'Let two or three prophets speak, and let the others weigh what is said.'

It is interesting to compare this process with the judging of prophets found in the Old Testament. There, a false prophet was to die (Deut 18:20). In order to qualify as a false prophet, one only needed to claim to be speaking for God and then to speak something which God had not commanded (Deut 18:20; cf. Jer 23:16). In Deuteronomy 18:22, one false prediction would mean that the prophet had spoken 'presumptuously'; his word was something the Lord had not spoken. So he would die for speaking falsely in the name of the Lord and thereby misrepresenting the Lord.

It was probably because the Old Testament prophet was in a position of speaking with God's absolute authority, that the penalty was so severe. The prophet was to be speaking God's words ('I will put my words in his mouth' Deut 18:18, RSV; 'my words which he shall speak in my name' Deut 18:19, RSV). To disobey the words of a true prophet would bring punishment from God (Deut 18:19). Since such a prophet would have exercised tremendous authority, it was important to safeguard the prophetic office with stiff penalties for impostors.

There is no such picture in 1 Corinthians. Rather, as we have seen, the congregation would simply evaluate the prophecy and form opinions about it. Some of it might be very valuable and some of it not. Now this process is understandable only if there is a difference in the kind of speech envisioned by the Old Testament and that in 1 Corinthians.

While the Old Testament prophets claimed to be speaking God's very words, it is inconceivable that Paul or the Corinthians thought that God's words needed to be evaluated to see whether or not they were true or useful. So the prophets at Corinth must not have been thought to speak with divine authority attaching to their actual words. Their prophecies were subject to evaluation and questioning at every point.[26]

1 Corinthians 14:30: Prophecies which were intentionally neglected

After giving instructions that two or three prophets could speak, Paul guarantees that an orderly pattern will be followed: 'If a revelation is made to another sitting by, let the first be silent' (1 Cor 14:30, RSV).

This verse pictures a situation something like the following: while one prophet is speaking, another suddenly has something 'revealed' (*apokaluptō*) to him (or her). This second prophet signals in some way, perhaps by standing, that he has something to say. Then the first prophet does not finish his prophecy but immediately sits down and is silent, allowing the second one to speak.

Prophecies which could be lost

The first thing we notice in this verse is that Paul seems to be totally unconcerned by the fact that the first prophecy might be lost for ever and never heard by the church. This attitude on Paul's part seems to fit the picture of New Testament prophecy which we saw in 1 Corinthians 14:29. For if prophets had been thought to speak the very words of God, we would have expected Paul to show more concern for the preservation of these words and their proclamation. If God actually were speaking his words through a prophet to the church, it would be important for the church to hear those words!

By means of contrast with Paul's attitude here, we can recall the situation in Jeremiah 36, where Jehoiakim shows callous disregard for the prophetic words written for him to read (Jer 36:23–25), and is sentenced to greater punishment as a result (Jer 36:30). Yet Paul in 1 Corinthians 14:30 advocates a system whereby some of the words the first prophet was to say would *never* be heard by the church.

Now if New Testament prophets had been thought to speak with absolute divine authority attaching to their very words, this verse would be very hard to understand. How could Paul direct that God's words be lost?

However, if the New Testament prophets were only thought to be speaking merely human words to report something which God had brought to mind, Paul's instructions would be quite reasonable: many Christians had things to contribute to the worship service (1 Cor 14:26), and there was only a limited amount of time. Therefore, as many people as possible should be allowed to contribute, in order that through the diversity of contributions everyone present would be edified in some way (1 Cor 14:31).

Of course, there would be times when someone would come with 'a hymn, a teaching, a revelation, a tongue, an interpretation' (1 Cor 14:26)—or a prophecy—which, because of time, could not be used. But that did not matter. What was important was that all things were done for edification (1 Cor 14:26).

At this point one might object that the words of the first prophet need not be lost: he would simply hold his peace until the second prophet had finished, and then he would resume his speech.

But this objection does not adequately account for Paul's words. For if the first prophet was expected to resume speaking, why then would Paul command this *first* prophet to be silent at all? If the first prophet could retain his revelation and speak later, then so could the second prophet. And in that case it would make much more sense for the second prophet to wait, instead of rudely interrupting the first prophet and making him give his speech in two parts.

In order for Paul's instruction to be understandable, then, we have to suppose that he assumed that the first prophet would *not* resume speaking after the second prophet had stopped: the remainder of the first prophet's prophecy would be intentionally neglected, and probably never heard by the church.

Does a 'revelation' imply divine authority?

The second point of interest for us in 1 Corinthians 14:30 is the term translated 'revelation'. In fact, the Greek term used here is a verb (*apokalyptō*), and the verse is more literally translated, 'If (something) is revealed to another one sitting, let the first be silent.'

As I shall argue in chapter 5, below, this term 'reveal' (*apokalyptō*), along with evidence in 1 Corinthians 14:32–33, indicates that it is a specific revelatory activity of the Holy Spirit which gives rise to any prophecy by a New Testament prophet. Paul pictures some kind of process whereby the prophet is spontaneously made aware of something which he feels God has caused him to think about.

But it is precisely at this point that a problem arises. Someone might argue that the fact that New Testament prophecy is based on a 'revelation', from God *necessarily implies* that the prophet was speaking with divine authority attaching to his very words.

This, in fact, does not need to be the case. Several instances of the terms 'to reveal' (Greek *apokaluptō*) and 'revelation'

(Greek *apokalupsis*) show that the *report* of a 'revelation' can often be thought to have only the authority of merely human words—similar, for example, to the authority one would accord a sermon, or the advice of a mature Christian, etc. These should by no means be ignored, but neither should they be thought to have authority equal to Scripture itself in our lives.[27]

For example, in Philippians 3:15 (RSV), Paul encourages his readers to be zealous for continual growth and effective service for Christ, and then says, 'If in anything you are otherwise minded, God will reveal [*apokaluptō*] that also to you.' In other words, if any of the Philippians strayed from their high calling, God would make known to them their error; he would 'reveal' it to them.

But we cannot suppose that whenever some Philippian Christian reported to his neighbour that God had 'revealed' some sin in his life, that the conversation (the *report* of such a 'revelation') with the neighbour would have absolute divine authority attaching to the actual words spoken. Rather, the 'revelation' would be reported in merely human words, the prophet's own words, not God's very words.[28]

Similarly, in Romans 1:18 (RSV) Paul writes that 'the wrath of God is revealed (*apokaluptō*) from heaven against all ungodliness and wickedness of men'. This revelation of God's wrath was plain for all people to see, but certainly, when people discussed what God had revealed to them, Paul would not have claimed for these discussions the special category of divinely authoritative actual words.

Then in Ephesians 1:17 we read a prayer that God would give the readers a 'spirit of wisdom and of revelation (*apokalupsis*, a cognate noun) in the knowledge of him', so that they would know more of the benefits which were theirs as Christians. Once more, it would not be possible to think that every time a believer gained new insight into his privileges as a Christian and reported it to a friend, the actual words of that speech would have been thought to be God's very words. It would be the *report* of something God had 'revealed' to the Christian, but the report would only come in merely human words.

Finally, in Matthew 11:27, Jesus says that if anyone knows the Father, it is because the Son has revealed (*apokaluptō*) the Father to him. Now if someone wanted to argue that a report of a 'revelation' is always couched in words that are the very words of God, then this statement would require us to say that *any* believer reporting how he came to know God would be speaking with absolute divine authority in his actual words— but this is clearly an impossible situation.

So the terms 'reveal' and 'revelation' by themselves by no means indicate that prophets in 1 Corinthians 14 were thought to speak with a divine authority of actual words. Specifically, the term *apokalyptō* in 1 Corinthians 14:30 does not require us to think that a Christian prophet who reported something God had revealed would be speaking the very words of God.

D. A. Carson rightly observes:

> When Paul presupposes in 1 Corinthians 14:30 that the gift of prophecy depends on a revelation, we are not limited to a form of authoritative revelation that threatens the finality of the canon. To argue in such a way is to confuse the terminology of Protestant systematic theology with the terminology of the Scripture writers.[29]

1 Corinthians 14:36: No words of God from the Corinthian prophets

After a brief section about women speaking in the church (1 Cor 14:33b–35), Paul says, 'Or from you did the word of God go forth, or unto you only has it come?' (1 Cor 14:36). This verse has Paul taking the offensive against the Corinthian church and denying them the right to establish rules for church worship contrary to the ones he has just laid down.

Paul asks two rhetorical questions, and he implies that the answer to both of them is negative. When he says, 'Or from you did the word of God go forth?' he implies that the word of God has *not* gone forth from them—in other words, they have not been speaking words with absolute divine authority, like Paul has. Therefore they should be subject to Paul's apostolic directions, not think that some of their prophets could give directions of equal authority. The word of God 'came forth' from the apostles, not from any prophets in local churches such as Corinth.

Now the RSV and NIV translate this verse to ask, 'Did the word of God *originate* with you'—in other words, were you the original source of the gospel message? Of course they were not. Therefore (so this interpretation goes), they could not make rules to override Paul's commands.

Even if this is the meaning of the verse ('Did the gospel originate with you?'), the implication is clear: no one at Corinth (including the prophets) could make rules which would compete with Paul's words in authority. And this would imply that no prophets at Corinth could speak 'words of the Lord' as the apostles could.

But there are reasons to question whether the verse means, 'Did the gospel originate with you?' First, the gospel did not originate with Paul either (it came from Jesus Christ, and then first through the apostles at Pentecost, but not from Paul in any case). Therefore, saying that the gospel did not originate with the Corinthians would not show that the Corinthians were inferior to Paul in authority.

Moreover, the common Greek word which Paul used (*exerchomai*) simply means 'go out', and there is no necessary sense of 'original source' or 'first point of origin' attaching to the word. The same word is commonly used of reports about Jesus which 'go out' from various cities, but in no case is one of the cities the original source of the message about Jesus (see Mt 9:26; Mk 1:28; Lk 4:14; 7:17; Jn 21:23; compare another passage about a message 'going out' in Rom 10:18).

And Paul could easily have said, 'Did the word of God (or: the gospel) *first* go forth from you?' if he had meant this. But that is not what he said. He simply said, 'Did the word of God go forth from you?' and implied that it did not—that is, that it never had gone forth from them. No one at the church in Corinth gave forth words of God.

But there is still another implication in this question. Let us assume for a moment that prophets in Corinth *were* able to speak with a divine authority of actual words, perhaps not even for the whole Christian world, but simply words which would have absolute divine authority for the Corinthian church alone. If this were the case, then we would certainly assume that they would be able to speak this kind of a 'word of the Lord' on such a secondary issue as the conduct of the worship service. Of course this was important, but it was hardly on the same level as defining major doctrines for the entire Christian world, for example. Yet Paul denies them even this ability; they are unable to do what they want concerning the conduct of worship; they must obey Paul and others who are able to speak with greater authority. So 1 Corinthians 14:36 makes it very unlikely that anyone at Corinth, even any prophet, was able to speak with absolute divine authority.

1 Corinthians 14:37–38: Prophets with less authority than an apostle

In 1 Corinthians 14:37–38, Paul is writing to a community where several prophets were active, and he still asserts his authority over the entire community, even over the prophets. These verses are thus the positive counterpart to verse 36. Paul writes:

> If any one thinks that he is a prophet, or spiritual, he should acknowledge that what I am writing to you is a command of the Lord. If any one does not recognize this, he is not recognized (1 Cor 14:37–38, RSV).

Paul is here claiming something more than the correctness of his own opinion. He is also claiming that anyone who disobeyed him would be disobeying a 'command of the Lord' and would be punished not by Paul but by God himself.

As we noted above in the discussion of apostolic authority, Paul's claim sounds very much like a claim that what he has written to Corinth has a divine authority of actual words. And this authority is set over against the authority of everyone at Corinth, including the prophets. According to Paul, the words of the prophets at Corinth were not and could not have been sufficiently authoritative to show Paul to be wrong. If he is claiming for himself a divine authority of actual words, he seems to be attributing to the Corinthian prophets something considerably less than that.

1 Corinthians 11:5: Women prophets who neither govern nor teach

Before leaving 1 Corinthians we note briefly that Paul assumes women could prophesy in church: 'Any woman who prays or prophesies with her head unveiled dishonours her head' (1 Cor 11:5, RSV). Yet in 1 Corinthians 14:34 (RSV) he says that women 'are not permitted to speak, but should be subordinate'.

Anticipating the discussion in Chapter 4, we can say briefly that the type of speech in view in 1 Corinthians 14:34 is not all speech but only speech which assumes authority over the men of the congregation, speech which is not 'subordinate'. (Note the strong contrast implied by the Greek word *alla* ['but']: 'to speak' in the sense forbidden by Paul is to act in a way which is exactly the opposite of being subordinate.)

Now if this interpretation is correct, then 1 Corinthians 11:5 can easily be reconciled with 1 Corinthians 14:34, provided that the type of prophecy done by women at Corinth did not involve authoritative speech, that is, speech which assumed the right to enforce obedience or belief. Now speech which purported to have a divine authority of actual words would have assumed that right, but the same would not be true of speech which just reported in merely human words something God had brought to mind. So it seems that the prophecy uttered by women at Corinth could not have claimed the extremely high authority of speech with a 'divine authority of actual words'. Thus, 1 Corinthians 11:5 is one more indication that prophets at Corinth were not thought by Paul to speak with a divine authority of actual words.

Conclusions from 1 Corinthians

We have now examined five different verses or short passages in 1 Corinthians. In each one there are indications that, in Paul's view at least, the prophets at Corinth did not speak with a divine authority of actual words, and were not thought by others to speak with an absolute divine authority.

In 1 Corinthians 14:29 it seems that the prophet's words could be challenged and questioned, and that the prophet could at times be wrong. Yet there is no indication that an occasional mistake would make him a 'false' prophet. In 1 Corinthians 14:30, Paul seems unconcerned that some of a prophet's words could be lost for ever and never heard by the church. In 1 Corinthians 14:36, he refuses the prophets the right to make rules for worship other than the ones he has given, and in 1 Corinthians 14:37–38 he seems to indicate that, in his opinion, no Corinthian prophet had a kind of divine authority equal to his own. Finally, in 1 Corinthians 11:5 and 1 Corinthians 14:34–35, Paul allows women to prophesy while denying to them the right to enforce obedience or belief on the congregation, and this would be consistent with a view that prophets spoke with something less than 'absolute' divine authority.[30]

These five passages, then, indicate that Paul thought of prophecy at Corinth as something quite different from the prophecy we see, for instance, in Revelation or in many parts of the Old Testament. There, a divine authority of actual words is claimed by or on behalf of the prophets. But the prophecy we find in 1 Corinthians, while it may have been prompted by a 'revelation' from God, had only the authority of the merely human words in which it was spoken. The prophet could err, could misinterpret, and could be questioned or challenged at any point.

It now remains to examine briefly the accounts of prophecy elsewhere in the New Testament, and to compare these accounts with our conclusions from 1 Corinthians.

4

New Testament Prophets in the Rest of the New Testament:

Speaking Merely Human Words To Report Something God Brings to Mind

Evidence from Acts

1. Acts 11:28: Agabus: Scene I

This scene takes place at Antioch, in the church which from Acts 13 to the end of the book will replace Jerusalem as the missionary centre of the early church. It is the church which a bit later would send out Paul and Barnabas on their first missionary journey. In fact, Barnabas and Saul (Paul) have just been teaching for a whole year in this church (Acts 11:25–26).

Then we read:

> Now in these days prophets came down from Jerusalem to Antioch. And one of them named Agabus stood up and foretold by the Spirit that there would be a great famine over all the world; and this took place in the days of Claudius. And the disciples determined, every one according to his ability, to send relief to the brethren who lived in Judea; and they did so, sending it to the elders by the hand of Barnabas and Saul (Acts 11:27–30, RSV).

The question is what kind of authority attaches to the prophecy of Agabus.

When Luke says that Agabus foretold 'by the Spirit' he uses a phrase (Greek *dia tou pneumatou*) which is never used in the

Greek Old Testament (the Septuagint) to refer to prophetic speech. The word *dia* ('through' or 'by means of') seems to signify 'the originator of an action',[31] and this construction would be well suited to express a rather loose relationship between the Holy Spirit and the prophet, since it allows room for a large degree of personal influence by the human person himself (note 'we are more than conquerors *through him who loved us*' in Romans 8:37 RSV; and 'guard *through the Holy Spirit* the good tradition that was entrusted to you' in 2 Timothy 1:14—both using the same grammatical construction).

A degree of imprecision is also suggested by the word translated 'foretold' (Greek *sēmainō*, 'signified, indicated'). This same word was used in extra-biblical literature (such as the Jewish writer Josephus or the secular writer Plutarch) of prophetic speech 'that simply gives a vague indication of what is to happen',[32] and we may conclude that absolute divine authority is neither required nor ruled out by this description.

Therefore, although the evidence in this passage is too slim to draw any certain conclusions, Luke's language is entirely compatible with a kind of New Testament prophecy similar to that in 1 Corinthians, prophecy which was based on a 'revelation' but not reported in divinely authoritative words. In fact, the vagueness attaching to the expressions 'signified, foretold' and 'through the Spirit' would seem to suggest—but only *suggest*—some lesser kind of authority.

2. Acts 13:2: Is this really prophecy?

This passage again is set in Antioch. There in this growing church 'there were prophets and teachers, Barnabas, Symeon who was called Niger, Lucius of Cyrene, Manaen a member of the court of Herod the tetrarch, and Saul' (Acts 13:1, RSV).

Then we read in verse 2 that while the prophets and teachers (named in Acts 13:1) were worshipping the Lord and fasting 'the Holy Spirit said, "Set apart for me Barnabas and Saul for the work to which I have called them"' (Acts 13:2, RSV).

Is this a report of a prophecy? People often assume that it is, especially since prophets are mentioned in verse 1.

However, it is not certain whether this passage does speak of prophecy. The fact that prophets and teachers are mentioned in verse 1 need only show that they were the leading men of the Antioch church, to whom such a revelation, whatever its form, would appropriately come.

More significant is the fact that Luke attributes these words not to a prophet but to 'the Holy Spirit'. If we examine several similar statements in Acts, we find that when this form of expression is used, *if no human spokesman is named* prophecy is not in view:

Acts 8:29 (RSV): 'And *the Spirit said* to Philip, "Go up and join this chariot"' (not prophecy).

Acts 10:19 (RSV): 'And while Peter was pondering the vision, *the Spirit said* to him, "Behold, three men are looking for you" (not prophecy).

Acts 18:9 (RSV): 'And *the Lord said* to Paul one night in a vision, "Do not be afraid, but speak and do not be silent..."' (not prophecy).

We could also compare:

Acts 15:28 (RSV): 'For it has *seemed good to the Holy Spirit* and to us to lay upon you no greater burden than these necessary things...' (no indication that this was a result of prophecy).

Acts 16:6–7 (RSV): 'And they went through the region of Phrygia and Galatia, *having been forbidden by the Holy Spirit* to speak the word in Asia. And when they had come opposite Mysia, they attempted to go into Bithynia, but *the Spirit of Jesus did not allow them...*' (no indication that this was a result of prophecy).

Acts 16:9 (RSV): 'And *a vision appeared to Paul* in the night: a man of Macedonia was standing beseeching him and saying, "Come over to Macedonia and help us"'. (not prophecy).

Acts 20:23 (RSV) is ambiguous (Paul speaking): '...*the Holy Spirit testifies to me* in every city that imprisonment and afflictions await me' (may include prophecies and/or other kinds of communications from the Holy Spirit as in the verses above).

Acts 23:9 (rsv) (some Pharisees speaking of Paul): 'What if *a spirit or an angel spoke to him*?'[33] (prophecy not mentioned or implied).

Now if Acts 13:2 is similar to several of these other examples, it would suggest that Luke is here speaking of a strong subjective sense of guidance from the Holy Spirit (such as in Acts 15:28) which gave a clear conviction in this matter to several or perhaps all of those 'worshipping the Lord and fasting'. It might even have included a vision or perhaps an inaudible voice which was 'heard' mentally by one or several members of the group, leading them quickly to some agreement on this guidance.

At any rate, Luke's failure to attribute the speech to any one of the prophets, coupled with his pattern elsewhere of attributing *non-prophetic* speech to the Holy Spirit, make it somewhat doubtful that prophecy is in view here.

3. *Acts 19:6: New Christians in Ephesus prophesy at conversion*

When Paul came to Ephesus he found some people who had heard (directly or indirectly) the message which John the Baptist preached, and had been baptized with the baptism of repentance and preparation for the Messiah which John had practiced. But these people had apparently not heard that Jesus was the one John was preparing the way for (Acts 19: 4–5), and they had 'never even heard that there is a Holy Spirit' (Acts 19:2).

Now Paul proclaimed to them the good news about Jesus, that he was the one they were looking for. Then:

> On hearing this, they were baptized in the name of the Lord Jesus. And when Paul had laid his hands upon them, the Holy Spirit came on them; and they spoke with tongues and prophesied. There were about twelve of them in all (Acts 19:5–7, rsv).

Here the verb 'prophesy' describes a speech activity which reminds us somewhat of the bands of prophets in the Old Testament. In any case, the prophesying here bears no resemblance to the messenger speeches in the Old Testament which were thought to possess absolute divine authority in the actual words spoken. And this is also certainly different from the divinely authoritative speech of Paul and the other apostles.

If the passage means that everyone was speaking in tongues and prophesying at the same time (a sense that is suggested by the combination of verb tenses in the Greek text), then no one's speech would have been heard distinctly.

On the other hand, even if it just means that these new Christians were continuing in a pattern of speaking in tongues and prophesying one at a time (a sense which is also possible from the Greek text), this would hardly be a case where 'divinely authoritative prophets' would provide 'charismatic leadership' in the church and fill the need for guidance in the absence of apostles, until the Scriptures were complete—for Paul the apostle was present with them (and was about to continue with them for over two years). There would hardly be any need for twelve additional sources of 'words of the Lord' when Paul himself was present with them. So the 'prophesying' here at Ephesus does not seem to have been of the type which possessed the absolute authority of God's very words.

4. Acts 21:4: Prophecies which Paul disobeys

In this passage Paul is nearing the end of his third missionary journey, and he is drawing near to Jerusalem. His ship lands at the port city of Tyre (in Syria, on the coast, somewhat northwest of Galilee). Paul and his companions had to wait there for several days while the ship unloaded its cargo, so they sought out the Christians there.

> And having sought out the disciples, we stayed there for seven days. Through the Spirit they told Paul not to go on to Jerusalem. And when our days there were ended, we departed and went on our journey (Acts 21:4–5, RSV).

This verse does not mention prophecy directly, but the parallel with Acts 11:28, where human speech activity 'through the

Spirit' is explicitly attributed to the prophet Agabus, suggests that these disciples were in fact prophesying. (In contrast to Acts 13:2, human spokesmen are here explicitly credited with the warning.)

But if this really is a report of prophesying, as it certainly seems to be, then it is very significant for understanding the nature of prophetic authority in ordinary New Testament congregations. It is significant because Paul simply disobeyed their words, something he would not have done if he had thought that they were speaking the very words of God.

On the other hand, if the disciples at Tyre had a gift of prophecy which was similar to what we found at Corinth and at Ephesus, and perhaps also at Antioch (see above), then Paul's disobedience to the prophecy would be entirely understandable.

In fact, we can surmise something of how such a prophecy would come about. Suppose that some of the Christians at Tyre had had some kind of 'revelation' or indication from God about the suffering which Paul would face at Jerusalem. Then it would have been very natural for them to couple their subsequent prophecy (their report of this revelation) with their own (erroneous) interpretation, and thus to warn Paul not to go.

In short, this passage indicates a type of prophecy which was not thought by Paul to possess absolute divine authority in its actual words: the prophets at Tyre were not speaking 'words of the Lord'.

Although he does not agree with the viewpoint on prophecy which I am arguing for in this book, it is significant that Richard Gaffin understands this verse to represent an unreliable human response to something revealed by the Holy Spirit:

> Luke's point is not the impaired validity and unreliability of their speech, in which nevertheless the Spirit is somewhat instrumental, but their recoil against what the Spirit had revealed to them of Paul's future. That revelation and their response to it must not be confused or merged in their speech-act.[34]

Here Dr Gaffin seems to understand the event in a way similar to what I expressed above. There is a revelation from the Holy Spirit to the disciples at Tyre, and in response to that revelation, they tell Paul not to go to Jerusalem. The difference in our viewpoints is that I would call the response or report of that revelation a 'prophecy', and Dr Gaffin would not. But whatever term is used, it is significant that we would both say that there can be a 'revelation' from the Holy Spirit to a person or persons, and also a spoken response to that revelation which can have 'impaired validity' and 'unreliability'. That is really the essence of what I am arguing for in this book, and what—it seems to me—the New Testament usually calls 'prophecy'. But if the *concept* be admitted even if it is called not 'prophecy' but 'an unreliable human speech-act in response to a revelation from the Holy Spirit', there does not seem to be much difference in our understanding at this point. Nor does there seem to be strong reason for saying such an 'unreliable human response to revelation from the Holy Spirit' could not occur today.

5. Acts 21:9: Philip's daughters as prophets

This brief passage follows close on the narrative above about Tyre. Continuing towards Jerusalem, Paul comes to another port city, Caesarea:

> On the morrow we departed and came to Caesarea; and we entered the house of Philip the evangelist, who was one of the seven, and stayed with him. And he had four unmarried daughters, who prophesied (Acts 21:8–9, RSV).

No indication is given of the content of their prophecies, but the fact that prophetic warnings to Paul about suffering in Jerusalem come just before (Acts 21:4) and just after (Acts 21:11) this passage makes us think that perhaps similar warnings were contained in the prophecies given by Philip's daughters.

In any case, this passage gives some brief confirmation to our discussion of 1 Corinthians 11:5 in chapter 3: if women were not allowed authoritative roles in congregational meetings in the first-century churches, then it seems unlikely that these women would be speaking with the same kind of absolute authority as the apostles. Much more likely is the possibility that they were 'prophesying' simply by reporting in their own words what God would bring to mind, and that these prophecies did not have the authority of words of the Lord.

6. Acts 21:10–11: Agabus, Scene II: A prophecy with two small mistakes

Following just after the verse mentioning Philip's daughters, two more verses describe another prophetic event which confronts Paul, still in Caesarea. Luke writes:

> While we were staying for some days, a prophet named Agabus came down from Judea. And coming to us he took Paul's girdle and bound his own feet and hands, and said, 'Thus says the Holy Spirit, "So shall the Jews at Jerusalem bind the man who owns this girdle and deliver him into the hands of the Gentiles"' (Acts 21:10–11, RSV).

There appear to be two competing factors in this passage. On the one hand, Agabus's introductory phrase, 'Thus says the Holy Spirit,' suggests an attempt to speak like the Old Testament prophets who said, 'Thus says the Lord...'

On the other hand, however, the events of the narrative itself do not coincide with the kind of accuracy which the Old Testament requires for those who speak God's words. In fact, by Old Testament standards, Agabus would have been condemned as a false prophet, because in Acts 21:27–35 neither of his predictions are fulfilled.

First, Agabus predicted that 'the Jews at Jerusalem' would 'bind' Paul (Acts 21:11; the Greek word for 'bind' here is deō). However, when Paul is actually captured in Jerusalem later in the same chapter, Luke tells us twice that it was not the Jews but the Romans who bound Paul: 'Then the tribune came up and arrested him, and ordered him to be bound [Greek deō] with two chains'

(Acts 21:33, RSV). Similarly, in reflecting on this event, 'the tribune also was afraid, for he realized that Paul was a Roman citizen and that he had *bound* [Greek *deō*] him' (Acts 22:29, RSV).

The second 'mistake' in Agabus's prophecy concerned the second detail which he predicted, the fact that the Jews would 'deliver' Paul into the hands of the Gentiles. Here the Greek word for deliver is *paradidomi*, 'to deliver, hand over'. Essential to the sense of this word is the idea of actively, consciously, willingly 'delivering, giving over, handing over' something or someone to someone (or something) else—this is the case in all of the other 119 instances of its use in the New Testament.

This word *paradidomi* is used, for example, of Judas 'delivering' Jesus into the hands of the Jewish leaders (Mt 10:4; 26:16, etc); of the Jews then 'delivering' Jesus into the hands of the Gentiles (Romans) (Mt 20:19); 'delivering' John the Baptist to prison (Mk 1:14); Moses 'delivering' laws to the people (Acts 6:14); or Paul 'delivering' teachings to the church (1 Cor 15:3). None of the other 119 instances of the word in the New Testament lacks the idea of an action that is consciously, intentionally done by the one doing the 'delivering'.

But in Luke's narrative following the prophecy of Agabus, he shows that the Jews do not 'deliver' Paul over to the hands of the Gentiles. Rather than intentionally 'giving Paul over' to the hands of the Gentiles (as the Jews had done with Jesus, for example), they tried to kill him themselves (Acts 21:31). He had to be forcibly *rescued from* the Jews by the tribune and his soldiers (Acts 21: 32–33), and even then 'he was actually carried by the soldiers because of the violence of the crowd' (Acts 21:35).

Now it might be argued that Luke has no intention of showing that Agabus gave an inaccurate prophecy. These are really only differences in detail, someone might say.

However, this explanation does not take full enough account of the fact that these are the *only* two details Agabus mentions—they are, in terms of content, the heart of his prophecy.

In fact, these details are what make it unusual as a prediction.

Probably anyone who knew how the Jews throughout the Empire had treated Paul in various cities could have 'predicted' with no revelation from the Holy Spirit at all that Paul would meet violent opposition from the Jews in Jerusalem. What was unique about Agabus' prophecy was this prediction of 'binding' and 'delivering into the hands of the Gentiles'. And on these two key elements, he is just a bit wrong.

Now it is especially in the case of prophetic pronouncement that accuracy in detail was an essential mark of authenticity. Note the following examples:

1 Kings 17:14: Elijah predicted that the jar of meal would not be used up and the jug of oil would not run dry. In 1 Kings 17:16: this prediction comes true.

Josh 6:26 (RSV): Joshua predicted that of the man who rebuilds Jericho: 'At the cost of his first-born shall he lay its foundation, and at the cost of his youngest son shall he set up its gates.' In 1 Kings 16:34 both predictions come true for Hiel of Bethel.

1 Kings 21:23: Elijah predicted that the dogs would eat Jezebel within the bounds of Jezreel. In 2 Kings 9:35–36 this prediction comes true.

1 Kings 13:2: a man of God from Judah predicted that someone named Josiah would be born to the house of David and would sacrifice the disobedient priests themselves upon the altar at Bethel. In 2 Kings 23:15–16, 20 this prediction comes true.

2 Kings 7:1: in famine-stricken, besieged Samaria, Elisha predicted that one day later, about the same time of day, a measure of fine meal would be sold for a shekel and two measures of barley for a shekel, at the gate of Samaria. In 2 Kings 23:16 this prediction comes true.

More examples could be given, but the pattern should be clear.[35] Regarding the mistakes in details in Agabus's prophecy, D. A. Carson writes, 'I can think of no reported Old Testament prophet whose prophecies are so wrong on the details.'[36]

Furthermore, Luke is aware of the legitimacy of making prophetic fulfilment explicit where it occurs:

Luke 4:21 Jesus claims that Isaiah 61:1–2 has been fulfilled in himself (cf. Lk 24:44).

Acts 1:16–20 Peter claimed that the predictions about Judas in Psalms 69:25 and Psalms 109:8 were fulfilled.

Acts 3:18 the predictions of 'all the prophets', that the Messiah should suffer, were fulfilled.

Acts 11:28 the prediction of Agabus, that there would be a famine over all the world, was fulfilled in the days of Claudius.

Acts 13:27, 29 the Old Testament prophets' predictions were fulfilled when the Jewish leaders condemned Christ and had him crucified.

Acts 13:33-35 the Old Testament predictions of Christ's resurrection were fulfilled (cf. Acts 2:25–31).

But in the case of this prediction by Agabus, even in contrast to the general prediction in Acts 11:28, Luke's silence about the 'fulfilment' is telling. Not only do we have an unfulfilled prophecy, but a prophecy whose two elements—'binding' and 'giving over' by the Jews—are explicitly falsified by the subsequent narrative.[37]

Two other considerations support this interpretation. First, the nature of the error itself. It is not that Agabus has spoken in a totally false or misleading way; it is just that he has the details wrong. But this kind of minor innaccuracy is exactly compatible with the type of prophecy we found earlier in 1 Corinthians, in which the prophet receives some kind of revelation and then reports it in his own words. He would have the general idea correct (Paul would be imprisoned at Jerusalem), but the details somewhat wrong.

In this case, for instance, the text could be perfectly well explained by supposing that Agabus had had a vision of Paul as a prisoner of the Romans in Jerusalem, surrounded by an angry mob of Jews. His own interpretation of such a 'vision' or 'intuitive insight' (from the Holy Spirit) would be that the Jews had bound Paul and handed him over to the Romans, and that is what he would (erroneously) prophesy.

Secondly, such a solution makes the Agabus narrative fit Luke's larger purpose in the section, which is no doubt to show the contrast between Paul's sure knowledge of God's will and resolute purpose to obey it in spite of personal danger (cf. Acts 20:22–24; 21:13), and the uncertain grasp of God's will possessed by the prophets and other disciples whom Paul meets (Acts 21:4, 12–14), and who try to dissuade him from going to Jerusalem. The close connection with the misleading instructions in Acts 21:4 is especially significant: both the prophecies in Tyre and the one in Caesarea are nearly right, but not completely so.

It seems, therefore, that the best solution is to say that Agabus had a 'revelation' from the Holy Spirit concerning what would happen to Paul in Jerusalem, and gave a prophecy which included his own interpretation of this revelation (and therefore some mistakes in the exact details). Luke then recorded Agabus's prophecy exactly, and recorded the subsequent events exactly, even including those aspects of the events which showed Agabus to be slightly wrong at some points.

The remaining difficulty with this interpretation of the text, however, is the introductory phrase Agabus uses, 'Thus says the Holy Spirit....' There are three solutions which might be proposed for this:

(a) Agabus claimed a divine authority of actual words for his prophecy and the minor discrepancies are not sufficient to nullify that claim, for he was generally correct.

In this case Agabus will be seen as an example of a prophet who is different from the prophets in 1 Corinthians. He will be more like the first type of prophet, such as John in Revelation, who claims an absolute divine authority.

My own problem with this view is that I find it hard to reconcile with the Old Testament pattern of precise fulfilment of prophecies (strictly speaking, Agabus predicted two events which 'did not come to pass' Deut 18:22) and with the fact that Luke so clearly describes the non-fulfilment of the two parts of the prophecy in the immediately subsequent narrative.

(b) 'Thus says the Holy Spirit' means here not that the very words of the prophecy were from the Holy Spirit, but only that the content generally had been revealed by the Spirit. In this case Acts 21:10–11 would fit the pattern of prophecy in 1 Corinthians.

A similar example of a 'prophecy' which is then summarized—but with markedly altered content—as something 'the Holy Spirit' was 'saying' is found in Ignatius's *Epistle to the Philadelphians* 7.1–2 (about A.D. 108). The prophecy itself, given by Ignatius, said, 'Give heed to the bishop, and to the presbytery and deacons.' But the summary of it which Ignatius gave, after affirming that he had 'no knowledge' of divisions in the church 'from any human being', was this: 'The Spirit was preaching, and saying this, "Do nothing without the bishop, keep your flesh as the temple of God, love unity, flee from divisions, be imitators of Jesus Christ, as was he also of his Father."' In this section, the phrase translated 'saying this' is *legōn tade*, the same two words used by Agabus in Acts 21:11 (*tade legei*, 'thus says...'). Yet the phrase hardly introduces a direct quotation—it is a greatly expanded interpretation. The Holy Spirit was saying 'approximately this' or 'something like this'.

And similar examples of this phrase (Greek *tade legei*) introducing statements from 'the Lord' are found in *The Epistle of Barnabas* 6:8; 9:2 and 9:5—in every case they introduce extremely free paraphrases with interpretation of the Old Testament, except in 9:5, where no Old Testament quotation even seems to be in view. It is clearly possible, therefore, that Agabus' introductory statement to him meant nothing more than, 'This is generally (or approximately) what the Holy Spirit is saying to us.'

The problem with this solution is that this phrase, Greek *tade legei*, is used frequently in the Greek translation of the Old Testament (the Septuagint) to introduce the words of the Lord in the Old Testament prophets ('thus says the Lord...'). On the other hand, it is also used to introduce statements from many other people, not always with direct quotations, so perhaps it need not always signify that the actual words of the person quoted would follow. Moreover, the exact words used by

Agabus, 'Thus says the Holy Spirit,' are never elsewhere used
to introduce Scripture or Old Testament prophetic speech
which consisted of the very words of God.

(c) A third possibility is that Agabus, perhaps in trying to
imitate the Old Testament prophets, or perhaps not fully
understanding the nature of his prophetic gift, wrongly used an
introductory statement which was inappropriate to his status as
a prophet with lesser authority. The statement might have
given the impression that he was speaking the very words of
God, while in fact he was not. Since we know very little else
about him, it would be precarious to conclude that such a misunderstanding of his role would have been impossible. And
Luke does seem almost to point out the mistakes in his
prophecy. In this case his prophecy would be like those in 1
Corinthians.

The problem with this solution is that it is hard to imagine
that Agabus would have been active in the Jerusalem church
for several years, in the presence of several of the apostles, and
still have a misunderstanding of his prophetic gift, and of the
clear difference between his prophesying and the absolutely
authoritative words of the apostles.

After considering these three solutions I tend to think the
second one is most likely, and has the least difficulties. Others,
however, may find one of the other two more persuasive. In
any case, this passage is one of the more difficult to classify in
one category or the other.

Evidence from other New Testament books

1. *Matthew 10:19–20*

In this passage Jesus says:

> When they deliver you up, do not be anxious how you are to speak
> or what you are to say; for what you are to say will be given to you
> in that hour; for it is not you who speak, but the Spirit of your
> Father speaking through you (Mt 10:19–20, RSV).

If this passage be understood to refer to New Testament prophecy, then it clearly belongs in the first category, that of prophecy which is thought to have a divine authority of actual words. Verse 20 ('for it is not you who speak, but the Spirit of your Father speaking through you') makes this claim especially clear. The same is true of parallels to this passage in Mark 13:11 and Luke 12:11–12.

But are these passages talking about New Testament prophecy as it occurred in local congregations? They seem rather to be saying something particularly about the apostles,[38] for in all three cases these words of Jesus are addressed to the twelve disciples (who would be the 'apostles').

This is especially clear in Matthew's account. He introduces this section on the mission of the Twelve with the following words:

> And he called to him his twelve disciples and gave them authority over unclean spirits, to cast them out, and to heal every disease and every infirmity. The names of *the twelve apostles* are these.... (Mt 10:1–2, RSV).

Similarly, in Mark 13:11, the statement is set in the context of a private talk to 'Peter and James and John and Andrew' (Mark 13:3, RSV). Luke 12:11–12 is in the context of things he said 'to his disciples first' (Lk 12:1, RSV). So in no case do these statements about being given words to say from the Holy Spirit seem to have direct application, at least, to people other than the apostles.

2. Romans 16:26

When Paul says that 'the mystery which was kept secret for long ages' is 'now disclosed and through the prophetic writings is made known to all nations' (Rom 16:25–26, RSV), some might argue that he is speaking of the writings of the New Testament prophets.

However, this does not seem to be the sense of the verse.

This statement comes one verse before the end of Romans, and its wording is quite similar to Paul's statement at the very beginning of the book, in Romans 1:2 (RSV), where he says that God promised the gospel beforehand 'through his prophets in the holy scriptures'. But there Old Testament prophets are clearly meant.

Furthermore, Paul always (thirteen of thirteen other times) uses 'scripture' (Greek *graphē*) to refer to Old Testament Scripture. And evangelistic preaching of the 'mystery of Christ' at the time Romans was written was primarily by oral preaching, not by circulating written prophecies. When Paul says that the mystery of Christ is made known 'through the prophetic writings' (Rom 16:26, RSV), he means that the apostles and others are using the Old Testament prophecies in their preaching, to show that these prophecies are speaking of Christ (cf. Acts 2:14–36; 8:32–35; 17:2–4; 18:28; 28:23; etc).

This passage, therefore, does not tell us about the New Testament gift of prophecy.

3. *1 Thessalonians 5:19–21: prophecies which must be sifted*

Paul writes to the Thessalonians: 'Do not quench the Spirit, do not despise prophesying, but test everything; hold fast what is good, abstain from every form of evil' (1 Thess 5:19–22, RSV).

The close connection between 'do not despise prophesying' (v. 20) and 'test everything' (v. 21) means that prophecies are most naturally included in the 'all things' of verse 21. Prophecies (especially) are to be 'tested', and out of the testing will come some things that are 'good'. To those, the Thessalonians are to 'hold fast'.

The conjunction 'but' connecting verses 20 and 21 brings out the contrast more clearly: 'Do not despise prophesying, *but* test all things; hold fast to what is good.'[39]

We should notice here that Paul does not say, 'Test all persons,' or, 'Test all prophets,' but rather, 'Test all *things*.' Again, the procedure he commands makes this something different from the Old Testament where every *prophet* was tested and found 'true' or 'false', but not every prophecy of a true prophet was tested in this way. Paul's command rather puts this kind of prophecy in the same category as the prophecies at Corinth, where every *prophecy*, but not every prophet, was tested.[40]

This process of evaluating prophecies to sort the good from the bad is exactly parallel to what we found in 1 Corinthians 14:29, and provides additional confirmation that in Thessalonica as well as in Corinth Paul did not think that the prophets spoke with a divine authority of actual words.

Moreover, the bare fact that Paul would even have thought it necessary to warn a church—a church which highly regarded the word of God (1 Thess 2:13)—not to 'despise' prophesying is an indication that the Thessalonians themselves were far from regarding prophecies as absolutely authoritative actual words of the Lord.

4. *1 Peter 4:11*

After telling his readers that they should use their gifts for one another 'as good stewards of God's varied grace' (1 Pet 4:10, rsv) Peter then explains, 'whoever speaks, as one who utters oracles of God' (1 Pet 4:11, rsv). But here Peter is not saying that everyone who speaks in the church service (teaching, preaching, prophesying, sharing testimonies, etc) is speaking the very words of God. He is rather speaking of the solemnity of purpose and care with which all congregational speech should be uttered—people should speak as carefully as they would if they were uttering the very 'oracles of God'.

Once again, this passage does not speak to us directly about the nature of the gift of prophecy in the New Testament, or about its authority.

5. *Apostolic preparations for their absence*

In addition to the verses we have considered so far, there is one other type of evidence which suggests that New Testament con- gregational prophets spoke with less authority than New Testament apostles or Scripture. The problem of successors to the apostles is solved not by encouraging Christians to listen to the prophets but by pointing to the Scriptures.[41]

So Paul, at the end of his life, emphasizes 'rightly handling the word of truth' (2 Tim 2:15, RSV), and the 'God-breathed' character of 'Scripture' for 'teaching, for reproof, for correction, and for training in righteousness' (2 Tim 3:16, RSV). Jude urges his readers to 'contend for the faith which was once for all delivered to the saints' (Jude 3, RSV). Peter, at the end of his life, encourages his readers to 'pay attention' to Scripture, which is like 'a lamp shining in a dark place' (2 Pet 1:19–21, RSV), and reminds them of the teaching of the Apostle Paul 'in all his letters' (2 Pet 3:16, RSV). John urges his readers to keep 'the words of the prophecy of this book' (Rev 22:7, RSV). In no case do we read exhortations to 'give heed to the prophets in your churches' or to 'obey the words of the Lord through your prophets', etc. Yet there certainly were prophets prophesying in many local congregations after the death of the apostles. It seems that they did not have authority equal to the apostles, and the authors of Scripture knew that.

Prophecy in early church history

1. *Didache 11*

After this lengthy investigation of the authority of the gift of prophecy in the New Testament, there is one further passage— this one outside the New Testament—which, some may think, indicates that the gift of prophecy enabled those who had it to speak with absolute divine authority like the Old Testament prophets and the New Testament apostles. That passage is in the *Didache*, chapter 11: 'Do not test or examine any prophet who is speaking in a spirit (or: in the Spirit), 'for every sin shall be forgiven, but this sin shall not be forgiven' (*Didache* 11:7).

It is very difficult to decide when the *Didache* was written or how representative it is of life in the early church—there is no scholarly agreement on the matter, and the composition itself does not contain enough internal clues to allow us to make a very certain decision.

In this passage, the reference to the sin against the Holy Spirit shows that these prophets were thought to be speaking with a divine authority that extended to their actual words. Even to *evaluate* (Greek *diakrinō*) anything they said 'in the Spirit' was to sin against the Holy Spirit. A prophet's speech, in this case, was beyond challenge or question (except for a few forbidden things detailed in the following lines, such as asking for money 'in the Spirit'!).

But this passage almost directly contradicts Paul's instructions in 1 Corinthians 14:29. Paul says to *evaluate, weigh* what the prophets say. Using the same Greek word (*diakrinō*), the *Didache* says *not* to evaluate the prophets when they are speaking in the Spirit.

This is only one of several places where the *Didache* says things which are contrary to or at least add greater restrictions to teachings or instructions found in the New Testament (compare *Didache* 1.6 [let alms sweat in your hands until you know to whom you are giving]; 4.14 [confession of sins in the congregation required]; 6.3 [food offered to idols prohibited]; 7.1–4 [baptism in running water; fasting before baptism]; 8.1 [fasting on Wednesdays and Fridays commanded; prohibited on Mondays and Thursdays]; 8.3 [praying the Lord's prayer required three times a day]; 9.1–5 [unknown communion service given as pattern; unbaptized persons excluded from communion]; 10.7 [prophets can hold communion services however they want to]; 11.5 [apostles cannot stay in a city more than two days]; 16.2 [no salvation 'unless you be found perfect at the last time']).

Therefore, although the *Didache* does contain much interesting and even useful material, it clearly differs from the New Testament at several points. Because there are so many differences with New Testament teaching, the *Didache* seems to have been written by someone who was out of touch with mainstream apostolic activity and teaching. It is not a reliable guide to the teachings or practice of the apostles in the early church.

Regarding the gift of prophecy, it seems to make the same kind of mistake others have made, too readily equating the New Testament gift of prophecy with Old Testament prophecy, and attributing to it an absolute, unchallengeable kind of authority.

Of course, once the author of the *Didache* thought of prophecy in this way, it was only natural for him to forbid the very kind of evaluation of prophecies which Paul, with a less authoritative view of New Testament prophecy, commanded.

2. Subsequent early church history: why did prophecy eventually diminish? Was it totally lost?

This investigation has taken us through all the relevant New Testament material on the authority of the gift of prophecy and its relationship to the Old Testament prophets and New Testament apostles. It is not within the scope of our purpose here to survey all the material on prophecy from the early history of the church, but one general comment is in order.

If we assume for a moment that this study is correct in seeing a diminished authority for New Testament prophecy, so that it did not equal Old Testament prophetic speech or New Testament apostolic speech, it must still be admitted that such a distinction between types of authority is a fine one and one which might easily be blurred or forgotten. It would eventually be quite easy for some Christian prophets, whether for good or ill motives, to begin to claim not only that they had received a 're-velation' from God or Christ, but also that they spoke with the very words of God when giving their prophecies.

This was in fact apparently what happened, at least in Montanism and probably in many other cases as well. Of course, if these prophets began to promote heretical ideas, the reaction of the rest of the church would eventually be to drive them out altogether: someone who claims to be speaking God's very words would eventually be accepted or rejected; he (or she) could not be merely tolerated.

Yet along with this rejection of prophets who misunderstood their status there could easily come a rejection of prophecy altogether, so that a failure on the part of the church itself to recognize this diminished authority in the gift of prophecy might have contributed significantly to a total rejection of prophecy in the church. Then coupled with this factor might also be a gradual decrease in belief in the supernatural generally—a sort of decrease in the intensity and vitality of personal faith. This explanation is of course only a suggestion, but it does seem consistent with other surveys of the historical evidence from the early church.[42]

Now if prophecy was rejected by most of the church, it might just cease to function, at least as prophecy. Bruce Yocum notes that 'prophecy and other charismatic gifts flourish in an atmosphere of expectant faith.'[43]

Yet something else may happen. Experiences similar to prophecy, yet not recognized as such, may continue to be given by the Holy Spirit to believers throughout all ages. Roy Clements suggests that that was in fact what happened:

> It seems to me that among Christians who have known a personal work of the Holy Spirit in their lives one finds in every generation testimony to leadings, insights, hunches, premonitions, which are probably identical to the kind of Christian awareness that Luke in Acts regularly ascribes to the Spirit.... And when such leadings include the element of public announcement I believe they amount to what the New Testament calls 'prophecy', even if that is not what we call the phenomenon in our church tradition these days.[44]

Summary

An investigation of other passages in the New Testament has given further understanding of the gift of prophecy in the New Testament, and further evidence to distinguish the 'prophetic' activity of the apostles from the ordinary functioning of the gift of prophecy in local congregations.

On the one hand, there is 'apostolic' prophecy, with absolute divine authority in the actual words used. Any instances of prophecy with this kind of absolute divine authority seemed to be regularly associated with the apostles, as in Matthew 10:19–20 (and parallels), Ephesians 2:20 and 3:5, and Revelation.[45]

On the other hand, there is 'ordinary congregational prophecy', prophecy for which no absolute divine authority is indicated. Christian men and women who experience this ordinary functioning of the prophetic gift are found in several New Testament congregations, and would include the prophets in the church at Corinth (1 Cor 14:29, 30, 36, 37–38; 11:5), the disciples at Tyre (Acts 21:4), the prophets in the church at Thessalonica (1 Thess 5:19–21), Philip's four daughters (Acts 21:9), the disciples at Ephesus (Acts 19:6), and probably Agabus in Acts 11:28 and 21:10–11. If these examples represent ordinary congregational prophecy, then this category would also include cases where there is not enough evidence to make decisions about specific cases, such as prophecy in the church at Rome (Rom 12:6), and, Paul seems to imply, 'in all the churches of the saints' (1 Cor 14:33).

Do those in the charismatic movement today understand prophecy to have such lesser authority? Though some will speak of prophecy as being the 'word of God' for today, there is almost uniform testimony from all sections of the charismatic movement that prophecy is imperfect and impure, and will contain elements which are not to be obeyed or trusted.

The Anglican charismatic leaders Dennis and Rita Bennett write:

> We are not expected to accept every word spoken through the gifts of utterance…but we are only to accept what is quickened to us by the Holy Spirit and is in agreement with the Bible….one manifestation may be 75% God, but 25% the person's own thoughts. We must discern between the two.[46]

Assembly of God leader Donald Gee says:

> It seems very difficult for some people to recognize any source of

prophetic utterance except the divine or the satanic. They refuse to see the important place of the human spirit. As a matter of fact there can be a whole range of degrees of inspiration, from the very high to the very low....The majority of prophecies which we feel compelled either to reject as such, or else receive with great reserve, emanate from the human spirit.[47]

And Bruce Yocum, the author of a widely-used charismatic book on prophecy, writes:

Prophecy can be impure—our own thoughts or ideas can get mixed into the message we receive—whether we receive the words directly or only receive a sense of the message ....(Paul says that all our prophecy is imperfect).[48]

Similarly, George Mallone says::

Prophecy today, although it may be very helpful and on occasion overwhelmingly specific, is not in the category of the revelation given to us in Holy Scripture....A person may hear the voice of the Lord and be compelled to speak, but there is no assurance that it is pollutant-free. There will be a mixture of flesh and spirit.[49]

Now it must be admitted that some confusion arises when charismatics call prophecy 'the word of the Lord' but then say it is not exactly the word of the Lord, but that confusion seems to come from the lack of a clear distinction between Old Testament and New Testament prophecy. In actual practice, no responsible charismatic leader says that prophecy today is equal in authority to Scripture, or should be treated as such.

Yet just here is a point of real misunderstanding in the current discussions over prophecy. Those who argue that prophecy has ceased continue to insist that any prophecy in New Testament times or today must have absolute divine authority. For example, one writes: 'The words of the prophet are words of God and are to be received and responded to as such.'[50]

So it seems to me that often those who hold a 'cessationist' view (that prophecy has ceased and is not for today) are arguing against a view of prophecy which no responsible charismatic holds. And it is a view of prophecy which seems inconsistent with many New Testament passages. I think that is why many charismatics (and non-charismatic evangelicals) do not really feel the force of the anti-charismatic arguments. It would seem more productive (if one wishes to bring responsible criticism against the charismatic movement) to argue against the continuation of the *lesser* kind of prophecy which the most responsible charismatic spokesmen are claiming does exist and function today.

Charismatic writer Donald Bridge puts it well:

> If prophecy is assumed to be directly inspired by God, authoritative and infallible, then clearly there can be no prophecy today. The Bible is complete.... However, there is no need to force all prophecy into such a definition.... What authority does prophecy carry? The same authority as that of any other Christian activity in the church, like leadership, counselling, teaching....If it is true, it will prove to be true. Spiritual people will respond warmly to it. Wise and proven leaders will approve and confirm it. The enlightened conscience will embrace it.[51]

Application for today

If our understanding of the authority of ordinary Christian prophecy is correct, then the primary application to our lives today would be to encourage ourselves not to make the same mistake some made in the early church by overvaluing prophecy and thinking of prophecies as the very words of God. For if that happens (as it sometimes does today), then prophecy will be rejected altogether by some (who see it as a competitor with Scripture as a source of God's words for our lives) and too highly esteemed by others (who see it as the actual words of God and fail to exercise proper discernment over it, sometimes giving prophecy more importance than Scripture in their daily lives, and sometimes even being led astray by the mistaken, human interpretations which come with it).

At this point it is appropriate to make a brief comment regarding the charismatic movement today. Although most charismatics would agree that prophecy today is not equal to Scripture in authority, it must be said that in practice much confusion results from the habit of prefacing prophecies with the common Old Testament phrase, 'Thus says the Lord' (a phrase not used by any congregational prophets in the New Testament churches). The modern use of this phrase is unfortunate, because it gives the impression that the words which follow are God's very words, whereas the New Testament does not justify that position—and, when pressed, most responsible charismatic spokesmen would not want to claim it for every part of their prophecies anyway. So it seems that there would be much gain and no loss if that introductory phrase were dropped.

This suggestion is similar to that of others in the charismatic movement. Timothy Pain says that prophecies should not be 'prefixed with, "Thus says the Lord," or "O my children"! It is much better, in humility...to prefix to the prophecy the words, "I think the Lord is suggesting something like..."'[52]

Assembly of God leader Donald Gee says, 'We hear to a point of weariness the phrase, "I the Lord say unto you." ....it is not essential. The message can be given in less elevated language.'[53]

And in his recent book *Signs and Wonders Today* charismatic writer Donald Bridge seems to agree:

> Nor is there any biblical reason to suppose that prophecy will always be prefaced by, 'Thus saith the Lord', or delivered in the first person singular as if God were directly addressing the listeners....Indeed, such a custom may serve only to confuse 'normal' prophecy with inspired canonical prophecy in the Bible, and discourage the hearers from that very 'weighing' exercise that God requires of them.[54]

In conclusion, there is a danger that prophecy will be overvalued, and there is the opposite danger that it will be rejected altogether. To avoid both of those common errors, we should understand the authority of prophecy correctly, as something which God can use to bring things to our attention, but as something which nonetheless can contain human interpretation and mistakes. It must therefore be subject to Scripture, and must be regulated and tested according to Paul's instructions in 1 Corinthians 14. In brief form, therefore, a modern application of this chapter would be just what Paul told the Thessalonians: 'Do not quench the Spirit, do not despise prophesying, but test everything; hold fast what is good' (1 Thess 5:19–21, RSV).

5

The Source of Prophecies:

Something God Brings to Mind

In the previous chapters we were concerned with the words spoken by a prophet. Were they the words of God or merely the prophet's own words? Did they have absolute divine authority or were they subject to evaluation and sifting by the congregation?

Now we turn to a different subject, the *source* of a prophet's message. How does a prophet know what to say? And what does he think or feel before and during the time he speaks? Is he fully in control of himself or does he experience moments of near-ecstasy?

The important differences between Old Testament prophets and New Testament prophets which we saw in chapters 2–4 should warn us against too quick a jump from a description of the psychological state of the Old Testament prophets to that of the New Testament prophets. Our primary source of information will be the text of the New Testament itself.

1 Corinthians 14:30: Prophecy must be based on a 'revelation' from God

When Paul gives specific instructions to regulate prophetic speech in the congregation, he begins by saying, 'Let two or three prophets speak, and let the others weigh what is said' (1 Corinthians 14:29, RSV). Then, to ensure against disorder, he continues, 'If a revelation is made to another who is seated, let

the first be silent. For you are all able to prophesy one by one...'
(1 Cor 14:30–31).

Apparently Paul is speaking about a situation where the first
prophet would be standing while he spoke (a common practice:
note Lk 4:16; Acts 1:15; 5:34, 11:28, 13:16) and the rest of the
congregation would be sitting listening to him (cf. Acts 20:9;
Jas 2:3). Then suddenly something would be 'revealed' to one
of the seated listeners. He or she would somehow have to signal
this fact to the speaker, perhaps by standing up also, or by
motioning with the hand. Then the first speaker would be silent
and allow the second to speak his prophecy.

This glimpse of the procedure to be followed by prophets at
Corinth allows us to make several observations about the
psychological state of the prophet and the 'revelation' which is
said to come to him.

The revelation comes spontaneously

The thought that occurs to a prophet is pictured as coming to
him *quite spontaneously*, for it comes while the first speaker is
talking. So this prophecy does not seem to be a sermon or les-
son which had been prepared beforehand; it comes rather at
the prompting of the Holy Spirit.

The revelation comes to an individual

This 'revelation' is something that is seen as coming *to an individual person* ('to another sitting by'), not to the entire congregation. Thus the prophecy seems to be not simply a comment
on some new fact which had just been disclosed by the first
speaker, but is rather based on something which has come privately to the mind of the second prophet, without the rest of the
congregation having been aware of it.

The revelation is from God

The 'revelation' which comes to the prophet is thought by Paul
to be of divine, not human, origin. This is evident, first, from
the fact that the word Paul uses for 'revelation' (Greek

apokaluptō) and its related noun (*apokalupsis*) together occur forty-four times in the New Testament, and they never refer to human activity or communication.[55] Rather, whenever the New Testament speaks of a 'revelation', it is always given by the activity of God (Mt 11:25; 16:17; Gal 1:16; Phil 3:15), of Christ (Mt 11:27; Gal 1:12), or of the Holy Spirit (1 Cor 2:10; Eph 3:5), or is a result of events brought about directly by them (especially the Lord's return: Rom 2:5; 8:19; 1 Cor 1:7; 1 Pet 1:7, etc). So this 'revelation' is something which has a divine origin.

Second, Paul's method of argument in 1 Corinthians 14:29–33 also shows that he has in mind a 'revelation' which is divine in origin, and specifically one which comes from the Holy Spirit. But in order to demonstrate this, it is necessary first to determine the meaning of 'the spirits of prophets are subject to prophets' in verse 32 (RSV).

The most likely interpretation is to understand 'spirits' as a reference to the workings of the Holy Spirit in various prophets. A similar reference is found in 1 Corinthians 14:12 (RSV). 'Since you are eager for manifestations of the Spirit,' is literally, 'Since you are eager for *spirits*' (Greek *pneumata*).

Another somewhat parallel example is found in 1 John 4:2 (RSV): 'By this you know *the Spirit* of God: *every spirit* which confesses that Jesus Christ has come in the flesh is of God.'

And yet another related expression is found in Revelation 3:1; 4:5; and 5:6, where 'the seven spirits of God' apparently refers to the various manifestations or workings of the Holy Spirit (compare also 'the seven spirits who are before his throne' in Revelation 1:4, RSV).

Moreover, there are some reasons in the context of 1 Corinthians 14:32 which indicate that 'the spirits of prophets' means 'the workings of the Holy Spirit in various prophets'.

(a) 1 Corinthians 14:33 (RSV), 'For God is not a God of confusion but of peace,' is the reason Paul gives to provide a support or ground for verses 31–32. Now this verse speaks about the character of God. As such, it makes very good sense if verse 32 is describing the activities of the Holy Spirit. Paul would reason: the Holy Spirit will subject his inspiration to the prophet's own timing, and thus will never force a prophet to speak out of turn, because it is not in the nature of God to inspire confusion; it would contradict his own character.

If, on the other hand, verse 32 is a reference to human spirits, it is hard to see how the description of God's character in verse 33 could serve as the ground for verse 32: a statement about God's character would not allow Paul to draw conclusions about the actual behaviour of men.

(b) It is understandable why Paul used 'spirits' here instead of 'the Holy Spirit'. It would have been misleading for Paul to say 'the Holy Spirit is subject to prophets', for that is not true as a general statement, but only in the issue of deciding when a prophet should speak. 'Spirits' fits Paul's purposes better, since it has a more limited reference to the Spirit's specific workings.

(c) There are two possible objections to Paul's rule in verse 30 for which verse 32, understood in this way, would give an effective answer. First, someone might argue that he was forced to prophesy. When the Holy Spirit came upon him with a revelation, he simply could not restrain himself—he had to speak. Paul's answer is that the Holy Spirit remains subject to the prophets; he will never force a prophet to speak. Secondly, someone might object that he could not wait his turn to speak; if he did, the message might be irrevocably lost. To this verse 32 replies that the Holy Spirit is not so impetuous and uncontrollable as that. He is subject to the wise timing and oversight of the prophets.

It is not inconsistent with New Testament teaching to say that the Holy Spirit as He works in a believer's life is 'subject to' or 'subjects himself to' the believer. This same verb (Greek *hypotassō*) is often used of voluntary submission which is not the necessary result of inferior power. It is used in Luke 2:51 of the submission of Jesus to his parents, and in 1 Corinthians 15:28 of the submission of the Son to the Father. So also in this passage, Paul is showing that the Holy Spirit will not force a prophet to speak, but allows the prophet himself to determine when he will speak. This is a voluntary submission in one particular function for the sake of order, and implies no theological statement about the prophet as somehow superior to the Holy Spirit.

The best solution, then, is to say that 'spirits of prophets' in verse 32 means 'the workings of the Holy Spirit in the prophets'.

We can now paraphrase this section:

> If a revelation is made to another sitting by, let the first be silent, for ... the Holy Spirit working in the prophets subjects himself to the prophets, for God is not a God of confusion but of peace.

So Paul is arguing that the *first* prophet should be silent because the Holy Spirit will not force him to continue speaking. This again assumes that the 'revelation' which comes to the prophet comes from the Holy Spirit, and comes so directly that the manner in which it comes reflects both the character of God ('God is not a God of confusion but of peace' [1 Cor 14:33, rsv]) and the personal volition of the Holy Spirit ('the spirits of prophets are subject to prophets' [1 Cor 14:32, rsv]).

The revelation gives insight from God's perspective

The kind of revelation which comes to a prophet is not just any kind of magical disclosure or mysterious insight, but would put the issue in a heavenly or divine perspective. This is evident both from the fact that it is the *Holy Spirit* who does the 'revealing', and from the restriction of the 'reveal/revelation' word group to activities of the one true God (in New Testament usage of the terms)—other terms are used for pagan practices.

This means that the prophets of whom Paul spoke in 1 Corinthians 14:30 did not simply engage in fortune-telling and divination, announcing unrelated, hidden facts to satisfy curiosity or avarice, knowing something only from the perspective of this world. Rather, the 'revelations' they were given enabled them to see facts in relation to God's purposes, and to report that information in such a way that the church might be built up, encouraged and consoled (1 Cor 14:3).

This is important for distinguishing New Testament prophecy from pagan fortune-telling or soothsaying, in which special knowledge of hidden facts was used for personal benefit or in the service of false religion (cf. Acts 8:6ff.; 16:16ff.).

By way of application, we can say that New Testament prophecy would not include things like ESP, astrology, and other occult practices, in so far as they claim to divulge hidden or future facts but do so without placing these facts in the perspective given by the one living and true God, and without using these facts in submission to him.

The revelation is recognizable to the prophet

This final observation concerns *the force with which the 'revelation' came to a prophet.* Paul seems to think of this revelation as a momentary and quite recognizable occurrence, for it happens spontaneously and with such force that it justifies the interruption of a prophet who is already speaking (1 Cor 14:30). In fact, it sometimes came so forcefully that the Corinthians were in danger of thinking they could not resist the Holy Spirit; Paul had to reassure them that the Spirit subjects himself to them in this matter (1 Cor 14:32).

But how would a person know if what came to mind was a 'revelation' from the Holy Spirit? Paul did not write specific instructions; nonetheless, we may suppose that in practice such a decision would include both an objective and a subjective element. Objectively, did the revelation conform with what the prophet knew of the Old Testament Scriptures and with apostolic teaching? (Cf. 1 Cor 12:3; 1 Jn 4:2–3; and, in the Old Testament, Deut 13:1–5.)

But there was no doubt also a subjective element of personal judgement: did the revelation 'seem like' something from the Holy Spirit; did it seem to be similar to other experiences of the Holy Spirit which he had known previously in worship? (Cf. 1 Jn 4:5–6; Jn 10:1–5, 27.) Beyond this it is difficult to specify much further, except to say that over time a congregation would probably become more adept at making evaluations of prophecies, and individual prophets would also benefit from those evaluations and become more adept at recognizing a genuine revelation from the Holy Spirit and distinguishing it from their own thoughts.

On the other hand, we must stop short of saying that this experience was so strong it was somehow 'ecstatic'. Paul assumes the prophet will know what is going on around him, and will be able to control himself (see below for more discussion on this).

Such a revelation apparently could come in the form of words, thoughts, or mental images which God brought to mind. Yet chapters 3 and 4 (above) caution the prophet against claiming certainty that the very words are God's words. (In fact God *can* cause words to come to mind which he does not want us to take as his own words.)

How much does the prophet know?

This brings us to another question: How much does the prophet know about what is in the 'revelation'? Is his or her knowledge clear or fuzzy, broad or narrow? Two passages in 1 Corinthians 13 help us on this question.

1 Corinthians 13:8–13: We see in a mirror dimly

In 1 Corinthians 13 Paul is attempting to show the superiority of love over temporary gifts such as prophecy or tongues. But in order to show this, he must demonstrate that love will endure beyond the time when prophecy, tongues and other gifts have ceased. So in this section he says that prophecy will cease (1 Cor 13:8) *because* it is imperfect (verse 9). It is imperfect *because* we see in a mirror dimly (verse 12):

> Love never ends; as for prophecies, they will pass away; as for tongues, they will cease; as for knowledge, it will pass away. For our

knowledge is imperfect and our prophecy is imperfect; but when the perfect comes, the imperfect will pass away....For now we see in a mirror dimly, but then face to face. Now I know in part; then I shall understand fully, even as I have been fully understood (1 Cor 13:8–10; 12, RSV).

The mirror imagery suggests both *indirectness* and *incompleteness* (one does not see everything, but only those things within the borders of the mirror) in the knowledge that comes through this revelation. But it need not suggest that the image is distorted—mirrors in antiquity could have rather high standards of clarity.

If we apply this to prophecy, it means that the prophet does not see God face to face or speak with him directly, but only receives revelation from God in some kind of (here undefined) indirect manner. It also means that what the prophet sees or learns is only a glimpse of some reality, but not the whole picture. The expression 'dimly, in a puzzling way' indicates that what the prophet sees or learns, or the implications of what is 'revealed', are often difficult to understand (cf. Jn 11:50; 1 Pet 1:11).

That this is the correct understanding of Paul's metaphor is made more clear by an examination of 1 Corinthians 13:9: 'For we know in part and we prophesy in part.' Here it is precisely the *limitations* of prophecy which are in view, and thus it is the way in which a mirror *limits* one's vision which Paul emphasizes.

This sentence in verse 9, 'For we know in part and we prophesy in part,' in itself also describes a way in which prophecy is imperfect. The phrase 'in part' refers primarily to a quantitative imperfection in prophecy: it only gives *partial knowledge* of the subjects it treats. Agabus might come to know something about the future (Acts 11:28; 21:11), but he cannot see all of it. The prophets at Tyre are given a glimpse of Paul's suffering (Acts 21:4) but they cannot foresee all of it. The prophets at Corinth may have some of the secrets of an unbeliever's heart revealed to them (1 Cor 14:25), but they cannot know the unbeliever's heart completely.

This is why prophecy will 'pass away' or 'be rendered useless' (1 Cor 13:8); it is only a temporary and partial substitute for the full and complete means of attaining knowledge which we will have when Christ returns. When that perfect means of knowing comes, the imperfect ways will pass away (1 Cor 13:10).

To summarize this passage: prophecy is imperfect (i) because it gives only a glimpse of the subjects it treats ('in part', verse 9); (ii) because the prophet himself only receives some kind of indirect revelation, and a limited one at that ('we see in a mirror', verse 12); and (iii) because what the prophet does receive is often difficult for him to understand or interpret ('dimly', verse 12).

What can we conclude from this? Apparently that the prophet *may not always understand* with complete clarity just what has been revealed to him, and at times *may not even be sure* that he has received a revelation.

1 Corinthians 13:2: Understanding mysteries and knowledge

Paul writes, 'If I have prophecy and know all mysteries and all knowledge ... but have not love, I am nothing' (1 Cor 13:2).

This verse does not mean that every prophet has an understanding of 'all mysteries and all knowledge', for Paul is using hypothetical superlatives in his argument. He takes several examples of gifts (prophecy, faith, self-sacrifice) and argues that even if developed to their greatest possible degree, they would be worthless without love: 'If I have *all* faith, so as to remove mountains ... If I divide into fragments all my possessions ... if I deliver my body to be burned' (the ultimate in self-sacrifice).

So Paul is simply saying that the ultimate result of prophecy developed to its fullest possible extent would be a knowledge of all mysteries and all knowledge. This is not now the case with any living prophet, according to Paul, for 'we prophesy in part' (1 Cor 13:9) and so only at Christ's return will we know fully 'even as we are known' (1 Cor 13:12).

Nevertheless, this passage does make clear by implication that knowing 'mysteries' and 'knowledge', even if only in part, is a normal component of the gift of prophecy. So there is a benefit which comes to the prophet as a result of his having the gift of prophecy: when he receives a revelation, he then understands and knows more than he would have otherwise.

'Mysteries' here are 'the secret thoughts, plans, and dispensations of God which are hidden from the human reason ... and hence must be revealed to those for whom they are intended' (BAGD, 530). Therefore this verse gives further confirmation to our earlier understanding of 'revelation' as an essential element of prophecy. But the verse will not allow us to go beyond this and define with much certainty the precise content of the 'mysteries and knowledge'.

Is prophecy 'ecstatic'?

All of this discussion about the revelation which comes to the prophet would be incomplete without an enquiry into the degree of control and awareness of surroundings which a prophet had when he or she received such a revelation. Was the prophet in a trance of some kind? Did he lose any measure of self-control, or become temporarily unaware of his surroundings? These matters all relate to the question of prophetic ecstasy.

The meaning of 'ecstatic'

The English word 'ecstasy' can be used to mean several different things. For our purposes in this study, we are concerned with four specific questions in the general area of ecstatic experience:

(a) Was the prophet forced to speak against his will?

(b) Did the prophet lose his self-control and begin to rave violently or in a disorderly, disruptive way?

(c) Did the prophet speak things which made no sense to him?

(d) Was the prophet for a time unaware of his surroundings? For the purpose of this study, we can consider a prophet to be in an *ecstatic* state if any one of these four conditions is true of him. On the other hand, merely (i) prophesying in an excited state, or (ii) speaking with strong emotion, or (iii) having a high level of concentration or awareness of the meaning of his words, or (iv) having an unusually strong sense of the presence and the working of God in his mind, are not sufficiently abnormal states to warrant the use of the term 'ecstatic'.

1 Corinthians 12:1–3: Christian prophecy is different from pagan prophecy

At the beginning of the long discussion of spiritual gifts in 1 Corinthians 12–14, Paul distinguishes *Christian* experience of spiritual gifts from the kinds of spiritual influences experienced by *unbelievers*. He writes:

> Now concerning spiritual gifts, brethren, I do not want you to be uninformed. You know that when you were heathen, you were led astray to dumb idols, however you may have been moved. Therefore I want you to understand that no one speaking by the Spirit of God ever says 'Jesus be cursed!' and no one can say 'Jesus is Lord' except by the Holy Spirit (1 Cor 12:1–3, RSV).

Here Paul recognizes their pagan background, and because of that he concludes that they need instruction about spiritual gifts—otherwise, they would be 'uninformed' or 'ignorant'. They previously followed 'dumb idols' who could not speak words of instruction to their followers or through their followers.

The Corinthians may have experienced some very strange things in pagan worship services (including perhaps some cries of 'cursing' during religious ecstasy). But Paul says this will not happen with genuine Christian prophecy. If someone appears to be under some kind of spiritual influence and then begins to curse Jesus, it is simply not from the Holy Spirit. That kind of thing does not happen with the Holy Spirit's gifts.

For our purposes here, we should notice that Paul clearly distinguishes pagan 'spiritual' experiences from Christian ones. Therefore, any ancient evidence showing 'ecstatic' prophesying by *non-Christians* would not really tell us about the nature of *Christian* prophecy. The evidence for that must come instead from the New Testament itself.

1 Corinthians 14:29–33: Orderly, reasonable conduct

Within this passage alone we find several considerations which indicate that Paul thought none of the four criteria of ecstasy to be true of the Corinthian prophets.

(a) That the prophet was not forced to speak against his will is shown by the fact that he could stop his prophecy to allow another to speak (1 Cor 14:30b), that the second prophet apparently did not suddenly burst into speech but rather signalled that he was ready to prophesy and then waited for the first prophet to stop (verse 30a), that all prophets were able to prophesy in turn (verse 31), and that the Holy Spirit subjected himself to the prophet in such a way that he could act in a restrained and orderly manner (verse 32).

(b) That the prophet did not lose his self control or begin to rave violently is made clear by Paul's argument in 1 Corinthians 14:33 when he says that the result of the Spirit's working in a prophet is not 'disorder' (or 'frenzied disturbance' Greek *akatastasia*), but peace (v. 33), as well as by verse 32 where it is made explicit that the prophet himself retains control of the situation, because the Holy Spirit is subject to him.

(c) Although there is no explicit statement that a prophet understood what he was saying, it is clear that the hearers understood, for they were to evaluate what was said (1 Cor 14:29), and they would all learn and be encouraged by the prophecies (v. 31). If the hearers all understood and learned from the prophecy, then certainly the prophet himself understood what he was saying.

(d) Since the first prophet was able to recognize from some clear signal that someone else had received a revelation and was ready to prophesy (1 Cor 14:30), it is clear that Paul assumed him to be well aware of his surroundings, not out of touch with reality at all. This was true not only while a man was prophesying, but also while he was receiving a revelation, for the second prophet knew enough to wait his turn while someone else was speaking, so that they could prophesy 'one by one' (1 Cor 14:30–31).

1 Corinthians 14:3–4

Here we find more evidence for the intelligibility of the prophet's words, for he speaks 'to men' and the result is that they are strengthened, encouraged and comforted (v. 3). The contrast here is between speech in tongues which no one understands (v. 2) and prophecy which is understood by the hearers.

1 Corinthians 14:23–25

Whereas an unbelieving visitor might level the charge of madness against the congregation if all spoke in tongues (v. 23), this would not be true in the case of prophecy: even if *all* prophesied (v. 24), a situation which might well have been thought to give opportunity for some ecstatic outbreaks, the result would not be confusion but very understandable speech which would convince the visitor of his sin (v. 25).

1 Corinthians 14:40

When Paul commands that all things (including prophecy, v. 39) be done 'in a fitting and orderly way' (New International Version), he assumes that the prophets would behave not in an ecstatic manner, but as people who were very much in control of themselves.

Objection: Perhaps Paul was trying to correct actual prophetic ecstasy at Corinth

Someone might argue, in spite of all of this evidence, that although Paul *wanted* prophets to behave in the way we have outlined, in fact the prophets at Corinth were engaged in some quite ecstatic behaviour, and Paul was attempting to correct their disorder in this epistle.

However, before Paul gives the instruction in 1 Corinthians 14:29–33 he already assumes that prophecy at Corinth was commonly understood to be very intelligible and quite beneficial to the hearers (1 Corinthians 14:3–4, 23–25). The problem—if we can define it with any certainty—was perhaps a very simple one, namely, that more than one prophet would try to speak at once (1 Cor 14:30–31), and perhaps that some claimed they could not refrain from speaking (v. 32).

Paul's response is that the Corinthians are able to control themselves, for this is the way the Holy Spirit *always* acts: he creates peace, not confusion, and is subject to the prophet (vv. 32–33). So the claim that some prophets were unable to exercise self-control was simply not true, according to Paul. His reply both corrects the Corinthian disorder and shows that Christian prophecy itself is by nature non-ecstatic.

Other New Testament verses

Very briefly we can note here some other New Testament verses which might relate to the problem of prophetic ecstasy.

(a) *Acts 19:6* Here speaking in tongues and prophesying are closely joined as if they might be a single experience. But the text itself gives no indication of any ecstatic experiences here. And with regard to precisely the one characteristic by which tongues might be termed 'ecstatic' (its unintelligibility, my criterion [b]), Paul, in the more full discussion in 1 Corinthians, clearly differentiates tongues from prophecy (cf. 1 Cor 14). So we do not find New Testament evidence for tongues as ecstatic in any sense that would bear on the question of prophecy.

(b) *2 Corinthians 12:1–4* Paul says that he was 'caught up to the third heaven' and experienced 'visions and revelations of the Lord' (vv. 2, 1, RSV). The experience was 'ecstatic' in sense (v. 4): he was for a time so unaware of his surroundings that he did not know whether he was in the body or out of the body (v. 2). Might this be an example of New Testament prophetic ecstasy?

This section is not really relevant to our investigation of the New Testament gift of prophecy because (a) the 'revelations' Paul received were specifically *not* given in order that he might prophesy (that is, report them to others): he heard things which are not permitted for men to speak (v. 4), and was so reticent about even mentioning the experience that he waited fourteen years (v. 2) and then spoke of it in the third person (vv. 2–5); furthermore, (b) such an experience seems to Paul to be extremely unusual, and not the normal experience of prophets or any other Christians, for he says the revelations were of an extraordinary character (v. 7), and relates that experience only as a last-ditch attempt to show his superiority over the false apostles, and thus as something of which he 'might' boast (vv. 5–6). So this experience cannot be taken as characteristic of New Testament prophecy.

Conclusion on prophetic ecstasy

An examination of data in 1 Corinthians and then elsewhere in the New Testament indicates that certainly at Corinth, and quite probably elsewhere in the New Testament church, prophets did not have ecstatic experiences while prophesying.

Is prophecy miraculous?

In connection with this discussion of a 'revelation' from the Holy Spirit as the source of a prophecy, it is appropriate to ask whether prophecy is in fact a 'miraculous' gift. Or is it a non-miraculous or more ordinary gift? Does the fact that it is based on a revelation from the Holy Spirit make it miraculous?

1 Corinthians 12:8–11

Here it is helpful to look at the gift of prophecy as it appears in the list of gifts in 1 Corinthians 12:8–11. Paul writes:

> To one is given through the Spirit the utterance of wisdom, and to another the utterance of knowledge according to the same Spirit, to

another faith by the same Spirit, to another gifts of healing by the one Spirit, to another the working of miracles, to another prophecy, to another the ability to distinguish between spirits, to another various kinds of tongues, to another the interpretation of tongues. All these are inspired by one and the same Spirit, who apportions to each one individually as he wills (1 Cor 12:8–11, RSV).

In this passage, prophecy (v. 10) is one of the abilities which are empowered (or 'inspired') by the Holy Spirit (v. 11). But we should also observe that prophecy is not unique in this sense, for all the gifts Paul lists are included in the empowering work of the Holy Spirit mentioned in verse 11. The fact that prophecy originates with the Holy Spirit only puts it on a par with these other gifts.[56]

What do we mean by 'miracle'?

The question of whether prophecy is 'miraculous' may be answered in different ways, depending on the sense in which 'miracle' is used:

(a) If 'miracle' is defined the way people sometimes understand it, that is, as 'a direct intervention by God in history' then the answer must be that prophecy cannot be distinguished from other gifts in this way. This is true for two reasons:

(i) Paul makes no distinction in the kinds of working of the Holy Spirit (such as 'direct' and 'indirect') in various gifts, but emphasizes that they *all* are brought about by the working of the Holy Spirit (1 Cor 12:11). Now Paul is arguing against the pride and jealousy concerning spiritual gifts which troubled the Corinthian church. He is trying to show how all the gifts are valuable because they all are from the Holy Spirit. It would destroy the force of his argument if it could be claimed that some gifts are 'more directly' from the Holy Spirit or more a result of the Holy Spirit's own activity than others.

(ii) Paul himself lists the various gifts and offices in different ways at different times, showing no awareness of any 'miraculous versus non-miraculous' distinction in categories of gifts: faith, and words of wisdom and knowledge are listed alongside of gifts of healing and workings of acts of power (1 Cor 12:8–10); 'helps' and 'administrations' are mixed in between gifts of healing and kinds of tongues (1 Cor 12:28); hymns, lessons, revelations, tongues and interpretations can be mentioned in the same breath (1 Cor 14:26); revelation, knowledge, prophecy and teaching all come together (1 Cor 14:6).

Thus if one wanted to argue that prophecy is a 'miraculous' gift because it resulted from the direct activity of the Holy Spirit, then he would have to argue that *all* the gifts are 'miraculous' in that sense. But this would void the term 'miracle' of any value for distinguishing some kinds of activities from others.

(b) There is another possible definition of 'miracle', however. If a 'miracle' is defined as 'something which *arouses awe and wonder* in people because of its apparent contradiction of normal laws of natural human or physical behaviour,' then prophecy would be considered a miraculous gift on the basis of 1 Corinthians 14:22–25: prophecy is a 'sign' for believers (v. 22), an evident demonstration that God is working among them, and also an amazing process that evokes wonder from an unbeliever (v. 25). Because it is a less common way for God to work in the world, it is more clearly seen as an indication of divine activity.

So prophecy is at least sometimes a 'miraculous' gift in terms of the response it elicits from people, but any attempt to classify it as 'more directly' from God than some other gifts is not persuasive in terms of the text of Scripture itself.

Summary

The reception of a 'revelation' from God was the source of a prophecy. The Pauline terms for such revelations, and the context in which Paul speaks of them, enable us to say that the revelation came quite spontaneously (but privately) to an individual, was of divine origin, was seen from a divine perspective, and probably took the form of words, thoughts or mental pictures which suddenly impressed themselves forcefully on the mind of the prophet.

But prophesying, like other gifts, is only 'partial' or is 'limited' as a source of knowledge. Both the revelation received by a prophet and the resulting prophecy will give only partial information about the subject, and will sometimes be difficult to understand or interpret.

Since there are indications in 1 Corinthians that the prophet was not forced to speak against his will, did not lose his self-control or rave violently, did not speak things which made no sense to him, and was not unaware of his surroundings, the gift of prophecy should not be termed an 'ecstatic' gift, nor was prophesying an 'ecstatic' activity.

Prophecy is not any more 'miraculous' than other gifts if 'miracle' means something which comes 'directly' from God. But if 'miracle' means something which arouses awe and wonder because it is a less common way for God to work in the world, then 1 Corinthians 14:22–25 would allow us to call prophecy 'miraculous.'

Application for today

If we are to see the gift of prophecy functioning in our churches today, we must first believe that it is possible that God would give us such 'revelations' from time to time, and, second, we must allow ourselves to be receptive to such influences from the Holy Spirit, especially at times of prayer and worship.

In practical terms, this would mean allowing more time for 'listening' for God or 'waiting' on him, mixed in and added to our regular times of Bible reading, intercessory prayer, and verbal praise. Then also, some of our more informal times of corporate worship should allow for periods of quietness and receptivity to such promptings from the Holy Spirit. If God should bring something to mind in these times, then the person receiving such a revelation should tell the congregation what it is.

Yet, as we saw in chapters 3 and 4, this report should not be thought of as 'God's very words', nor should the speaker preface his or her remarks with words which would give that impression, such as, 'Thus says the Lord,' or, 'Hear the words of God', etc.—those statements should be reserved for Scripture, and Scripture alone. Something like, 'I think the Lord is showing me that...' or, 'I think the Lord is indicating that...' or, 'It seems that the Lord is putting on my heart a concern that...' would all be much more appropriate, and far less misleading.

Many of us have experienced or heard of similar events today—for example, an unplanned but urgent request may have been given to pray for certain missionaries in Japan. Then, much later, those who prayed discovered that just at that time the missionaries had been in an awful accident or at a point of intense spiritual conflict, and had needed those prayers. Paul would call the sense or intuition of those things a 'revelation', and the report to the assembled church of that prompting from God would be called a 'prophecy'. It may have elements of the speaker's own understanding or interpretation in it and it certainly needs evaluation and testing, yet it has a valuable function in the church nonetheless.

This brings us to the next point: though such revelations from God are valuable, they are also limited. They must never compete with Scripture in the authority or importance we attach to them, and they must never be allowed to function without continuing evaluation by the church, especially those in leadership. All must recognize that the revelation is partial, and may not be clear to the person prophesying, and may contain elements of mistaken understanding or interpretation on the part of the person prophesying.

Since prophesying was not an ecstatic activity, the scriptural rules for orderly conduct should be followed, and no one should be allowed to think that he or she will be forced by the Holy Spirit to prophesy, or will lose self-control or awareness of the surrounding circumstances. Prophecy may involve heightened awareness of God's purposes, but it does not therefore involve diminished awareness of the ordinary situations of life.

6

Prophecy and Teaching:

How Are they Different Gifts?

Our study to this point has shown that the New Testament gift of prophecy has less authority than Old Testament prophetic speech and New Testament apostolic speech (chapters 3 and 4). It has also concluded that the source of prophecy was a 'revelation' from God, or specifically from the Holy Spirit.

Now a related question arises: What is essential for a prophecy? In other words, just what is it that makes something a prophecy and not some other kind of speech activity? More specifically:

(1) Is a 'revelation' *necessary* for there to be a prophecy?

(2) Does a 'revelation' by itself constitute a prophecy, or is it also necessary that the revelation be reported in some way?

These questions can best be answered in connection with an investigation of another gift, the gift of teaching, and a comparison between prophecy and teaching. Therefore this chapter will first discuss the essential nature of prophecy, and then, by way of comparison, the essential nature of teaching.

The essential nature of prophecy

What is necessary for a prophecy to occur? What factors make the difference between something that is a prophecy and something that is not? The New Testament seems to indicate two factors that are essential to prophecy:

(1) a revelation from the Holy Spirit (= the source of the prophecy);

(2) a public report of that revelation (= the prophecy itself).
This section will discuss these two points in order.

A 'revelation' is necessary for a prophecy

That a 'revelation' from the Holy Spirit was necessary for a
prophecy to occur is seen from the following considerations:

(a) As we saw in the previous chapter, in 1 Corinthians
14:29–33, Paul assumes that the person about to prophesy is
the person who has received a 'revelation' (v. 30). No other
valid reason is given for silencing the first prophet and allowing
the second to speak. The probable implication is that nothing
but a 'revelation' could qualify the second speaker as a
prophet.

Then also when Paul argues that the Holy Spirit at work in
prophets is subject to the prophets themselves (v. 32), he
specifically has in mind the activity of the Holy Spirit in impart-
ing a 'revelation' (v. 30). Verse 32 is a general statement which
applies to all prophets, just as verse 31 explicitly includes all
who prophesy. It does not seem possible that some prophet at
Corinth could have avoided Paul's instructions by claiming that
verses 30–33 did not apply to him, because he normally
prophesied *without* ever having a 'revelation.' Rather, Paul
assumes that his instructions apply to all the prophets, and thus
that all prophesy on the basis of 'revelations' imparted to them
by the Holy Spirit.

(b) A similar indication is found in 1 Corinthians 14:24–
25, where Paul pictures the following situation in the congregation:

> But if all prophesy, and an unbeliever or outsider enters, he is con-
> victed by all, he is called to account by all, the secrets of his heart
> are disclosed; and so, falling on his face, he will worship God and
> declare that God is really among you (1 Cor 14:24–25, RSV).

In this case, those who prophesy make a public disclosure of
the secrets of a visitor's heart (v. 25a). The visitor responds in
a way that indicates that, at least in his view, only God could

have made these things known to the prophets (v. 25b). And apparently *everyone who prophesies* contributes to this act of conviction and investigation ('he is convicted by all', v. 24, RSV). So again Paul assumes that all who prophesy have received a 'revelation'.

(c) In the rest of the New Testament, all the examples of Christian prophecy about which we have enough information to make a decision also imply the prior reception of some kind of 'revelation'. In Acts 11:28 and again in Acts 21:10–11, Agabus' predictions are descriptions of future events, and thus based on something that had been revealed to him.

It is possible, though not certain, that the same is true of the Ephesian 'disciples' in Acts 19:6, where they began to speak with tongues and to prophesy as soon as Paul had laid his hands on them and the Holy Spirit had come upon them. The spontaneity of the event and their ignorance of even the rudiments of Christian teaching (Acts 19:2) show that this prophesying (whatever form it took) was not intelligent Christian preaching but rather was the result of some extraordinary working of the Holy Spirit, and thus probably the result of a 'revelation'.

Finally, in the mention of apostolic prophecy in Ephesians 3:5, the same requirement holds true: a revelation concerning the Gentile inclusion is specifically said to be given to apostles and prophets by the Holy Spirit.

Elsewhere the New Testament speaks of pre-Pentecost prophecy as well. This material must be treated with more caution because it may not be the same in all respects as specifically *Christian* prophecy in the church after Pentecost, but it does give us an idea of the kinds of abilities which were thought to characterize those who could be designated 'prophets'. In several cases, the distinguishing characteristic of a prophet is the possession of information which could only come through a 'revelation'.

For example, in Luke 7:39, the Pharisee assumes that a prophet could know about the life of someone he had just met—presumably by receiving a 'revelation'. And in John

4:19, when Jesus startles the woman at the well with knowledge of her previous life, she says, 'Sir, I can see that you are a prophet.' In Luke 22:63f., the guards blindfold and beat Jesus, then cruelly demand of him, 'Prophesy! Who hit you?', apparently employing a popular conception of a prophet as one who can know things through 'revelations' and need not rely on ordinary means of acquiring information. In Acts 2:30f., where David is said to have foreseen and therefore spoken of the resurrection, he is specifically designated as a prophet. In John 11:51, Caiaphas is said to predict both the fact and the meaning of Jesus' death. 'This he did not say of himself, but ... he prophesied'—here prophesying is specifically contrasted to speaking 'of oneself', from one's own knowledge.

In addition to these examples, there is the negative consideration that we find no example in the New Testament of a prophet simply speaking on the basis of his own knowledge or ideas instead of on the basis of some kind of 'revelation'.

However, someone may object at this point that the fact that people 'learn' from prophecy (1 Cor 14:31) makes it equal to teaching, or to 'Bible teaching'. But this conclusion is not correct, for people can learn from many things: someone's prayer, someone else's kind behaviour or even another person's encouraging smile. These activities may be called 'teaching' in some broad sense, but they are not 'teaching' in the sense in which Paul uses the word in the New Testament to refer to the explanation and application of Bible passages to the church.

(d) Although the previous chapter has shown that one cannot always depend on the phenomena of Old Testament prophecy to provide parallels with New Testament prophecy, at this point there is some similarity: the possession of a revelation from God was what distinguished true from false prophecy in the Old Testament. A false prophet was one who spoke when the Lord had given him nothing to speak (Deut 18:20), who spoke from his own mind (Ezek 13:3; Jer 23:16ff.), or who spoke by a lying spirit (1 Kings 22:23). But a true prophet was one to whom God had revealed his secret (Amos 3:7).

In this connection it is interesting to note the way true and false prophets are distinguished in 1 John 4:1–6. A false prophet (v. 1) is one who speaks by a spirit which is not of God, the spirit of the Antichrist (v. 3). So even the false prophet speaks by a 'revelation' of sorts, but it is from an evil spirit, not from 'the Spirit of God' (v. 2).

The answer to our first question, therefore, must be clearly positive. A 'revelation' from the Holy Spirit is necessary for a prophecy to occur. If there is no such revelation, there is no prophecy.

A report of the revelation is necessary for a prophecy

What if someone receives some kind of revelation from the Holy Spirit, but gives no indication of that revelation to anyone else? Is the receipt of a revelation by itself enough to be considered a prophecy? The answer to that question must be negative.

There are many instances in the New Testament where a 're-velation' is given for the private benefit of the individual recipient, and he does not subsequently report it in a public proclamation. When Jesus said that his teachings had been 'hidden ... from the wise and understanding' and 'revealed ... to little children' (Mt 11:25, 27), it did not mean that everyone who understood Jesus' teaching was a prophet. Whenever God revealed to one of the Philippian Christians some lack of Christian maturity in his or her life (Phil. 3:15), it did not mean that a Christian was therefore a prophet. When the Christians in Ephesus and the surrounding cities received a 'spirit of revelation' in the knowledge of Christ (Eph 1:17), they did not all automatically become prophets. (Cf. Jn 12:38; Rom 1:17, 18; Gal 2:2; Eph 1:17.)

Furthermore, other examples could be cited where people received some kind of special revelation but are not thereby said to be prophets, or to prophesy. The 'revelations' can take the form of dreams (Mt 1:20; 2:12–13, 19, 22; 27:19), visions (Mt 17:9; Lk 1:22; Acts 7:31; 9:10, 12; 10:3, 17, 19; 16:9; 26:19;

2 Cor 12:1), or trances (Acts 10:10; 22:17).

This means that the reception of a 'revelation' alone would not constitute a person a prophet. Only where the revelation is also proclaimed to others, as in 1 Corinthians 14:29–33 or the examples with Agabus or the prophets at Tyre, is a prophecy said to occur. In fact, it is the telling of the revelation which is itself called the 'prophecy'.

The essential nature of teaching

What then is the gift of teaching? Is it always different from prophecy, or might some prophecies also be called 'teachings'? Can any speech activity reporting a spontaneous, personal 'revelation' be called not a prophecy but a 'teaching'?

An investigation of the New Testament data on 'teaching' will show it to be clearly distinct from prophecy—'teaching' is based not on a 'revelation' but on Scripture, and generally results from conscious reflection and preparation.

Teaching is based on Scripture, not on a spontaneous revelation

In contrast to the gift of prophecy, we find that no human speech act which is called a 'teaching' (Greek *didaskalia* or *didachē*) or done by a 'teacher' (*didaskalos*), or described by the verb 'teach' (*didaskō*), is ever said to be based on a 'revelation' in the New Testament. Rather, 'teaching' is often simply an explanation or application of Scripture.

This is evident in Acts 15:35 (RSV), where Paul and Barnabas and 'many others' are in Antioch 'teaching and preaching *the word of the Lord*'. And at Corinth, Paul stayed one and a half years 'teaching *the word of God* among them' (Acts 18:11, RSV). The readers of the epistle to the Hebrews, though they ought to have been teachers, needed rather to have someone to teach them again 'the first principles of *God's word*' (Heb 5:12, RSV). Paul tells the Romans that the words of the Old Testament *Scriptures* were 'written for our instruction (or 'teaching', Greek *didaskalia*)' (Rom 15:4, RSV), and writes to Timothy that 'all scripture' is 'profitable for teaching (*didaskalia*)' (2 Tim 3:16, RSV).

Of course, if 'teaching' in the early church was so often based on Scripture, it is not surprising that it could also be based on something equal to Scripture in authority, namely, a received body of apostolic instructions. So Timothy was to take the teaching which he had received from Paul and commit it to faithful men who would be able to 'teach others also' (2 Tim 2:2, RSV). And the Thessalonians were to 'hold firm to the trad-·itions' which they were '*taught*' by Paul (2 Thess 2:15).

Far from being based on a spontaneous revelation which came during the worship service of the church (as prophecy was), this kind of 'teaching' was the repetition and explanation of authentic apostolic teaching. To teach contrary to Paul's instructions was to 'teach' different or heretical doctrine (Greek *heterodidaskalō*) and to fail to give heed to 'the sound words of our Lord Jesus Christ and the *teaching* which accords with godliness' (1 Tim 6:3, RSV). In fact, Paul said that Timothy was to remind the Corinthians of Paul's ways 'as I *teach* them everywhere in every church' (1 Cor 4:17, RSV). Similarly, Timothy was to 'command and teach' (1 Tim 4:11, RSV) and to 'teach and urge' (1 Tim 6:2, RSV) Paul's instructions to the Ephesian church.

The difference with prophecy is quite clear here: Timothy wasn't to *prophesy* Paul's instructions; he was to *teach* them. Paul didn't *prophesy* his ways in every church; he *taught* them. The Thessalonians were not told to hold firm to the traditions which were 'prophesied' to them but to the traditions which they were 'taught'.

Thus it was not prophecy but *teaching* which in a primary sense (from the apostles) first provided the doctrinal and ethical norms by which the church was regulated. And as those who learned from the apostles also taught, their *teaching* guided and directed the local churches.

Among the elders, therefore, were 'those who labour in the word and *teaching*' (1 Tim 5:17), and an elder was to be 'an apt teacher' (1 Tim 3:2, RSV; cf. Tit 1:9)—but nothing is said about any elders whose work was prophesying, nor is it ever said that an elder has to be 'an apt prophet' or that elders should be 'holding firm to sound prophecies'. In his leadership function Timothy was to take heed to himself and to his 'teaching' (1 Tim 4:16), but he is never told to take heed to his prophesying. James warned that those who *teach*, not those who prophesy, will be judged with greater strictness (Jas 3:1).

Teaching is always named as a separate gift from prophecy

One further observation also indicates that we should expect that teaching would be different from prophecy: they are listed as separate, distinct gifts whenever the New Testament talks about different kinds of spiritual gifts (Eph 4:11; Rom 12:6; 1 Cor 12:28). This would make us suspect that any definition that viewed them as the same activity had not quite understood them in the New Testament sense.

The difference between prophecy and teaching

In conclusion, *teaching* in terms of the New Testament epistles consisted of repeating and explaining the words of Scripture (or the equally authoritative teachings of Jesus and of the apostles) and applying them to the hearers. In the New Testament epistles, 'teaching' is something very much like what is described by our phrase 'Bible teaching' today.

By contrast, no prophecy in New Testament churches is ever said to consist of the interpretation and application of texts of Old Testament Scripture. Although a few people have *claimed* that the prophets in New Testament churches gave 'charismatically inspired' interpretations of Old Testament Scripture,[57] that claim has hardly been persuasive, primarily because it is hard to find in the New Testament any convincing examples where the 'prophet' word group is used to refer to someone doing this kind of activity.

Rather, a prophecy must be the report of a spontaneous

revelation from the Holy Spirit. So the distinction is quite clear: if a message is the result of conscious reflection on the text of Scripture, containing interpretation of the text and application to life, then it is (in New Testament terms) a *teaching*. But if a message is the report of something God brings suddenly to mind, then it is a *prophecy*. And, of course, even prepared teachings can be interrupted by unplanned additional material which the Bible teacher suddenly felt God was bringing to his mind—in that case, it would be a 'teaching' with some prophecy mixed in.

The difference between prophecy and preaching

In modern English, the word 'preaching' is generally used to mean the same thing as the New Testament meant by 'teaching'. Therefore, this does not need to be a separate subject—all the things said about 'teaching' in the previous section apply to 'preaching' as well.

However, it may be helpful at this point to mention two charismatic leaders who see the difference between prophecy and teaching (or 'preaching') to be very similar to what we found in the New Testament.

British Anglican charismatic Michael Harper writes:

> A preacher usually prepares, speaks and expounds from the Word of God. But a prophet speaks directly under the anointing of the Holy Spirit. Both have a part to play in the edification of the Church—but they should not be confused.[58]

And American Episcopalian charismatics Dennis and Rita Bennett say:

> Prophecy is not 'inspired preaching'... in preaching, the intellect, training, skill, background, and education are involved and inspired by the Holy Spirit. The sermon may be written down ahead of time, or given on the spot, but it comes from the inspired intellect. Prophecy, on the other hand, means that the person is

bringing the words the Lord gives directly; it is from the spirit, not the intellect.[59]

Why does Paul allow women to prophesy but not to teach?

The differences between prophecy and teaching with respect to authority in the congregation

Once we have understood 'prophecy' and 'teaching' not according to some twentieth-century English language definitions but according to the way they are spoken of in the New Testament itself, it is possible to understand how it was entirely consistent for Paul to permit women to prophesy (1 Cor 11:5) but not to teach (1 Tim 2:12) in the public assemblies of the New Testament churches.

Teaching provided normative doctrinal and ethical guidance for the church. Those who publicly taught in churches spoke not with authority equal to Scripture itself, but with authority that, in practical terms, provided the doctrinal and ethical summaries of scriptural teachings and the practical applications of Scripture by which the church was directed. Scripture was the final authority, but teachers—more than prophets or evangelists or those with any other gift—were the ones who regularly had the responsibility to show how Scripture, the church's absolute authority, was to be interpreted and applied in each local congregation. To teach in the church was to exercise at least a *de facto* leadership and authority (and often a publicly recognized and acknowledged leadership and authority) which strongly influenced the doctrinal and ethical convictions of the church.

Whether many or most teachers were also elders, or whether all teachers were also elders, is difficult to decide with certainty. But it is clear that there is a very close connection between the role of elder and the role of teacher, a connection made appropriate by the leadership which teachers in fact exercised in the congregation.[60]

But New Testament church prophecy had no such authority.

Those who prophesied did not tell the church how to interpret and apply Scripture to life. They did not proclaim the doctrinal and ethical standards by which the church was guided, nor did they exercise governing authority in the church. (For this last point see chapter 9 below.)

Prophets in New Testament churches rather reported in their own words something which, it seemed to them, God had forcefully brought to mind. So *teaching* based on the written word of God had far greater authority than occasional prophecies which the speaker *thought* were from God. Prophecies were subordinate to the authoritative *teaching* of Scripture, and, to be accepted, would have had to be in conformity to the received *teaching* of the church. But the reverse was not true: teachings did not have to conform to any collection or summary of prophecies that had been spoken in the church.

What about prophets preceding teachers in 1 Corinthians 12:28?

Someone may object at this point that the ordering of gifts in 1 Corinthians 12:28 (RSV), 'first apostles, second prophets, third teachers,' indicates that prophets had greater authority than teachers in the church (cf. also Eph 4:11). However, the list in 1 Corinthians 12:28 is not an ordering according to authority: note that later in the list 'administrators' are put next to last, and 'helpers' come before 'administrators'.

As the discussion in chapter 3 indicated (see pp. 68–69), the ranking in this passage is not one of authority. Rather, Paul goes on to explain the meaning of 'first ... second ... third ... then ... then ...' in the following verses. At the end of the list he encourages the Corinthians to 'earnestly desire the greater gifts' (1 Cor 12:31), and, after explaining the crucial importance of love in chapter 13, he returns to the idea of 'greater' gifts in 1 Corinthians 14:1–5, showing that prophecy is 'greater' (Greek *meizōn*, the same word used in 1 Corinthians 12:31) than uninterpreted tongues (1 Cor 14:5) because in prophecy the church is 'edified'. Therefore 'greater' in this context means 'contributing more to the edifying of the church', and the list in

1 Corinthians 12:28 should be understood (at least in the first four kinds of persons mentioned) as a listing according to value in edifying the church. This understanding is consistent with Paul's overall concern in 1 Corinthians chapters 12—14, 'Let all things be done for edification' (1 Cor 14:26, RSV).

Is Paul's teaching consistent with itself?

Today, there are differing views among Christians about appropriate roles for women in the activities of the church. However, whatever a person may think about this question as it applies to the contemporary situation, it should still be possible to see consistency, not contradiction, in Paul's instructions. 1 Timothy 2 indicates that Paul is concerned to preserve male leadership, headship, or governing authority in the church. He therefore prohibits women from teaching or having authority over men.[61] But praying and prophesying in church do not involve the speaker—male or female—in assuming functions of leadership or governing authority. There is therefore no reason to keep them from these activities; rather, they should be encouraged.

Summary

Prophecy, not only in 1 Corinthians but in the entire New Testament, has two distinctive features. First, it must be based on a 'revelation': if there is no revelation, there is no prophecy. Second, it must include a public proclamation. The mere reception of a revelation does not constitute a prophecy until it is publicly proclaimed.

Teaching, on the other hand, is always based on an explanation and/or application of Scripture or received apostolic doctrine; it is never said to be based on a revelation. That is why teaching has so much more authority for governing the congregation, and it also explains why Paul was perfectly willing to have women as well as men prophesy in the assembled congregation, while he restricted the authoritative teaching functions to men only.

Application for today

If the understanding of the gift of prophecy which has been proposed in this study is correct, it could do much to overcome the problem of 'spectator Christianity' in contemporary churches. This is because the activity of Bible teaching in the congregation is generally restricted to one or a few recognized church leaders. So as long as participation in the worship service is primarily determined by who is able to teach Scripture to the assembled congregation, there will be only limited participation by women, by children, and even by most (non-teaching) men.

But the gift of prophecy is much different, and carries no such restrictive use. Instead, *all Christians* are given permission to prophesy in church if God so prompts them (cf. 1 Cor 14:31). We should therefore expect, if opportunity for such prophesying were given, that our worship services would include much broader participation by *both women and men* in order that '*all* may learn and *all* be encouraged' (1 Cor 14:31, RSV).

Finally, a note of encouragement. It may be that the absence of prophecy in many churches today is not due primarily to the absence of revelations from the Holy Spirit, but rather to the failure of believers to recognize those revelations when they come and to understand that they are given for the benefit of the whole congregation—they have not fulfilled their purpose until they are reported to others! Perhaps church leaders today can do more to encourage Christians to mention such promptings from the Lord when they occur—no doubt in a hesitant and uncertain way, at first, but nevertheless with an attitude of seeking to help and edify the congregation in this way if that should be what the Holy Spirit wants.

Some may be uneasy about this—who knows what will happen? Yet if there are mature, biblically sound leaders in the congregation, and if they are ready to evaluate the prophecy publicly if they sense a need to do so, no harm will be done. In fact, there may begin to be times when the Holy Spirit gives unusual confirmation of his working by simultaneously revealing the same theme or idea to several different people in the congregation. At other times there may be prophecies which in the space of a few words strike through calloused hearts and bring tears of repentance, or heartfelt songs of hope and praise. In fact, the overall result will most likely be a greatly increased sense of the living presence of the Lord in the midst of His people, an exciting new depth of awareness in which everyone present 'will worship God and declare that God is really among you' (1 Cor 14:25, RSV).

7

The Content of Prophecies:

What Did the Prophecies Say?

The New Testament contains much material about the gift of prophecy, but very few actual prophecies are recorded. Is there any way, then, for us to find out the content of these prophecies? What did they actually say? What kinds of statements did they contain? What topics did they talk about?

In fact, there is an even better way to find out the content of congregational prophecies than by examining some or even several quotations of actual prophecies, and that is to examine New Testament statements about the purpose and function of the gift of prophecy in general—what is it intended to do, and what does it actually accomplish? These general statements about the gift should give us a more accurate picture of the contents of prophecies than looking at a few examples when we would have no way of knowing if the examples were themselves representative of the use of the gift as a whole.

So our initial purpose in this chapter is to find out the function and purpose of prophecy. How does the New Testament see it as bringing benefit to the church? Once again we shall study the relevant passages in 1 Corinthians first, and then examine the related passages elsewhere in the New Testament.

1 Corinthians 14:3: Anything that would build up, encourage, or comfort

The primary text here is 1 Corinthians 14:3 (RSV): 'He who

prophesies speaks to men for their upbuilding and encouragement and consolation.' In this context Paul is arguing that the
Corinthians, in seeking spiritual gifts, should seek especially to
prophesy (1 Cor 14:1). To prove this point, in verses 2–5 he
contrasts tongues and prophecy: no one understands the person speaking in tongues, so he is not speaking to men but to
God (v. 2). But by contrast, he who prophesies is speaking to
men so that they can understand, and by a prophet's words the
hearers receive edification, encouragement and comfort (v. 3).
While the tongue-speaker edifies himself, the prophet edifies
the church (v. 4). This is the reason prophecy is superior to
tongues: it brings more benefit to the church (v. 5).

This context suggests that prophecy was to be used for others

This context shows that Paul sees prophecy as an essentially
public gift. There is no indication that a prophet would prophesy in private for his own personal benefit. If he did, his
prophecy would be on the same level as the tongues in 1
Corinthians 14:4 (RSV) ('He who speaks in a tongue edifies himself'), and this would not be the kind of prophecy the Corinthians were especially to seek (v. 1). So unless prophecy functions
in the assembled meeting of the church (or, presumably, a
smaller meeting of some part of the church), it loses its pre-
eminence among the gifts.

While the context of 1 Corinthians 14:3 demonstrates the
necessity for prophecy to function publicly, the three specific
terms used by Paul in this verse define more precisely the wide
range of functions that prophecy was thought to have. Paul
says, 'He who prophesies speaks to men for their *upbuilding*
and *encouragement* and *consolation* (1 Cor 14:3, RSV).

The terms used show a broad range of 'edifying' functions

The first word, 'upbuilding' (or 'edification'; Greek *oikodomē*)
is said to be the result not just of prophesying but of many
different human activities: church discipline brings edification
(2 Cor 10:8, 13:9), not offending others by what we eat brings

edification (Rom 14:19), self-denial for the benefit of one's neighbour will bring edification (Rom 15:2), and acting in love will 'build up' or edify others (1 Cor 8:1).

When the church comes together, any legitimate speech activity can result in edification: a hymn, a teaching, a revelation, a tongue, an interpretation—all give 'edification' (1 Cor 14:26). In fact, according to Ephesians 4:29 (RSV) ('Let no evil talk come out of your mouths, but only such as is good for *edifying*'), all Christian speech, even that of ordinary conversation, should bring about this kind of edification. It is a general term which refers to any kind of help towards growth in Christian maturity—and prophecy is one of the activities which contribute to the edification of Christians in the church.

The second term, *encouragement* (Greek *paraklēsis*) can mean 'comfort' (from sorrow: Lk 2:25; 6:24; 2 Cor 1:3–7) or 'encouragement' (to those who are discouraged: Rom 15:4, 5; 2 Cor 7:4, 13) or 'exhortation or appeal' (that is, an urging of someone to do something: 2 Cor 8:17; 1 Thess 2:4; Heb 12:5; 13:22). Yet it has a weaker force than 'command', for Paul contrasts this verb 'appeal, exhort' with the verb meaning 'command': 'I am bold enough in Christ to *command* you ... yet ... I prefer to *appeal* to you' (Philem 8–9, RSV).

It is probable that the range of meanings 'comfort— encouragement—exhortation' was not neatly divided in the minds of Paul's readers, so any New Testament use—like this one in 1 Corinthians 14:3—which is not further defined by context, might be thought to encompass a variety of speech activities which could include any or all of these elements. This word, then, is not very restrictive in meaning, and would allow for prophecy to include a variety of kinds of speech which would bring the hearers at times 'comfort', at times 'encouragement', and at times 'exhortation'.

Concerning the last term, 'consolation' (Greek *paramuthia*), it is difficult to find much difference in meaning from the second term, 'encouragement'. It is 'difficult to find a convincing criterion by which to draw any sharp line of demarcation. Both are characterized by the twofoldness of admonition and comfort.'[62]

Taken together, these three terms indicate that prophecy cannot be distinguished from other speech activities simply by means of its functions, for there is no one function that will serve as a distinguishing characteristic. Every function of prophecy (edification, encouragement, exhortation, consolation) is also a function of several other activities, such as teaching, preaching, singing 'psalms and hymns and spiritual songs' (Col 3:16, RSV), and engaging in ordinary Christian conversation (Eph 4:29).

It is interesting to notice that the common conception of a prophet as one who predicts the future plays no part in Paul's definition at this point. It is not, as we shall see later, that prediction was excluded from prophecy, but rather that prediction was not an end in itself; it was only valuable as it served the purposes outlined in 1 Corinthians 14:3 (RSV): 'upbuilding and encouragement and consolation'.

Why then is prophecy so important a gift?

How, then, is prophecy different from other speech activities in the New Testament church? What made prophecy so valuable that Paul wanted it to be sought above all the other gifts? The answer is found not in the function of prophecy but in the fact that prophecy is based on a divine 'revelation' (see chapter 5).

Because of this revelation, the prophet would be able to speak to the specific needs of the moment when the congregation assembled. Whereas the teacher or preacher would only be able to obtain information about the specific spiritual concerns of the people from observation or conversation, the prophet would have in addition the ability to know about specific needs through 'revelation'. In many cases the things revealed might include the secrets of people's hearts (cf. 1 Cor 14:25), their worries or fears (which need appropriate words of comfort and encouragement), or their refusal or hesitancy to do God's will (which need appropriate words of exhortation).

Sometimes the prophet might have only the need revealed to him, and sometimes only the word of exhortation or comfort, for Paul does not restrict the content of revelation so closely as that, and either possibility would fulfil the purposes defined in 1 Corinthians 14:3. Nor can we say that the prophet would always know to which person in the congregation his or her words applied. At times, that may have been revealed to him, while at other times the prophet, like a preacher, may not have known who in the congregation was helped by a specific prophetic word of exhortation or encouragement. Indeed, many times the words of a prophet would perhaps edify several people at once, or perhaps everyone present.

Prophecy, then, is superior to the other gifts because the revelation on which it depends allows it to be suited to the specific needs of the moment, needs which may only be known to God (cf. 1 Cor 14:25; Rom 8:26–27). In this way, prophecy is supremely qualified to be speech which edifies, speech which 'fits the occasion, that it may impart grace to those who hear' (Eph 4:29, RSV).

1 Corinthians 14:31: Might prophecy include teaching, since people could 'learn' from it?

Paul says that if a revelation is made to another sitting by, the first (prophet) should be silent: 'For you are all able to prophesy one by one, in order that all may *learn* and all may be encouraged' (1 Cor 14:31).

Does the word 'learn' here imply that prophecy also had a teaching function, perhaps even one that included rather standard kinds of doctrinal instruction?

This is not necessarily the case, because people can 'learn' from many things in addition to formal Bible teaching or doctrinal instruction. The term 'learn' (Greek *manthanō*) can often mean 'to learn how to act, to learn knowledge that will affect one's manner of life' (Mt 11:29; Rom 16:17; 1 Cor 4:6; Eph 4:20; Phil 4:9, 11; 1 Tim 5:4; Tit 3:14; Heb 5:8).

So Paul's use of 'learn' in 1 Corinthians 14:31 is entirely appropriate to any prophecy in which the hearers are edified, encouraged, exhorted or comforted. In every case, the hearers would be 'learning', and though this process may have included the reception of doctrinal material, it would always have been used in order to bring about spiritual growth or 'edification'. The emphasis of the prophecy would have been on immediate practical application to the hearers' lives. So 1 Corinthians 14:31, then, does not mean that a prophet performed the same kind of function as a teacher, but only that people would 'learn' from both activities.

1 Corinthians 13:2: Prophesying with or without love—a crucial difference

Paul warns the Corinthians that they may have amazing and highly developed spiritual gifts, but even then, they would be 'nothing' if they did not use these gifts in love. Specifically with respect to prophecy, he says, 'And if I have prophecy, and understand all mysteries and all knowledge, and if I have all faith, so as to remove mountains, but have not love, I am nothing' (1 Cor 13:2).

To be 'nothing' when one prophesies without love may refer either to the benefits to others or to the benefits to oneself. If it refers to the benefits to others, Paul would be saying that a prophet without love has no good effects (similar to the noisy gong or clanging cymbal in 1 Corinthians 13:1, which are meaningless and disruptive). This would probably be because even though the speaker prophesies something the Holy Spirit has given through a 'revelation', he or she does not take care that the words are spoken with kindness (1 Cor 13:4), and without arrogance or disorderliness (1 Cor 13: 5).

This then would be another indication of the great degree of freedom enjoyed by New Testament prophets: apparently their own choice of words, of tone, and of attitude would determine the effectiveness of their prophecies. The prophecy would be a result both of the 'revelation' received by the prophet and of the words with which the prophet chose to report it.

But if being 'nothing' when one prophesies without love means that there are no benefits to oneself, then Paul would be saying that a loveless prophecy brings him no credit in the eyes of God, even though it may do some good for others (similar to giving away his goods in 1 Corinthians 13:3).

It does not seem that the context gives us enough information to choose between these two interpretations (and, in fact, that may not be necessary, since both could be intended as well—'nothing' for the prophet or for others!). The main point is clear: it is essential to prophesy with love.

At this point it is appropriate to put this part of 1 Corinthians 13 together with the very practical application Paul gives it in 1 Corinthians 14. Paul sees the main result in this: the prophet who acts in love will take care that his speech always edifies his hearers. Thus, the prophet prophesying in love

(a) will wait his turn (1 Cor 14:31 RSV, 'You can all prophesy one by one.' Compare 'is not ... rude' in 1 Cor 13:5, RSV);

(b) will speak to others for their benefit and seek their good (1 Cor 14:3 RSV, 'He ... speaks to men for their upbuilding and encouragement and consolation.' Compare 'does not insist on its own way' in 1 Cor 13:5, RSV);

(c) will willingly submit his prophecy to evaluation and scrutiny by others (1 Cor 14:29 RSV, 'Let the others weigh what is said.' Compare 'is not ... boastful' in 1 Cor 13:4, RSV);

(d) will gladly give way and allow another to prophesy instead of himself (1 Cor 14:30 RSV, 'Let the first be silent.' Compare 'is not jealous ... does not insist on its own way' in 1 Cor 13:4–5, RSV);

(e) and even when speaking of the sins of others will presumably not do it in the kind of triumphant, haughty manner which would provoke alienation and withdrawal by the outsider, but rather with the kind of compassion which would evoke worship of God (1 Cor 14:24–25 RSV, 'He is convicted by all, he is called to account by all, the secrets of his heart are disclosed.' Compare 'does not provoke to wrath ... does not rejoice at wrong' in 1 Cor 13:5–6).

In short, the prophet prophesying in love would continually seek to use his gift to benefit others and not himself. This could not be done mechanically, but must be the result of an inward attitude of love for others in the congregation. Only then would prophecy be of greatest benefit to the church according to the 'more excellent way'.

Functions of prophecy mentioned outside 1 Corinthians

Acts 15:32: Judas and Silas as prophets

After the decision of the Jerusalem Council in Acts 15, two members of the church in Jerusalem, Judas and Silas, 'leading men among the brethren' (Acts 15:22, RSV) were sent with Paul and Barnabas to convey the results of the decision to the church in Antioch. After they had delivered the letter from Jerusalem, Judas and Silas stayed with the church for a while longer. Luke tells us, 'And Judas and Silas, who were themselves prophets, exhorted the brethren with many words and strengthened them' (Acts 15:32 , RSV).

This verse confirms but does not add to what we learned about the function of New Testament prophecy from 1 Corinthians 14:3–5, since 'exhorted' represents the Greek term *parakaleō*, the cognate verb to 'encouragement' (Greek *paraklēsis*) in 1 Corinthians 14:3. The other word, 'strengthen', is a general term which occurs only in Acts, but is very similar in sense to the noun 'upbuilding' (Greek *oikodomē*) in 1 Corinthians 14:3.

Acts 11:27–30 and 21:11: The two prophecies of Agabus

In both of these cases Luke shows Agabus predicting some future event. This is an indication that prediction of the future was one function of prophecy, but the other texts we have examined, both in 1 Corinthians and in Acts, show that prediction should not be considered the only function of prophecy, and indeed not even its primary function.

In both of these cases in Acts, Luke is careful to show how the predictions served to encourage, exhort or strengthen the church. In Acts 11, the prophecy seems to have led to preparation and perhaps even to some collection before the famine began (v. 29), so that the church at Antioch was enabled by the prophecy to be of greater usefulness than they would have been without this special bit of 'advance information'. In Acts 21, the prophecy allowed the church at Antioch to know roughly what would happen to Paul, and thereby they were afforded an opportunity to see the strength of Paul's resolve to follow willingly in the steps of Jesus even when facing suffering and perhaps death. In seeing this, the church would no doubt have been encouraged and strengthened to imitate Paul's courage and obedience.

In each case the prophetic gift was necessary for a particular purpose. No other gift would have sufficed, for it was specifically knowledge of some future event which was needed in each case, and only prophecy, based as it was on a revelation from the Holy Spirit (see chapters 5 and 6 above), could provide this knowledge.

In neither case, however, was prediction an end in itself. The New Testament always shows prophetic prediction as simply one of several kinds of means to a greater end, the encouragement and edification of the church.

1 Timothy 1:18: Prophecies indicating Timothy's gifts and areas of effective ministry

The verse reads, 'This command I commit to you, Timothy, my son, in accordance with the former prophecies about you, in order that by means of them you may fight the good fight.'

Here Timothy is given a command which in some way corresponds to previous prophecies about him. Paul commands him 'in accordance with the former prophecies.' Yet the precise way in which the prophecies and the command corresponded is not specified by Paul.

The command or 'charge' which Paul gave Timothy at this time was to 'remain at Ephesus' in order to 'charge certain persons not to teach any different doctrine...' (1 Tim 1:3, RSV), yet it probably also included the directions for the operation of the church found in 1 Timothy 2:1 and following. In short, Paul was commanding Timothy to continue to take a leadership role, as an 'apostolic assistant' to Paul, in the teaching and administration of the church.

Apparently this role of governing and teaching included tasks which required precisely the kinds of gifts that the prophecies had mentioned in connection with Timothy—gifts, for example, of sound judgement, or mature understanding of Scripture, or unusual insight into people's abilities and motivations, or effectiveness in prayer, etc. Remembering these prophecies would encourage him: '...in order that by them [i.e., encouraged by them] you may fight the good fight.'

In this case, then, prophecy apparently provided knowledge of a future type of ministry, or knowledge of abilities which Timothy or others previously may not have recognized (which is quite similar). Thereby the prophecies encouraged Timothy to strive diligently towards the indicated goal, or perhaps brought to his attention gifts of which he was previously unaware, or of which he had thought himself unworthy because of youth or inexperience. In doing this the prophecies then would have enabled him to develop and use gifts which would otherwise have remained dormant.

Once again, then, the uniqueness of prophecy is found in its dependence on 'revelations' (either about unknown facts or about future events), and its purpose is to strengthen the ministry of the church in some specific way.

1 Timothy 4:14: A spiritual gift given through prophecy

In the midst of a string of personal instructions to Timothy (1 Tim 4:6—5:2), Paul writes, 'Do not neglect the gift you have, which was given you through prophecy when the council of elders laid their hands upon you' (1 Tim 4:14).

There is not enough evidence in the context to decide with certainty what this gift was, and the word 'gift' (Greek *charisma*) in the New Testament has a broad range of meanings. But the phrase 'through prophecy' suggests that the verse is talking about the same situation as that referred to in 1 Timothy 1:18, 'the former prophecies about you.' In that case, it is possible that the gift mentioned here is a special ability in administration or church rule, in sound teaching, or in solving church disputes and silencing false teachers—in other words, a gift which would equip Timothy for the kind of work outlined in this epistle.

The phrase 'through prophecy' here indicates the means or instrument by which the gift was given. This is not at variance with the idea that gifts are given by God, because this Greek construction (*dia* + genitive) is often used to indicate a human or 'natural' cause of a gift which at the same time is said to be divinely given (note Acts 7:25: God was giving deliverance 'through' the hand of Moses, and Acts 8:18: the Holy Spirit was given 'through' the laying on of the apostles' hands). In fact, Paul uses this same construction in 2 Timothy 1:6 (RSV) to mention a gift that was given Timothy 'through the laying on of my hands'.

So this verse does not suggest that the prophetic words themselves were of such power that they created a gift in Timothy or somehow by themselves bestowed an ability on him, any more than Acts 8:18 implies that there was some magical power in the hands of the apostles which allowed them to bestow the Holy Spirit (as Simon falsely thought, Acts 8:19). Rather, this verse indicates a more loose connection, suggesting perhaps that prophecies were spoken at the same time the gift was given to Timothy, and that the prophecies indicated what kind of gift God was giving him.

In this way, the prophecies would have the function of making known to everyone present, including Timothy, what otherwise would have remained completely unknown until the gifts could be noticed in practice. Prophecy which functioned in this way would clearly benefit the church, for it would encourage Timothy to begin to use and develop his new abilities, and would encourage the other hearers to provide him opportunities where he could do so.

The book of Revelation: Does it indicate anything about the content of ordinary congregational prophecies?

The entire book claims to contain revelations of 'what must soon take place' (Rev 1:1; 4:1; 22:6), and thus must be based on knowledge which could not be obtained by ordinary means. Even in the letters to the seven churches, where a disclosure of the future is not in view, John is given special information about the inward spiritual state of the churches (Rev 2:4, 23; 3:1, 9, 17), or at least an authoritative evaluation of the churches which required a divine revelation. But, as with other New Testament prophecy, attaining this special knowledge of the future or of hidden facts is not an end in itself. It is repeatedly made the basis for direct *exhortation* of the readers (Rev 2:5, 10, 16, 25; 3:2–5, 11, 18; 13:10; 14:7, 12; cf. Rev 1:3; 22:7).

Furthermore, the book frequently takes the opportunity to *comfort* believers who are undergoing trouble or persecution by proclaiming the sovereign rule of God in history, the certainty of his final triumph over evil, and the preservation and ultimate triumph of God's people with him (Rev 1:5; 2:26–27; 5:10; 6:10; 15–17, 11:15-18; 14:13; 17:14; 19:20–21; 20:6, 9—14; and chapters 20—22). Thus it is a prophecy whose function is to encourage, comfort and exhort those who read it—a similar function to what we found elsewhere with prophecy, even though here it is uniquely authoritative 'apostolic prophecy'.

Other possible functions

Several other possible functions for prophecy might be proposed, but for each one the evidence is so slight that only tentative conclusions are possible.

(a) *Did prophecies give inspired interpretation of Old Testa-*

ment Scripture? As was mentioned briefly in chapter 6, E. Earle Ellis sees exposition and interpretation of Scripture as a function of Christian prophets in Acts. However, he can show no examples where the person expounding Scripture is doing so specifically in the role of a prophet, and not in the role of a teacher or apostle or evangelist. Everyone expounding Scripture in Acts has one of these other roles. So the argument is not really persuasive.

Of course, this negative conclusion does not mean that prophecies would never include Scripture quotations and applications. These things may well have been part of prophecies, and perhaps even fairly frequently. But it is important to emphasize that where such exposition was based on preparation and reflection instead of on a spontaneous revelation, the New Testament writers would call it 'teaching', not prophecy.

(b) *Did prophecies include prayer and praise?* The previous study has indicated that prophecies generally could be thought of as God-to-man communication, since they had to be based on a revelation from God. But we might ask whether prophecies might sometimes include the man-to-God activities of prayer and praise.

The only possible direct support for this suggestion would be found in Luke 1:67, where Zechariah 'prophesied' his song of praise. Although this pre-Pentecost prophecy fits the pattern of Old Testament prophecy more than the New Testament gift, it does contain much praise, the content of which had been revealed to Zechariah as he was 'filled with the Holy Spirit' (Luke 1:67, RSV).

From a contemporary perspective, Bruce Yokum's interesting discussion of 'the forms of prophecy' includes not only prophecies that take the form of prayer, but also mentions 'prophecy in song'.[63]

And John Macarthur, though he does not agree with the continuation of prophecy today, mentions some claims that songs such as Bill and Gloria Gaither's 'The King is Coming' or

George Matheson's 'O Love That Will Not Let Me Go' were written as a result of what the authors perceived to be an unusual influence of the Holy Spirit bringing the words suddenly to mind.[64]

The major difficulty for the idea that prayer and praise are prophetic functions is 1 Corinthians 14:3 (RSV): 'He who prophesies speaks to men ....' Strictly interpreted, this would mean, 'He who prophesies speaks *only* to men.' However, Paul's concern here might simply be to emphasize that prophecy is able to be understood by men, or is primarily for their benefit. In that case, if prayer or praise was prompted by revelation, and if it served also to edify the hearers (because they silently participated in it; compare 1 Corinthians 14:16), there would seem to be no reason why it could not have been called 'prophecy'—perhaps 'prophetic praise' or 'prophetic prayer'. The essential elements would be that it was based on a 'revelation', that it be spoken publicly, and that it bring about an edifying result.

(c)*Did prophets add new 'sayings of Jesus' to the gospels?* A common idea in New Testament scholarship in this century has been that New Testament prophets, under the influence of the Holy Spirit, received actual words from the risen Lord Jesus which they then uttered in the congregation. These words were remembered and perhaps even written down as authoritative sayings of Jesus and, with the passage of time, some of them found their way into the gospel stories being circulated about the *earthly* life of Jesus.

According to this view, eventually some of these sayings spoken by prophets in the early church came to be presented in the written gospels as words spoken by the earthly Jesus, not as the prophetic words which they really were. Those who hold this position say that including such new 'sayings of Jesus' in the gospels was not really a serious mistake, because they *were* words of Jesus anyway, even if not words spoken during Jesus' earthly life.

This theory has come under strong criticism, however, and

many New Testament scholars have found it unpersuasive. Some of the most telling objections are these:[65]

(i) Prophecies in the Bible are never anonymous, as these would have to become before they could be thought to be 'sayings of Jesus'; rather, prophecies in the Bible are always attributed to the prophet through whom they were spoken.

(ii) If the words only gradually became part of the historical tradition, then at first the church clearly *distinguished* between recent 'charismatic' sayings of the prophets and 'authentic' historical words actually spoken by Jesus while on earth. But if this distinction was maintained at first, there is no reason why it should not have been maintained throughout the early years of the church until the gospels attained their final form.

(iii) If sayings of the risen Lord through the prophets were thought just as valuable as historical sayings of Jesus, then there would have been no reason for projecting them back into the context of Jesus' earthly life.

(iv) The theory neglects the concern of the early church, and especially the apostles, to safeguard the traditions about Jesus and prevent unwarranted corruption (cf. 1 Cor 7:10, 12, 25).

(v) The actual evidence claimed for showing such activity by prophets in the early church is slim and unpersuasive. The idea is *suggested* by some scholars and *assumed* by several others, but it is never really proven.

Concerning the book of Revelation, where we do have sayings of the risen Christ recorded, it is important to note that John is certainly not typical of other New Testament prophets (see chapter 4 above), and also that each prophetic saying is carefully preserved in a context which makes clear that the words come from the risen Lord and through a particular prophet who is clearly identified. In sum, primary evidence which clearly supports the theory has simply not been found. There is no proven instance where a prophetic saying has became a part of a historical narrative.

In addition to these other objections, it is now possible to offer another observation, based on our analysis of the gift of prophecy in the New Testament church. We have found that it was not the task of prophets at Corinth or in other local congregations to create actual 'words of the risen Lord'. Far from being interchangeable with the historical words of Jesus to which the community was subject, these prophecies were themselves subject to the community (1 Cor 14:29; 1 Thess 5:20–21). So this view of prophetic contributions to the gospels fundamentally misunderstands the nature of the gift of prophecy as it functioned in early Christian congregations.

Therefore it is appropriate to conclude that the theory of prophetic contributions to the gospel tradition both lacks sufficient convincing evidence and is contrary to much of what we do know about early Christian prophets and the churches in which they lived.

The 'form' of prophecies: Did they contain typical words and phrases, or distinctive patterns of speech?

Some people have thought that prophetic sayings would take certain set 'forms' or patterns of speech—often beginning or ending with the same words, for example, or often being spoken in poetry, or containing warnings of God's judgement, etc.

However, the tremendous variety in subject matter which we have found for New Testament prophecies, plus the fact that the prophet expresses the prophecy in his or her own words, make it unlikely that any one item, or any one pattern of expression, would repeat itself with unusual frequency in church prophecies.

Nevertheless, there is one thing that can be said about the form of expression prophecies would take. They would be spoken in language that the hearers could understand—otherwise, they would not fulfil their function of 'building up' or 'edifying' the church.

Moreover, the words and language used would be that chosen by the speaker—a fact consistent with what we have in the

New Testament showing that the *report* of a revelation is spoken in merely human words. Bruce Yokum mentions a bilingual Pentecostal group where no one seemed troubled about a request from leaders of the meeting that everyone prophesy in English, not in Spanish.[66] Yokum says:

> The language we use in prophecy is under our control. Prophecy comes through a *particular* human being, and it will be expressed in the language of that person.... We are responsible for the language we use in prophecy.[67]

Before reading 1 Corinthians 14, one might think that even prayer which the congregation did not understand, such as a prayer to God spoken in tongues, could have 'built up' or 'strengthened' the church, especially if it was a prayer for the church. But Paul thinks otherwise: 'He who speaks in a tongue edifies himself' (1 Cor 14:4, RSV), and the contrast is with the one who 'prophesies' and thereby 'edifies the church'. In order for the church to be edified in public assembly, the members have to hear and *understand* something that is spoken.

Again in 1 Corinthians 14:16–17, Paul says that if a person 'does not know' what is spoken in a prayer, he is not edified by that prayer (v. 17). So prophecy does not benefit the church in a mysterious, indiscernible way. Rather, people are helped by prophecies specifically as they gain new understanding and encouragement from what the prophet says.

Thus New Testament prophecy at Corinth was far removed from the frenzied, unintelligible utterances of 'inspired speech' in pagan Greek religion, such as the Pythia (the 'inspired' woman speaker) in the Oracle at Delphi, for example. Furthermore, New Testament prophecy would not have been couched in the notoriously ambiguous phraseology of the 'prophets' who 'interpreted' the Pythia's response at Delphi. According to Paul, speech which could not be undertsood simply did not edify.

Summary

Paul defines the functions of prophecy very broadly in 1 Corinthians 14:3. Its functions included 'building up, encouragement, and comfort'—results which could be achieved not only by prophecy but also by a wide variety of other speech activities. In order to accomplish these purposes, prophecy would not function privately but for the benefit of others. The great importance of prophecy came from the fact that it was based on something that had been revealed by the Holy Spirit, and this often allowed it to speak powerfully to the needs of the moment in the congregation.

Prophecies could include predictions of the future, even though this was not an essential component of prophecy, or perhaps even a frequent one. Prophecies could also indicate a person's spiritual gifts or areas of effective ministry, and might even do so in connection with the giving of the gift that was being mentioned in the prophecy. While prophecies were generally seen as communication from God to man, there is no reason to deny that prophecies could also include occasional elements of 'prophetic praise' and 'prophetic prayer'—praise and prayer whose content was based on something revealed spontaneously by the Holy Spirit.

Even though people would 'learn' from prophecy, its content would not ordinarily include what the New Testament would call 'teaching' (or Bible teaching), nor was it the function of prophecy to give 'inspired interpretations' of Old Testament Scripture. Some scholars have suggested that New Testament prophets received new messages from the risen Christ which then eventually found their way into the gospels and were recorded there as 'sayings of Jesus' while he was on earth, but this theory lacks persuasive historical evidence to support it and is contrary to what we have found about the nature of the gift of prophecy in early Christian congregations.

An accompanying attitude of love for others was essential for the right use of prophecy, and can be seen to underlie many of Paul's directions about how prophecy should function.

The New Testament does not lead us to expect to find any distinctive speech forms for prophecy, but it does require that prophecies be spoken in an intelligible way, not in incoherent or mysterious speech which would only puzzle, not edify, the hearers.

Application for today: What kinds of content can be in prophecies?

We have now reached a point in our study where we can give a rather broad but nevertheless useful description of the content of prophecy if it follows the guidelines indicated by the New Testament. We can also now give some more examples of the types of things a prophet might say. The results of chapters 3–7 will contribute to various parts of this description.

No claims to be speaking God's words

This restriction is derived from the discussion in chapters 3–4, where the New Testament data was seen to indicate that a prophecy would be the speaking of merely human words to report something God brings to mind.

In practical terms, this means that even if a prophecy contains words of ethical instruction ('You shouldn't go to London,' or, 'You should leave your job and devote all your time to preaching,' or, 'You should marry Philip'), these instructions should not be considered divine obligations (i.e. to disobey them would not be thought the same as disobeying God), but they should be viewed as the prophet's own fairly accurate (but not infallible) report of something he thinks (though not with absolute certainty) has been revealed to him by God. The person or persons to whom the prophecy was directed should respond in much the same way they would respond to preaching or to personal advice (since both sermons and advice are often given by those who think their words generally reflect

God's will also): in all three cases, the hearer(s) should evaluate (cf. 1 Cor 14:29) the prophecy, the sermon, or the advice for conformity to Scripture, to received teaching, and to facts which they know to be true.

Because New Testament prophecies do not speak with the very words of God, the content of the prophecy should not include a preface like, 'Thus says the Lord,' which would mislead hearers into thinking that the prophecy had or was claiming authority equal to the very words of God in Scripture. Of course, some of the very words in a prophecy *may* have been revealed by God, but it would be unwise and misleading for any prophet today to claim certainty that this was so. And even if God did bring some specific words to mind, the New Testament gives us no warrant for saying that God wants us to hear those words as his own words, carrying his own absolute authority. If the prophecy is from God, he will make it 'hit home' in the hearts of the hearers.

Material that has come through a revelation

Generally, this revealed material will consist of facts which could not be known by ordinary means. It may include prediction of the future (Acts 11:27–30; 21:11), the disclosure of the secret sins or anxieties or problems hidden in a man's heart (1 Cor 14:24–25), or the disclosure of certain gifts for ministry possessed by someone in the congregation (1 Tim 1:18; 4:14). But often the prophecy would include simply the statement of a known fact or verse of Scripture.

For example, someone might say, 'God has brought to my mind a verse of Scripture and I feel I must say it: "Honour your father and mother."' Then someone else might admit that the prophecy had called to mind a scriptural principle which encouraged him to make a particular decision with regard to his own life. Or again, someone might say, 'The Lord has put on my mind a tremendous concern for the Christians in the Philippines. I think we should pray for them now.' Then later it might be learned that that day a new onslaught of persecution had begun against believers in some section of the Philippines.

In both of these cases the information contained in the prophecy was not entirely hidden information which could only have been known by revelation. The members of the congregation would have agreed that it was good to honour one's father and mother and to pray for Christians in other cities. In these cases the revelation to the prophet was indispensable because it allowed those particular items of information (rather than some others) to be called to the attention of the congregation at those particular times (rather than at some other times). And the fact that these thoughts came spontaneously and forcefully to mind caused the prophet to think that they came from God and were not the product of his own evaluation of the situation at hand (in which case it would have been a 'teaching' or perhaps simply an 'exhortation').

Content that will edify others

Here I am using 'edify' in a very broad sense, to include anything which contributes to the spiritual growth of anyone present, or anything implied by 'upbuilding, encouragement, and consolation' in 1 Corinthians 14:3. This means that the prophecy will not include abstruse doctrinal discourses which the hearers are unable to apply to their own lives, or bits of 're- vealed' factual information (even true information, 1 Cor 8:1) which have no usefulness for the hearers' lives. Rather, the prophecy must affect the lives of the hearers in a positive way. In order to be edifying, it must suit the needs of the moment.

So a prophecy might include a simple reminder, such as, 'The Lord delights in our praise,' or, 'The Lord Jesus Christ is present with us,' or, 'God has sent his angels to protect us.' Or it might include an exhortation, such as, 'We need to be still before the Lord for a time,' or, 'Are we really putting the Lord's priorities on our use of time?' or, 'I think there may be someone here who is neglecting his or her family because of a desire to be promoted at work,' or, 'Does someone here need prayer for courage but is hesitating to ask?' These are not unusual or profound statements, but they are nevertheless the kind of thing the Holy Spirit can use to bring much needed blessing to individuals in a church.

Once I was talking with a man I had recently met. I was much younger than he, but I could sense that he was quite troubled about something. He had mentioned difficulties in his family, but I sensed a prompting from the Holy Spirit to change the subject, and, without really knowing why, I asked, 'How are things at your job?' The Holy Spirit evidently spoke to his heart with this simple question, because immediately he began to cry, exclaiming, 'That's the problem, that's the real problem....' We were then able to pray for a resolution of the real source of the difficulty.

Perhaps most Christians have experienced something like this at one time or another. The Lord has brought something to mind, and when it was spoken to someone else it brought forth an immediate response of surprised agreement, or comfort, or repentance, or encouragement. The New Testament writers would call this 'prophecy'. If we are receptive to such promptings, and if the Lord is pleased to give them to us, it will no doubt open the door to many more opportunities for effective ministry, bringing upbuilding, encouragement, exhortation and consolation to God's people. Within the limitations mentioned above, such a prophecy could speak to any subject and contain any kind of material which would contribute to its purpose.

8

Prophecy as a Sign of God's Blessing in a Church

(1 Cor 14:20–25)

Introduction

In the middle of Paul's instructions about the use of prophecy and tongues in the church he includes a six-verse admonition to the Corinthians (1 Cor 14:20–25), in which he says that they should not think in childish ways but should be mature, and then concludes by saying that they should seek to prophesy, because unbelievers will be driven away by tongues (without interpretation), but they will be convicted by prophecy. To that extent the passage is clear.

The problem comes in the middle of the passage, where Paul quotes an Old Testament passage (Is 28:11–12) and then says that tongues are a 'sign' to unbelievers but prophecy is (a 'sign') for believers. Yet why does he then go on to say they should use prophecy, not tongues, when unbelievers are present (see 1 Cor 14:23–25)?

The passage begins as follows:

Brethren, do not be children in your thinking; be babes in evil, but in thinking be mature. In the law it is written, 'With other tongues and with lips of strangers I will speak to this people, and even then they will not listen to me,' says the Lord. So tongues are a sign not to believers but to unbelievers, but prophecy is (a sign) not to un-believers but to believers (1 Cor 14:20–22).

The meaning of the Old Testament quotation (Is 28:11– 12)

The context of Paul's quotation from Isaiah 28:11–12 is one of judgement on unbelievers in Israel. The Lord had repeatedly warned his people but they had refused to listen. So he was warning them now that he would send on them foreign invaders (the Assyrians) whose speech they would not understand:

> For with stammering lips and with other tongues he will speak to this people, to whom he said, 'This is rest; give rest to the weary; and this is repose'; but they were not willing to hear.

In the past the Lord had spoken clear and comforting words to the people. But they had stubbornly resisted his word. So as a result, Isaiah says that in the future the Lord will speak unclear words 'with stammering lips and other tongues', as a punishment for their hardness of heart. The 'stammering lips' and 'other tongues' are the lips and tongues of foreign (Assyrian) invaders, whom the people will not understand.

Paul's use of Isaiah 28:11–12

Paul's quotation of this verse is quite free, but not foreign to the context. '"With other tongues and with other lips I will speak to this people, and not even then will they obey me," says the Lord.'

Paul understands very well that when God speaks to people in a language they cannot understand, it is a form of punishment for unbelief. Incomprehensible speech will not guide but confuse and lead to destruction. And it is one of the last in a series of divine rebukes, none of which have produced the desired repentance and obedience ('and not even then will they obey me'). So Derek Kidner, commenting on Isaiah 28, can say, 'Paul's quotation of verse 11 in 1 Corinthians 14:21 is thus a reminder, true to this context, that unknown tongues are not God's greeting to a believing congregation but his rebuke to an unbelieving one.'

Are both prophecy and tongues called 'signs'?

What conclusion does Paul draw from this quotation? He says, 'Thus, tongues are a sign not for believers but for unbelievers...' (1 Cor 14:22, RSV). It is simply a misunderstanding of the grammatical construction used here when some translations render this as 'tongues are *for* a sign' (Authorized Version and New American Standard Bible), or even tongues are '*intended* as a sign' (New English Bible), because this construction (Greek *eis* + accusative with the verb 'to be') often can replace a predicate nominative with no real change in meaning.[68] Paul simply says, 'Tongues *are* a sign.'

But then what does he say about prophecy? Quite literally, he says, 'But prophecy not for believers but for unbelievers.' There is no verb in this half of the sentence, and the idea must be supplied by the reader.

Several translations make this read, 'But prophecy *is* not for unbelievers but for believers.'

This is certainly a legitimate option grammatically, for Greek sentences frequently leave out the verb 'to be' and expect it to be understood by the reader. But just putting the verb 'is' in this sentence changes the focus slightly from Paul's concern in the first half of the sentence. This makes the second half of the sentence concerned with benefit: prophecy gives benefit for believers, or is intended to be used for believers.

Yet Paul is not talking about benefit in the first half of the verse, he is talking about what is a 'sign'. If the context allows it, it is much better to retain this same subject in the second half of the sentence. This gives a more satisfactory contrast and doesn't import a new idea (the idea of who benefits from prophecy). If we retain the idea of 'sign' in the second half, Paul's sentence means: 'Therefore, tongues are a sign not for believers but for unbelievers ... but prophecy *is a sign* not for unbelievers but for believers.'

In addition to the fact that this translation allows the same subject to continue through the sentence, there is another reason why this sense seems the best. To say (with the Authorized Version and New English Bible) that prophecy is designed for believers but not for unbelievers does not adequately explain the 'therefore', with which Paul introduces verses 23–25. In those verses Paul argues specifically that prophecy *does* have a positive function for unbelievers. But on the translation that says prophecy is not for unbelievers, we have this strange reasoning:

(a) Prophecy is intended *not for unbelievers* but for believers;

(b) therefore, you should prophesy *to unbelievers*.

Such reasoning simply does not make sense, and a better solution is required.

We can conclude that, if an appropriate sense can be found for this translation, it is best to translate verse 22: 'Therefore, tongues are a sign not for believers but for unbelievers ... but prophecy *is a sign* not for unbelievers but for believers.'

The key to understanding this passage: 'Signs' can be positive or negative

Much confusion about this passage has resulted from an assumption that a 'sign' in Scripture must always function in the same way, usually in a positive way, as something that indicates God's approval or blessing. If this is so, it is hard to understand why tongues are a 'sign' for unbelievers but then Paul says tongues will drive unbelievers away.

This problem can be solved, however, by realizing that 'signs' in Scripture can be either positive or negative, and sometimes both. If we trace the Greek term used for 'sign' (Greek *sēmeion*) back into the Greek translation of the Old Testament (the Septuagint), we find many examples to show this.

In the Septuagint, the word 'sign' (Greek *sēmeion*) can often mean 'an indication of God's attitude'. These indications are either positive or negative: positive towards those who believe and obey God, but negative towards those who disbelieve and disobey him. Many signs are entirely positive:

the rainbow (Gen 9:12–14)

the blood on the doorpost (Ex 12:13)

the invitation from the Philistines to Jonathan (1 Sam 14:10)

the mark on the forehead (Ezek 9:4, 6)

or any other signs sought by people who feel forsaken by God (Ps 74:9; 86:17)

Other signs are entirely negative, since they show God's disapproval and warn of judgement unless repentance is quickly forthcoming:

Korah, Dathan, and Abiram (Num 26:10)

the bronze censers of these men (Num 16:38; cf. v. 40)

Aaron's rod (Num 17:10)

the fulfilled curses (Deut 28:46)

the defeat of Pharaoh Hophra (Jer 44:29)

Ezekiel's iron wall (Ezek 4:3; cf. also Ps 65:8, Is 20:3, 2 Macc 15:35)

But sometimes the term can be used of signs which are both positive and negative, indicating God's approval and blessing on his people and his disapproval and warning of judgement towards those who are disobeying him. This is especially true of the events of the Exodus: when God sent a plague of flies on the Egyptians but kept the flies out of the land of Goshen, it was a *sign* of blessing to Israel but disapproval and warning to the Egyptians (Ex 8:23). The same signs and wonders can be negative signs to Pharaoh (Ex 10:1–2; 11:9–10; Deut 6:22, 11:3; Neh 9:10) but positive signs to Israel (Deut 4:34–35; 6:22; 7:19; 26:8).[69]

In conclusion, 'sign', when used to mean 'an indication of God's attitude', can take either a positive sense (indicating God's approval and blessing) or a negative sense (indicating God's disapproval and imminent judgement).

Also in the New Testament, 'sign' (*sēmeion*) can mean 'an

indication of God's approval and blessing' (Acts 2:22, 43; 4:30; 5:12; 6:8; 15:12; Lk 2:34; Jn 2:11; 4:54; 9:16; the word is also used this way outside the New Testament: compare *Epistle of Barnabas* 4.14; *1 Clement* 51.5). It can also mean 'an indication of God's disapproval and a warning of judgement' (Lk 11:30; 21:11, 25; Acts 2:19; perhaps Mt 12:39 [cf. 12:41]; 16:4; compare the use in A.D.95 in *1 Clement* 11.2).

Summary of Paul's meaning

The preceding information indicates that when Paul says 'Tongues are a sign not for believers but for unbelievers' (1 Cor 14:22), he is using 'sign' in a familiar and well-established sense. Towards those who disbelieve, signs as indications of God's attitude in the Old Testament are always negative. They indicate God's disapproval and carry a warning of judgement. This was precisely the function of the 'other tongues' in Isaiah 28:11 and Paul quite naturally applies the term 'sign' to them.

But 'signs' for those who believe and obey God in the Old Testament are generally positive. They indicate God's presence and power among his people to bless them. Thus Paul can quite easily apply the term to prophecy in a positive sense. Prophecy is an indication of God's approval and blessing on the congregation because it shows that God is actively present in the assembled church.[70]

This means that the word 'therefore', in 1 Corinthians 14:23 is quite natural. We can paraphrase Paul's thought as follows:

When God speaks to people in a language they cannot understand, it signifies his anger and results in their turning farther away from him. *Therefore* (v. 23), if outsiders or unbelievers come in and you speak in a language they cannot understand, you will simply drive them away—this is the inevitable result of incomprehensible speech. Furthermore, in your childish way of acting (v. 20) you will be giving a 'sign' to the unbelievers which is entirely wrong, because their hardness of heart has not reached the point where they deserve that severe sign of judgement. So when you come together (v. 26), if anyone speaks in a tongue, be sure someone interprets (v. 27); otherwise, the tongue-speaker should be quiet in the church (v. 29).

Similarly with prophecy, verses 24–25 follow quite easily from the statement in verse 22 that prophecy is a sign to believers. Once again we paraphrase Paul's thought:

> Prophecy is an indication of God's presence among the congregation to bless it (v. 22). *Therefore* (v. 23), if an outsider comes in and everyone prophesies (v. 24), you will be speaking about the secrets of the outsider's heart which he thought no one knew. He will realize that these prophecies must be the result of God's working, and he will fall on his face and declare, 'Truly God is among you' (v. 25). In this way prophecy will be a sure sign to you that God really is at work in your midst.

Implications for the gift of speaking in tongues

It should be noted in connection with this passage that Paul's reaction to this recognition of the sign function of tongues is not to forbid tongues in public worship, but to regulate the use of tongues so that they will always be interpreted when spoken in public (1 Cor 14:27–28). This seems to be a very appropriate response, for it is only *incomprehensible* tongues which have this negative function towards unbelievers, both in Isaiah 28:11 and in 1 Corinthians 14:23. But when a speech in tongues is interpreted, it is no longer incomprehensible and it no longer retains this ominous sign function.

Therefore, it is important to realize that in 1 Corinthians 14:20–23 Paul is not talking about the function of tongues in general, but only about the negative result of one particular abuse of tongues, namely, the abuse of speaking in public without an interpreter (and probably speaking more than one at a time [cf. 1 Cor 14:23, 27]) so that it all became a scene of unedifying confusion.

Concerning the proper public function of the use of tongues

plus interpretation, or the proper private function of speaking in tongues, Paul is elsewhere quite positive (1 Cor 12:10–11, 21–22, 14:4, 5, 18, 26–28, 39). So to use Paul's discussion of an *abuse* of tongues in 14:20–23 as the basis for a general polemic against all other (acceptable) uses of tongues is quite contrary to the entire context in 1 Corinthians 12–14.

This crucial point, essential to understanding Paul's meaning here, is completely overlooked by some Reformed and dispensational interpreters of this passage. For example, the fact that Paul is talking not about tongues with interpretation but about *uninterpreted* tongues (which were *not able to be understood* by the hearers) is overlooked by O. Palmer Robertson,[71] and also by Zane Hodges.[72] Neither Robertson nor Hodges adequately takes account of the fact that at Corinth any unbeliever who entered, whether Jew or Gentile, would not understand what was spoken in tongues. Paul repeatedly says that uninterpreted tongues could not be understood by the hearers at Corinth (see 1 Cor 14:2, 9, 11, 14, 16, 19, 23, 28). In fact, Paul's main concern in 1 Corinthians 14 is to contrast intelligible with unintelligible speech.

In this connection, Robertson argues that tongues were a 'sign' of the transition between God's dealing with Israel and his dealing with all nations.[73] That might possibly be true in some contexts (such as Acts 22), but it is totally foreign to the context of 1 Corinthians 12–14, where Paul makes no mention of the Gentile inclusion or of judgement on the Jews—he contrasts not 'Jews' and 'Gentiles' but 'believers' and 'unbelievers'. And because he does not specify *Jewish* unbelievers, while there were certainly Gentile unbelievers visiting the church at Corinth as well, we must understand 'unbeliever' here as referring to unbelievers generally (*both* Jewish unbelievers and Gentile unbelievers). Paul is using Isaiah 28:11–12 not as a prediction about Jewish unbelievers, but as an example or illustration (with reference to unbelievers generally). Realizing this, Carson is right to conclude that Paul cannot be speaking here of tongues as a sign of a covenantal curse on unbelieving Jews.[74]

Moreover, neither Robertson, nor Gaffin, nor Macarthur, all of whom use this 'covenantal curse' interpretation to argue against tongues today, take enough account of the fact that Paul's solution in this passage is *not* to forbid the use of tongues altogether, but to direct that tongues be used with interpretation (1 Cor 14:27–28). Since Paul approves tongues *with* interpretation, they cannot be a judgement sign on unbelieving Jews.

Conclusion: How is prophecy a sign of God's blessing?

Returning now to a consideration of prophecy, we are in a position to understand 1 Corinthians 14:24–25 more clearly. 'If you all prophesy' in verse 24 is probably to be understood as a hypothetical situation which Paul need not have thought would ever actually occur (note 1 Cor 12:29, 'not all prophesy, do they?').

Nevertheless, if several people prophesy, the outsider is 'convicted' of sin and 'called to account' by several different people (1 Cor 14:24), presumably in different ways or with respect to different matters. In this way the secret sins of his heart are 'disclosed' (1 Cor 14:25).

But does this passage mean that *specific* sins of a *specific* individual are mentioned in the prophecies? Might it not mean rather that there is some general preaching about sin, and the Holy Spirit applies it specifically to an individual's heart, giving a sense of conviction of sin?

Although verse 24 might simply mean that the outsider hears some general prophecy or preaching and is inwardly convicted of his sin, this cannot be true of verse 25. Verse 25 must mean that specific mention of one or more of his particular, individual sins is made in the prophecies.[75]

This is true because of the meaning of the word used and because of the context. The word for 'disclosed' or 'become manifest' is the Greek term *phaneros*. Both this word (eighteen times in the New Testament) and its related verb, *phaneroō*, (forty-nine times in the New Testament) always refer to a public, external manifestation, and are never used of private or secret communication of information, or of the internal working of God in a person's mind or heart.

With regard to the context, the reaction of the outsider—'falling on his face he will worship God, declaring, 'Truly God is among you'—is not normally one that accompanies even good preaching, but Paul seems quite sure that it will happen. Now Paul might have thought this would happen occasionally with a mention of general kinds of sins, but the statement as it applies to every situation like this is more understandable if he thought the prophecies would contain something very striking and unusual, such as specific mention of the visitor's sins. The visitor will think that these Christians know things that could only have been revealed to them by God; they know the secrets of his heart! It seems to be the fact of knowledge acquired by 'supernatural' means, not merely the conviction of sin, which effectively convinces the outsider of God's presence.

I have heard a report of this happening in a clearly non-charismatic Baptist church in the United States. A missionary speaker paused in the middle of his message and said something like this: 'I didn't plan to say this but it seems the Lord is indicating that someone in this church has just walked out on his wife and family. If that is so, let me tell you that God wants you to return to them and learn to follow God's pattern for family life.' The missionary did not know it, but in the unlit balcony sat a man who had entered the church moments before for the first time in his life. The description fitted him exactly and he came forward and acknowledged his sin and began to seek God.

This is why it is prophecy (rather than some other gift) which Paul calls a 'sign to believers'. The distinctiveness of prophecy is that it must be based on revelation, and revelation as it functions in prophecy is always something which, Paul thinks, comes spontaneously and comes only from God (see Chapter 5). Where there is prophecy, then, it is an unmistakable sign or indication of God's presence and blessing on the congregation—it is a 'sign for believers'—and even an outsider who visits will be able to recognize this.

We can now summarize the function of prophecy in 1 Corinthians 14:20–25.

(i) Prophecy functions in evangelism to reveal the secrets of an unbeliever's heart and thereby to amaze him with the power of God at work and to convict him of his sins.

(ii) In doing this, prophecy also serves as a certain indication (sign) that God is present and at work in the congregation to bless it and cause it to grow.

By implication from Paul's example of the outsider we can further conclude that prophecy would also function from time to time to reveal the secrets of some *believer's* heart, convicting him of sin and calling him to repentance. Although Paul does not cite this explicitly as a function of prophecy, it is certainly consistent with the picture of prophecy which we have found in these verses, and would fit perfectly well with Paul's view of prophecy as resulting in edification and exhortation in 1 Corinthians 14:3–5. Furthermore, it would allow prophecy to function in this way as a sign for believers not just when an outsider comes in, but at any time. Thus Paul's statement 'but prophecy is a sign for believers' could be understood as a more general statement, not restricted to the specific application to which Paul puts it in 1 Corinthians 14:24–25.

Application for today

We should heed Paul's warning to the Corinthians and not be childish or immature when we think about our congregational worship. Specifically, we should not speak in tongues without interpretation, for that would be giving an inappropriate 'sign' of God's judgement on the unbeliever, driving him or her away. (Those churches which do allow speaking in tongues should do it in the orderly way described in 1 Corinthians 14:27, and always with interpretation, as in verse 28.)

Mature thinking about prophecy would see it as something to be encouraged in the congregation, even when unbelievers are present. If prophecy is encouraged and allowed to function, it will convict both unbelievers and believers of sin, and will bring to the congregation a much more vivid sense that God is truly among them. It will be a 'sign' of God's approval, of his presence, of his blessing on his people. We ought to see it as this and give thanks for it.

9

Prophets and Church Government:

Were Prophets 'Charismatic Leaders' in the Early Church?

Introduction: The source of this suggestion

Rather frequently one hears the claim that New Testament prophets gave leadership and direction to early churches 'under the influence of the Holy Spirit', and that the prophets by means of such 'charismatic leadership' were the main source of government in these early churches. It was only much later, according to this view, that more formal, rigid structures were established to govern the churches, and officers like 'elder' and 'deacon' became established—perhaps not until after A.D. 100, and at least not until after Paul's death in A.D. 64–68.[76]

It is important to realize that this claim about prophets providing 'charismatic leadership' depends on an assumption that church offices such as elder and deacon, especially in Pauline churches, were only established at a later date. For if there *were* elders and deacons in new churches from the very beginning, then they, not the prophets, would be exercising this governing role.

An evaluation of the evidence for a charismatic leadership role for early prophets

In order to evaluate this claim, two questions need to be addressed:

(1) Did formal church offices develop at once or only after one or two decades, or more, had passed?

(2) Did prophets exercise governing functions in early churches?

When did the offices of elder and deacon develop?

If we look again at the record of the early church in Acts, it will seem clear that there were elders at a very early date: Acts 14:23 (RSV) says that Paul and Barnabas 'appointed elders for them in every church, with prayer and fasting....' Now this is a reference to the churches of Derbe, Lystra, Iconium and Pisidian Antioch—on Paul's *first* missionary journey. There is no reason to think that he failed to follow a similar pattern in other churches as well, appointing elders shortly after the church was established.

In Ephesus, there were also elders in the church, for near the end of Paul's third journey he stopped in Miletus and 'sent to Ephesus and called to him the elders of the church' (Acts 20:17, RSV). Also, he wrote to Timothy in Ephesus (1 Tim 1:3) with instructions about how the church should treat elders (1 Tim 5:17–21; compare the material on 'overseers', another title for elders, in 1 Tim 3:1–7).

The church in Jerusalem also had elders (note Acts 15:2, 4, 6, 22, 23).

Now those who hold the view that prophets gave 'charismatic leadership' in the churches will respond that these verses about 'elders' early in the history of the churches are simply later additions to Acts, and do not really reflect the actual historical situation. But at this point the argument sounds disturbingly circular:

There were no official elders in Pauline churches during Paul's lifetime

Evidence for this: all the references to elders in Acts are later additions

Evidence that these are later additions: there were no official elders in Pauline churches during Paul's lifetime.

This is not the most convincing form of argument.

There are two other reasons given in support of this view of prophets as 'charismatic leaders'. First, it is argued that since every person had a 'charismatic' gift in these churches, there could be no specially privileged group such as elders.

However, the fact that all Christians in the early church had *gifts* does not mean that all had gifts to *rule*. Paul distinguishes various gifts, among them gifts of administration, teaching, and the ability to judge wisely (1 Cor 6:5). Those who had such gifts would no doubt have come into leadership roles very early in the history of each church, and there is no reason to see such gifts in conflict with the idea of formal 'offices' of elder and deacon—such gifts would have made some Christians well suited for those offices.

Richard Gaffin's comment is very appropriate at this point:

> Any tension or opposition between gift (the Spirit) and office is totally foreign to the New Testament. Any construction by which the Spirit as a principle of unstructured freedom and unformed spontaneity is set in conflict with considerations of established order and stable structure is not based on New Testament teaching.... The one and same Spirit is the Spirit of both ardor and order.[77]

A second argument is to note that there is an absence of any mention of elders in some churches, such as Corinth.[78] Surely, it is argued, Paul would have addressed the elders and told them to deal with the problems—if there were elders at Corinth.

But in response it must be said that the fact that Paul addressed the entire congregation at Corinth shows that the entire congregation needed instruction and rebuke—and that the elders had been unable to deal with the problem. In fact, the elders were no doubt part of the problem, since they had failed to solve it. It is not enough to show that sometimes Paul fails to mention elders or overseers—one would have to show that he fails to mention them in contexts dealing with ecclesiastical leadership where such mention would have been necessary or at least expected, and this has not been done.

Moreover, there is some early evidence that Paul appointed elders in Corinth. In 1 Corinthians 16:16 (RSV) he urges the church 'to be subject to such men' as the household of Stephanus, those who were 'the firstfruits' or 'first converts' (Greek *aparchē*) in the region of Achaia (1 Cor 16:15). Apparently echoing this statement, the epistle of *1 Clement* (written from Rome to Corinth, A.D. 95) reminds the Corinthians that the apostles

> preached from district to district, and from city to city, and they appointed their first converts (Greek *aparchē*), testing them by the Spirit, to be bishops and deacons of the future believers (*1 Clement* 42:4; cf. 44:1–3).

Finally, it must be noted that the evidence for an early establishment of the office of elder is very extensive in the New Testament. A summary of the verses relating to elders (or, what is apparently another term for the same position, 'overseers' or 'bishops') will show this:

Acts 14:23—in every church (first missionary journey).

Acts 15:2ff.—in Jerusalem.

Acts 20:17—in Ephesus.

Philippians 1:1—'overseers' and deacons in Philippi.

1 Thessalonians 5:12 (RSV)—'Respect those ... who are over you in the Lord and admonish you....'

1 Timothy 5:17 (RSV)—'Let the elders who rule well be considered worthy of double honour....'

Titus 1:5 (RSV)—'Appoint elders in every town as I directed you [in Crete].'

Hebrews 13:17 (RSV)—'Obey your leaders and submit to them; for they are keeping watch over your souls, as men who will have to give account.'

James 5:14 (RSV)—'Is any among you sick? Let him call for the elders of the church....'

1 Peter 5:1 (RSV)—'So I exhort the elders among you....'

Such pervasive evidence should not be lightly brushed aside in favour of a theory of how one thinks the church 'must' have developed. Especially significant is the statement in 1 Peter, which was addressed to perhaps scores of large and small churches in four provinces in Asia Minor: Peter in about A.D. 62–64 is assuming that the normal pattern of church government is government by elders.

In addition to all this evidence, there is the negative consideration that there is not much evidence anywhere in the New Testament that anyone *other* than apostles (or 'apostolic assistants' such as Timothy and Titus) and elders exercised ruling functions in the churches.

Did prophets exercise governing roles?

In addition to the evidence just mentioned, showing that elders exercised governing authority in the early churches, there is all the New Testament evidence about the actual function of prophets. The conclusions we have reached in the previous chapters showed that prophets could give words to encourage, edify, or console, but there was no evidence in the New Testament itself that they also fulfilled governing functions in the church. Of course, there may well have been elders who also had the gift of prophecy—and many other gifts as well. But there is still no clear evidence that New Testament prophets functioning *as prophets* ever thereby functioned as 'charismatic leaders' in the early church.

Acts 15:32 reports that after Judas and Silas had come with Paul and Barnabas from the Jerusalem Council to Antioch, and had delivered the decision of the Jerusalem Council to the church at Antioch, then, 'Judas and Silas, who were themselves prophets, exhorted the brethren with many words and strengthened them' (Acts 15:32, RSV).

Yet this passage is evidence against any charismatic rule by prophets, since the *ruling* function of Judas and Silas was to deliver a decision to Antioch which had been reached by the *apostles* and the *elders* (*not* the prophets!) in Jerusalem. And that governing decision of the apostles and elders had been reached in a decidedly non-'charismatic' way. (Note: 'after there had been much debate' in Acts 15:7 [RSV].) Judas and Silas did not come in their role as prophets but in their role as 'leading men' among the brethren in Jerusalem (Acts 15:22). (Indeed, the prophets at Antioch [Acts 13:1] had been manifestly unable to impose any 'charismatic' governing solution on the community there.) It is only when Luke wants to mention the non-ruling functions of exhorting and strengthening that he mentions that Judas and Silas were also prophets. Nowhere in the New Testament is any terminology related to ruling, leading, or governing functions applied to someone *because* he has prophetic ability.

Bruce Yocum's reflection on experience in the charismatic movement agrees with this conclusion:

> It is usually a mistake for prophets to be the ultimate authority in a group. A number of heterodox sects and groups have been led by 'prophets' whose 'inspired' statements led people astray.... It is the place of prophets to prophesy, but it is the place of the heads of the community to judge prophecy.[79]

Summary

The New Testament evidence repeatedly indicates that there were offices such as elder and sometimes deacon from the earliest period of establishment of New Testament churches. It also indicates a widespread assumption that there were elders, not prophets, carrying out governing functions in all the local churches for which we have evidence.

On the other hand, there is no convincing evidence that New Testament prophets in their role as prophets ever governed early churches through 'charismatic leadership' by means of prophetic declarations about the direction of the church. This theory is based on some people's ideas of how the church 'must have' or 'could have' developed, but it is not supported by the facts of the New Testament itself.

Application for today

We should expect that governance and administration of churches today will be carried out by those with gifts for leadership who have been established in the formal governing offices of the church, especially (to use New Testament terminology) the office of 'elder'. We should not think a church somehow more 'spiritual' or 'faithful to the early church' if it begins to look to prophetic pronouncements for its guidance and direction—indeed, that would make it *less* like the New Testament church!

Instead, governance is to come through the mature judgement of the rightfully chosen officers of the church, and usually as they act taking into account the collective wisdom of the entire church, and with the consent and support of the church as a whole. Some church officers may also have the gift of prophecy, along with other gifts, but the gift of prophecy in itself does not make them any more qualified to lead the church—that comes through the gifts and characteristics appropriate for church office as outlined in passages such as 1 Timothy 3:1–13 and Titus 1:5–9.

10

Can All Believers Prophesy?

We have now completed our analysis of the gift of prophecy in itself—what authority it had (chapters 1–4), what its source was (chapter 5), how it differed from the gift of teaching (chapter 6), what kinds of content prophecies contained (chapter 7), how it was a sign of God's blessing on a church (chapter 8), and whether the gift of prophecy in itself enabled prophets to govern churches in their earliest days (chapter 9).

But there remain two questions about who could use the gift of prophecy. First, could all believers prophesy, or was the gift restricted to only certain people in the congregation? We shall examine that question in this chapter. Second, could women prophesy freely in local congregations, or does 1 Corinthians 14:33b–35 put some restrictions on the use of the prophetic gift by women? We shall examine that question in the next chapter, chapter 11.

Is 'prophet' an office in the church or an informal designation?

The first step in determining who could prophesy in local churches is to find out whether the word 'prophet' referred to a special office in the church. If there was a formally designated church office called 'prophet', then the answer to our question is quite easy: those who held the office of prophet could prophesy in church.

What do we mean by office? It means that someone is

publicly recognized as having the right and responsibility to perform certain activities in the church. For example, if someone has the office of 'elder', he is recognized by the entire church as having the right to govern the church, and also having the responsibility to do so. Everyone in the church presumably knows who the elders are, and knows that others are not elders. When Paul lists the qualifications for being an elder (or 'overseer/bishop') in 1 Timothy 3:1–7 and Titus 1:5–9, and when he appoints elders in every church (Acts 14:23) or tells Titus to appoint elders in every town (Titus 1:5), it is evident that 'elder' is a recognized church office.

Similarly with the office of 'deacon': the deacons are officers in the church because it is public knowledge who the deacons are, and they are expected to fulfil certain administrative responsibilities in the church. The qualifications for deacons in 1 Timothy 3:8–13 (note Acts 6:3 also), and the fact that there was a clear ceremony of ordaining (or publicly setting apart) people for this office (Acts 6:6; cf. 1 Tim. 3:10) show that this was a distinct 'office' in the early church.

The question now is whether New Testament prophets were such a clearly-defined, publicly recognized group or not. Did the churches require some kind of formal recognition (such as a public announcement, or a vote of approval from the congregation, or perhaps an ordination ceremony) before people could be called 'prophets' in local churches? In other words, was there in some sense an 'office' of prophet in the New Testament churches?

The other alternative would be that the term 'prophet' was not used of an office but was only used in a *descriptive* or *functional* sense, so that anyone who prophesied might be called a 'prophet'.

This second situation was true of many other gifts in the New Testament. For example, someone who regularly helped others might be called a 'helper', someone who often taught (without formal public recognition by the whole church) might still be called a 'teacher', someone who often interpreted speaking in tongues might be called an 'interpreter', etc. In these cases, someone who had not received any kind of formal recognition still might have a descriptive noun applied to him or her.

When nouns such as 'helper', 'administrator', 'healer', 'tongue speaker', 'interpreter', etc, are used in a merely descriptive way such as this, it is helpful to refer to them as *functional* uses of nouns (since they simply describe *functions* which people perform), in order to distinguish them from nouns which are used as technical terms to describe some church office or some position which required more formal recognition.

Now with regard to the term 'prophet', there are several reasons why it seems to be used in such a functional sense both in 1 Corinthians and in the rest of the New Testament instances which mention congregational prophets.

First, even if someone argued that there was an office of 'prophet' in the church at Corinth, he would still have to admit that there were some who did not hold that office but who nevertheless prophesied occasionally. This would be inevitable in a church where everyone was encouraged to prophesy (1 Cor 12:31; 14:1, 5, 39). Some would hesitantly be trying to use the gift for the first time, while others would receive a revelation (1 Cor 14:30) only very infrequently. In any given congregation there would be all sorts of varying degrees of prophetic ability.

Now these people who prophesy infrequently are still called 'prophets' by Paul, for in 1 Corinthians 14:32 (RSV) he says, 'The spirits of prophets are subject to prophets.' By this he cannot mean only that those who are formally recognized as prophets are able to control themselves when they prophesy, for then his instructions would have no relevance for the novices (who no doubt needed instruction as much as anyone). 'Prophets' here must refer to all who prophesy, even occasionally, and therefore cannot be restricted to a special office in the church.

Then in 1 Corinthians 14:29 (RSV), 'Let two or three prophets speak, and let the others weigh what is said,' Paul cannot

simply be giving instructions concerning a special formally recognized group, for then he would be excluding from congregational participation those who had prophetic gifts but were not
formally recognized—something contrary to Paul's express
desire that all who have gifts be able to use them for the benefit
of all (1 Cor 12:7, 21, 26; 14:5, 12; cf. Rom 12:6). So once again,
Paul means by 'prophet' here anyone who has the ability to
prophesy, or simply anyone who received a revelation and
prophesied.

In 1 Corinthians 14:37, 'If any one thinks himself to be a
prophet, or spiritual,' Paul implies that there is an element of
subjective evaluation. Someone might 'think himself' to be a
prophet, while someone else might differ with that opinion. If
'prophet' had been a formal office, no such difference of opinion could occur, for everyone would know who was a prophet
and who was not. Paul could not say, 'If anyone thinks himself
to be an elder,' for example—either you were or you weren't!
Thus, 'prophet' here cannot be an office but must just refer to
someone who has the ability to prophesy or who prophesies
frequently.

This leaves only 1 Corinthians 12:28, which must be considered an ambiguous use of the term. The connection with
'apostles' might suggest that church officers are named here,
but that is not certain. 'Teachers' might simply be a functional
description of those who teach (as in 1 Timothy 2:7; 2 Timothy
1:11; Hebrews; 5:12; and perhaps James 3:1; cf. Titus 2:3 and
the general phrase 'he who prophesies' in Romans 12:7).
Moreover, in 1 Corinthians 12:31 (RSV), when Paul says, 'Earnestly desire the higher gifts,' it seems that he would like all the
Corinthians to strive to be 'prophets' in the sense of 1 Corinthians 12:28, a wish which would be unusual if by prophet he
meant some formally recognized function or office.

Elsewhere in the New Testament 'prophet' is generally used
in cases which are ambiguous enough to prevent us from deciding whether any kind of office or formally recognized position
is in view. Agabus is called a 'prophet' (Acts 11:27; 21:10), but

there is nothing in the context to show whether office or just function is intended. The same is true of Acts 13:1, where we read that there were 'prophets and teachers' in the church at Antioch.

In Acts 15:32 (RSV) Luke mentions Judas and Silas, 'who were themselves prophets'. But this hardly seems like a designation of office, since the earlier narrative of the Jerusalem Council mentioned only the offices of apostle and elder (Acts 15:2, 4, 6, 22), but not prophet—Luke mentions it here not in connection with any official duty but only when he reports that Judas and Silas 'exhorted the brethren with many words and strengthened them' (Acts 15:32, RSV).

In Caesarea, Philip had 'four unmarried daughters, who prophesied' (Acts 21:9, RSV), a statement which does not even use a noun but a verb to refer to their prophetic activity, and clearly suggests more a function than a formal office.

Ephesians 4:11 is also ambiguous. Paul writes, 'And he gave some apostles, some prophets, some evangelists, some pastor-teachers....' In this list, clearly 'apostles' refers to those in a specific, recognized office. But 'evangelists' is not so clear—we have no record of people being set apart or ordained to an office of evangelist in the New Testament, but only some references to people who are called evangelists, perhaps because the activity or function of evangelism was their primary area of service in the church. (The only other uses of the term 'evangelist' in the New Testament are in Acts 21:8, referring to Philip the evangelist, and 2 Timothy 4:5, where Paul tells Timothy to do the work of an evangelist.) Moreover, unlike apostle or elder or deacon, there is nothing inherent in doing evangelism which requires public recognition by the whole church. Anyone can do evangelism whether recognized by the church or not, but no one can govern the church without being publicly recognized before the whole church.

As for pastor-teachers, although this is the only New Testament occurrence of this combination term, this probably was a recognized office in the early church, perhaps the same as the

office of elder. Yet the fact that Paul does not use the term
'elder' (though there were elders at Ephesus: Acts 20:17)
suggests that perhaps he is focusing on activities rather than
office: those who do the work of apostles, those whose activity
is prophesying, those whose activity is evangelism, those who
do the work of pastoring and teaching. If Paul had written, 'He
gave some apostles, some prophets, some elders, some
deacons...,' then it would seem clearly to be a list of offices in
the church. But he did not write this, nor is there any such list
in the New Testament. 'Apostles, prophets, evangelists, pastor-teachers' is at most a mixed list of offices and functions, and
does not provide clear evidence that 'prophet' was a formal
office in any New Testament churches.

In addition to the foregoing analysis of specific verses mentioning prophets, there are some minor considerations against
the view that 'prophet' was a recognized office. First, there is
no hint in the New Testament about any ceremony of recognizing or installing somone in a prophetic office or to perform
some specific prophetic tasks (as with apostles, elders and
deacons in Acts 1:23–26; 6:6; 14:23; 1 Timothy 4:14; 5:22;
Titus 1:5; etc). Second, there does not seem to have been any
need for formal public recognition of those who were prophets,
for anyone who received a revelation could prophesy (1 Cor
14:31).

So 'prophet' appears to be not an office but a designation of
function in the New Testament. Those who prophesied frequently or appeared to have the gift of prophecy were called
'prophets'.

British charismatic leader Michael Harper, in a booklet that
is in many ways very helpful and balanced on the gift of
prophecy, nevertheless at this point makes what seems to me to
be a mistake in evaluating the New Testament evidence. He
sees a distinction (often mentioned by other charismatics as
well) between the 'office of prophet' which only a few occupied
and the more common 'manifestation of prophecy', which was
potentially for anyone. Then he says that 1 Corinthians 14:29

only allows 'two or three' who hold the *office* of prophet to prophesy, but 1 Corinthians 14:31 says (referring to the rest of the church) that 'all' can prophesy.[80] Yet this misunderstands 1 Corinthians 14:31. It does not mean that all present could prophesy at a church service, but only that all who do prophesy can do so 'one by one', in an orderly way (see discussion of this verse in 'Do all have the ability?' below).

More accurate, it seems to me, is the conclusion of Assembly of God writer Donald Gee:

> Although there appears to be a distinction between official prophets and those who prophesied, it is arbitrary to claim for the prophets anything more than that they were those who exercised a frequent and proved gift of prophesying.[81]

But having said this, we must also recognize that the term can have a *more broad* or *more narrow* meaning depending on the context in which it is used. For example, 1 Corinthians 14:32 (rsv), 'The spirits of prophets are subject to prophets,' must use 'prophet' to apply to anyone who prophesies even once. This is a very broad meaning, and the context makes it clear to the reader.

But in 1 Corinthians 14:37, 'If someone thinks himself to be a prophet, or spiritual,' a more narrow meaning of the term is required. Here an element of subjective personal evaluation is involved. Some people would consider a certain person a prophet, others would not. In such a case, whether or not the term 'prophet' would be applied to a particular person would depend on at least three variable factors:

(a) The frequency and scope of that person's prophetic activity: Someone who prophesied before the entire congregation very frequently and at great length would certainly be called a 'prophet', while someone who prophesied less frequently and more briefly (and perhaps before a smaller group of believers) might not be so called.

(b) The situation in that particular congregation: In a church where no one had prophesied for several months or years even

a novice in prophetic activity would be called a prophet, but in a church where many prophets were active, people would not call the beginner a prophet until he began to prophesy more often.

(c) The individual speech habits of believers in the congregation: Some would enthusiastically want to label any novice a prophet, but others would be more restrictive in their use of the term.

Both the broad and the narrow use here described comprise what may be called an *informal* recognition that certain people are prophets and others (at least for the present) are not. There seems to have been no congregational vote to determine who could be called prophets, nor do we see evidence of any public announcement that certain designated people could be called prophets. Rather, it probably was generally recognized by the believers that 'prophet' simply meant 'someone who prophesies'. Such a non-technical definition fits well with all the New Testament data.

Can all believers prophesy?

Now that we have established that 'prophet' apparently was not a formal office in the New Testament, we can look at the main question of this chapter: Can all believers prophesy?

In order to answer this question we must distinguish several specific meanings and answer the individual senses of the question one at a time:

1. Are all believers permitted to prophesy?
2. Does every believer have a potential ability to prophesy?
3. Does every believer have an actual ability to prophesy?
4. Does every believer have the ability to prophesy at will?

We shall examine these questions one at a time.

Do all have permission?

Paul places certain restrictions on the permission to prophesy. No one can prophesy when someone else is speaking (1 Cor

14:30–31), and the limitations of time would not seem to allow every single person in the congregation to prophesy at one meeting (1 Cor 14:29). But other than those restrictions there are no New Testament limitations on the permission to prophesy.[82] There was no special prophetic office such that only those who held that office could prophesy in church, nor is there any indication that only older, more mature, or more respected members of the congregation could prophesy. Rather, every believer who received a revelation and waited to speak in turn had permission to prophesy.

Do all potentially have the ability?

By this we mean to ask whether every believer might one day prophesy, or, negatively, if there were any believers who for some reason were disqualified from ever being able to prophesy. Here the answer must be that such potential ability was possessed by everyone in whom the Holy Spirit worked. The gifts are given, Paul says, to *each person* (1 Cor 12:7, 11) by the Holy Spirit, and it is only the free volition of the Spirit ('according as he wills', 1 Cor 12:11) which determines who received which gift. Any Christian might possibly receive the gift of prophecy. Furthermore, Paul urges all the Corinthians to seek to prophesy (1 Cor 14:1, 39), implying that there was for every one of them at least the possibility that they would receive this prophetic gift.

Do all actually have the ability?

In this case we are asking whether every believer did in fact receive the ability to prophesy. Here the answer must be negative. Although Paul *wants* every Christian in Corinth to seek after prophecy and other useful gifts, he still is very clear that there is no one gift which will be possessed by every believer (1 Cor 12:8–10, 12, 14, 17, 19–20, 29–30) and even specifies prophecy as a function not possessed by all (note: 'Not all are prophets, are they?' in 1 Corinthians 12:29).

It is not inconsistent for Paul to say that *not all* will be *able* to prophesy while at the same time telling them all to *seek* to do so. Paul did not know which of the Corinthians would be given the prophetic gift. He could not have singled out one group, such as adults, or leaders, or mature Christians, and told only these people to seek to prophesy, for then he would have arbitrarily excluded some potential prophets. His only alternative was to do exactly what he did: encourage *all to seek* the gift while at the same time exhorting those who do not attain it to be content and trust in God's wisdom concerning what is best for the church (1 Cor 12:11, 15–16, 18, 28 with 31).

Another objection might stem from Acts 19:6 (RSV), where a dozen Ephesian believers 'spoke with tongues and prophesied'. Although this prophecy is probably similar in many respects to the type of prophecy we find in 1 Corinthians, the fact that they all seem to have spoken in tongues and prophesied at once makes it quite different from the orderly congregational speech in 1 Corinthians. It appears rather as a dramatic and unique event confirming the giving of the Holy Spirit to the Gentiles, similar to the events in Acts 2:4 and 10:46, and this exact event need not have been repeated either in the founding of other churches or in the subsequent lives of these twelve at Ephesus as they began to function in the orderly worship of the assembled congregation.

A final objection can arise from 1 Corinthians 14:31, where Paul says, 'For you can all prophesy one by one, in order that all may learn and all may be encouraged.' Doesn't this verse say that all can prophesy?

In fact, the verse does not exactly say that. It says rather that all can prophesy *one by one*—in other words, that all are able to control themselves and act in an orderly manner. The 'one by one' comes early in the Greek sentence and intrudes between 'you are able' and 'to prophesy', thus guaranteeing that the reader will understand that it is not simply the ability to prophesy but the ability to prophesy one by one which is in view.

This verse, then, does not mean that all actually can prophesy, but just that everyone in the congregation is able to control himself if he ever does prophesy.

The last clause of 1 Corinthians 14:31, 'In order that all may learn and all may be encouraged,' shows the result of prophesying one by one. Everyone in the congregation would be helped or encouraged, because they could all hear and understand. The other situation, where several would prophesy at once, would allow few or none to learn and be encouraged, because no one would be able to hear or understand what was said. But if everyone who prophesies does so one by one, everyone will hear and understand the words, and everyone will thereby be encouraged and strengthened.

Therefore, several sections of 1 Corinthians 12–14 show quite clearly that not all believers had an actual ability to prophesy.

Can people prophesy whenever they want to?

In the earlier investigation of 1 Corinthians 14:30 (chapter 5), we found that a 'revelation' was thought to be something which came quite spontaneously to a prophet, that it came from God, and that without a 'revelation' there could be no prophecy. Thus, no prophet could conjure up a revelation of his own accord and then begin to prophesy. He or she had to wait until something was revealed by the Holy Spirit.

At this point there is a difference between prophecy and some of the other gifts mentioned by Paul. Gifts such as administration, teaching, helping, giving aid and (probably) speaking in tongues (1 Cor 14:15, 18, 28) could be used at will. The believer who had one of these gifts could put it to use at any time. But prophecy was more spontaneous and could only be used when the prophet received a revelation. It seems that no one had the ability to prophesy at will.

Should even new believers be allowed to prophesy?
(1 Cor 12:1–3)?

What about prophecy by new Christians, especially those from a clearly non-Christian or pagan background? Should the church wait for a time—say, a year or two—to see if their Christian profession is real and if they have enough doctrinal understanding, before allowing them to prophesy?

This problem apparently arose at Corinth, not only with prophecy but also with regard to spiritual gifts generally. Corinth was strongly influenced by pagan Greek religions, and Paul even says that idol worship in Corinth was really worship of demons:

> What pagans sacrifice they sacrifice to demons and not to God. I do not want you to be partners with demons. You cannot drink the cup of the Lord and the cup of demons. You cannot partake of the table of the Lord and the table of demons (1 Cor 10:20–21).

Now this background would influence the question of the use of spiritual gifts by new Christians, especially those from backgrounds of demon worship. Paul apparently recognizes this problem and gives an answer to it in his introduction to the discussion of spiritual gifts in 1 Corinthians 12–14. He writes:

> Now about spiritual gifts, brothers, I do not want you to be ignorant. You know that when you were pagans, somehow or other you were influenced and led astray to dumb idols. Therefore I tell you that no one who is speaking by the Spirit of God says, 'Jesus be cursed,' and no one can say, 'Jesus is Lord,' except by the Holy Spirit (1 Cor 12:1–3, New International Version).

Paul says, in effect, 'I know that you formerly served gods who could not speak, and, therefore, gods from whom you could have learned nothing. So you are ignorant about spiritual gifts. Therefore, I make known to you that no one speaking by the Spirit of God says, 'Jesus be cursed,' and no one can say, 'Jesus is Lord,' except by the Holy Spirit.' Understood in this way, the verses provide a fitting introduction to chapters 12–14, for here Paul can be seen to emphasize the fact that *every* Christian has the Spirit of God within, enabling him or her to make such a statement.

This fits well into what we can tell of the background of many Christians at Corinth. Perhaps the Corinthians had expressed to Paul a concern about the intermingling of idolatry and Christianity. There were several former idolaters in the church (cf. 1 Cor 6:9–11; 8:7), and those who caused the most suspicion could be put in roughly two categories:

(a) On the one hand, people who claimed to be inspired were perhaps coming to the worship services and giving a very impressive performance, maybe even prophesying with much emotion. Yet they were saying some very disturbing things, sometimes even blaspheming Christ. Might the Holy Spirit nevertheless be empowering them, if not in the blasphemy, at least in some of the other things they said?

Paul answers, 'No, these people are not speaking by the Spirit of God. If the Holy Spirit were at work in them, they simply would not say such a thing.'

(b) On the other hand, if the Corinthians were not to trust these people, it would be difficult for them to know whom to trust. A large segment of the church consisted of converted idolaters, some of them with as yet only marginal Christian understanding. How could it be determined that any former idolater was speaking the truth—or even that any of his gifts, whether they be prophecy, teaching, healing, tongues, administration or whatever, were to be trusted in the church?

To this Paul replies, 'You must not be overly suspicious and exclude true believers from the work of the church. Anyone who makes a true, sincere Christian confession has made it by the power of the Holy Spirit and should be fully accepted in the church.'

We cannot of course understand 1 Corinthians 12:3 to refer to a simple repetition of some magic formula (compare the false professions in Matthew 7:21–23 and 15:8). Rather, the confession 'Jesus is Lord' to which Paul refers must be viewed as a profession of personal faith, given credibility by some reasonable indication of accompanying sincerity and understanding. Similarly, the words 'Jesus be cursed' do not by themselves necessarily indicate unbelief, for they would have been pronounced by anyone at Corinth who read Paul's letter aloud. But if they seemed to indicate the speaker's own sentiments, then Paul would consider them an indication of unbelief.

Of course Paul was not proposing a 100% foolproof system, because it would not have been possible in every case for the Corinthians to tell if a man was sincere, especially with the confession of faith. But as a general rule, useful in most cases, Paul was saying: (1) blasphemy indicated unbelief and (2) a confession of faith indicated belief.

With this understanding of 1 Corinthians 12:3, we see that Paul does not have speech gifts alone in view in this section. Although the confession of faith and the blasphemy are speech activities, they function as indications of the presence or absence of the work of the Holy Spirit in a person's life. If someone confesses that 'Jesus is Lord,' it indicates that the Holy Spirit is at work within him (1 Cor 12:3) and thus that he is a member of the one body of Christ (1 Cor 12:13) and has gifts which are to be used for the benefit of that body (1 Cor 12:7, 11, 12–31). If a person blasphemes, it indicates that the Holy Spirit is not at work within him (1 Cor 12:3), and thus that he is not a member of Christ and does not at that time have gifts which benefit the church. (1 John 4:1–6 has a similar teaching.)

In conclusion, in a city full of idolatry, 1 Corinthians 12:1–3 distinguishes those who have spiritual gifts (believers) from those who do not (unbelievers). Those whose credible profession of faith in Christ marks them as true believers have the Holy Spirit within them. And if they have the Holy Spirit within them, then they also have a valuable gift or gifts to be used for the benefit of the body of Christ. Even new believers, then, will sometimes be given the gift of prophecy. Subject to the appropriate controls of the congregation (see especially 1 Cor 14:29–33a, and chapter 13, below), even new believers should be allowed to use this and any other gifts they have for the benefit of the body of Christ.

Is prophecy a temporary or a permanent gift?

There are two minor senses in which prophecy could be considered a *temporary* gift. In the first place no prophet could
prophesy at will (see discussion above, p. 201). A person could
only prophesy when he or she received a revelation. Even if a
person prophesied quite often, one might say that he did not
really 'possess' the gift, since he had to wait until the moment
the Spirit gave him a revelation.

In the second place Paul clearly recognizes the absolute
sovereignty of the Holy Spirit in the distribution of gifts. All the
gifts are 'empowered by the same Spirit while he is distributing
to each one as he wills' (1 Cor 12:11). So it is indeed possible
that the Spirit would give someone a special ability—for healing or for prophecy, say—for only a few moments and then
never give it to that person again.

But in spite of these two valid points, it is possible to speak
of prophecy generally as a *permanent* or at least *semi-permanent* gift. While admitting that no prophet can prophesy at will,
we nevertheless find indications in 1 Corinthians 12–14 that
there were people who were able to prophesy frequently over
an extended period of time. This fact need not contradict Paul's
insistence on the sovereignty of the Spirit in distributing gifts.
It may only mean that Paul recognized that the Spirit acted in
an orderly and regular way, not in one that was totally
haphazard and unpredictable.

In 1 Corinthians 14:37, 'if someone thinks himself to be
a prophet', the reference is not to the time at which the
person is prophesying but to the time at which Paul's letter
is being read. This implies that some people prophesied frequently enough to be considered prophets all the time, not
just when they were prophesying. Similarly, in 1 Corinthians 13:2, the phrase 'if I have prophecy' implies a continu-
ous possession of the gift. Then in 1 Corinthians 12:29, 'not
all are prophets' implies that some people prophesy with

enough regularity to be thought of as prophets.

The same seems to be the case with other gifts. Apparently when someone had the ability to interpret tongues that fact was known to the entire congregation, because the tongue-speaker was supposed to know whether an 'interpreter' was present, and, if not, to refrain from speaking in tongues in church (1 Cor 14:28).

A similar conclusion can be drawn from the body metaphor in 1 Corinthians 12:12–26. If members of the church are thought of like parts of the body, the picture is one of retention of functions over a period of time (for a hand continues to be a hand, a foot continues to be a foot, etc). However, this metaphor cannot be pressed too far, for it would then imply that no one could acquire other gifts or lose gifts or have more than one gift, etc.[83]

So the pattern seems to have been that prophecy was normally a permanent or at least semi-permanent gift, even though no one could prophesy at will and there may have been some people who prophesied once and never again.

Yet in all of this discussion, though it is not wrong to talk about 'having' one gift or another (Paul speaks this way in 1 Corinthians 12:30 and 13:2, Greek text), it is still good to remember the mature perspective of Richard Gaffin on the question of the possession of spiritual gifts generally:

> Probably the most important and certainly the most difficult lesson for us to learn is that ultimately spiritual gifts are not our presumed strengths and abilities, not something that we 'have' (or even have been given), but what God does through us in spite of ourselves and our weakness. 'My grace is sufficient for you, for my power is made perfect in weakness' (2 Cor 12:9, RSV).[84]

The gift of prophecy could vary in strength

With many of the gifts Paul lists it is evident that various people possessed different *degrees of ability* in any specific gift. For example, with gifts like teaching and administration, even

among those who were recognized as teachers and administrators there was no absolute equivalence in ability. Some were
better teachers than others, and some had stronger administrative ability than others, could effectively carry larger responsibilities, etc.

On the other hand, there were those who did not have gifts
of teaching or administration, and who therefore did no public
teaching or administrative work for the church. But even with
these people, of course, there were lesser degrees of teaching
ability, or administrative ability—even if these abilities were
only exercised in their own families or towards their own children, for example, and were not used for the church generally.
They did not have a gift of teaching, yet in some sense they
'taught', and it could be said that they had *something like* the
gift of teaching, only at a very low degree of development.

These two factors taken together—the degrees of ability
possessed by those who had a gift, and the small ability that is
something like the gift possessed by those who don't have it—
lead us to conclude that it is not exactly accurate to think of
these gifts in the New Testament church in terms of absolute
possession and absolute non-possession. It is more accurate to
think in terms of a progression along a scale of increasing intensity.

When Paul says, 'Not all are teachers' (1 Cor 12:29), he
means that not all have significant enough teaching abilities to
function as teachers in the congregation. But even this is a relative comparison: someone who had only a small degree of
teaching ability might nevertheless be recognized as a teacher
in a new congregation where everyone else had even less ability
than he did.

Paul also recognizes degrees of ability (or frequency of use)
with respect to tongues, saying, 'I speak in tongues more than
you all' (1 Cor 14:18, RSV). And other gifts such as faith or the
ability to speak words of knowledge or wisdom would naturally
vary in degree.

In the pastoral Epistles there are indications that an individual himself may increase or decrease at least some of his abilities for ministry, for Timothy is told not to neglect the gift that is in him (1 Tim 4:14) but to practise using it. In verse 15, 'practise these things' refers to the public reading of Scripture, preaching, and teaching in verse 13, and the gift mentioned in verse 14, as well as to 'speech and conduct, love...faith...purity' in verse 12. He is also told to 'rekindle' this gift (2 Tim 1:6), which suggests that Timothy had let it fall into disuse, and that it was only operative at a low degree of intensity at the time Paul was writing. But by 'rekindling' it Timothy could restore it to a more intense or powerful function in his life.

These are all texts which deal with gifts other than prophecy, so we cannot be sure without further thought and investigation that the gift of prophecy would also follow this pattern. But it seems likely that it would.

One indication of this is found in Romans 12:6 (RSV): 'if prophecy, in proportion to (his) faith...' This apparently means that some who had the gift of prophecy had a greater measure of faith (that is, a trust or confidence that the Holy Spirit would work or was working in them to bring a revelation which would be the basis of a prophecy).[85] Those to whom God had given a greater proportion of this specific kind of faith would prophesy more. But this would not be the basis for pride. Paul insists in the same context that differing measures of faith are given by God (Rom 12:3 [RSV]: 'according to the measure of faith which God has assigned him'), and that individual gifts 'differ according to the grace given to us' (Rom 12:6, RSV).

If prophecy is like the other New Testament gifts mentioned, and if it follows the pattern of 'degrees of faith' mentioned in Romans 12, then there would be greater and lesser degrees of prophetic ability, ranged all along a wide spectrum, in any given congregation. Prophets would differ in ability among themselves, and would also see changes in the extent of their own prophetic abilities over a period of time. Those with a high degree of prophetic ability would prophesy more frequently, at greater length, from more clear and forceful revelations, about more important subjects, and over a wider range of topics.

Is it right to seek the gift of prophecy?

There are certain statements of Paul's which so clearly emphasize the sovereignty of the Holy Spirit in bestowing gifts that, taken by themselves, they might cause us to adopt a fatalistic attitude towards the acquisition of the gift of prophecy. The Spirit 'distributes to each one as he wills' (1 Cor 12:11). God 'has placed the parts in the body, even as he willed' (1 Cor 12:18). 'God has put' people with various gifts in the church (1 Cor 12:28), etc. A believer reading only those verses might decide that there was absolutely nothing he or she could do to acquire the gift of prophecy except sit and wait, hoping that someday the Holy Spirit might see fit to give this gift.

However, there are other verses of Paul's which show that he expected the Corinthians to take some positive steps to seek out the gift of prophecy for themselves. 'Seek earnestly the greater gifts' (1 Cor 12:31). 'Seek earnestly the spiritual gifts, especially that you may prophesy' (1 Cor 14:1). 'Seek earnestly to prophesy' (1 Cor 14:39). Apparently Paul thought the Corinthians would understand how to do this, for he never gave a clear explanation of what this seeking would involve.

Nevertheless, there are various hints in the text which help us know that there were at least some steps Paul expected the Corinthians to take. We can examine those hints, both regarding the gift of prophecy and regarding other gifts, and summarize some of the things which might be involved in seeking spiritual gifts, especially the gift of prophecy.

Pray

A person could pray for the ability to interpret tongues (1 Cor 14:13), and so could no doubt also pray for the gift of prophecy.

Be content with present gifts

A believer should not wrongly evaluate the gifts he does have by being puffed up with pride (1 Cor 12:20–24) or full of jealousy over gifts he does not have (1 Cor 12.14–19). He should rest content that the present distribution of gifts has been made by God and should be thought good and right (1 Cor 12:18, 27–30). Therefore, he should make up his mind to be content if he does not receive the gift he asks for.

Grow towards Christian maturity

Paul links prophecy with general Christian maturity in 1 Corinthians 14:37 ('If any one thinks he is a prophet or spiritually mature'). In 1 Corinthians 2:6 it is the mature to whom Paul imparts a wisdom, and in 1 Corinthians 2:14 the immature man does not receive (an understanding of) the things of the Spirit of God. As it is with wisdom and understanding, so it may well be with prophecy. It is more often given to those who are mature.

Have right motives

In 1 Corinthians 14:1 Paul combines seeking the gift (prophecy) with maintaining the right motive (love). He reminds the Corinthians that they should strive to excel in building up the church (1 Cor 14:12), and in 1 Corinthians 12:31 he tells them to seek the 'greater' gifts, that is, those of most value to the church. Thus he implies that their overriding motive in seeking gifts should not be personal glory but the edification of the church.

Use present gifts.

If the Corinthians did have a proper motive for seeking prophecy and sincerely wanted to have that gift for the benefit of the church, then Paul would quite fairly expect to see that high motive manifested in the use of gifts which were presently possessed for the benefit of the church (1 Cor 14:12, 26). If someone failed to use his present gift for the benefit of all, or misused it so that it attracted attention to himself but did the church no good (as in 1 Cor 14:17), then it would be evident that his motives for seeking prophecy were not right.

And another note should be added here about the way we discover what gifts we presently have. Richard Gaffin puts it well:

> The way to determine our spiritual gifts is not to ask, 'What is my 'thing' spiritually, my spiritual specialty, that sets me apart from other believers and gives me a distinguishing niche in the church?' Rather the New Testament on the whole takes a much more *functional* or *situational* approach. The question to ask is, 'What in the situation in which God has placed me are the particular opportunities I see for serving other believers in word and deed (cf. 1 Peter 4:10f.)?' 'What are the specific needs confronting me that need to be ministered to?' Posing and effectively responding to this question will go a long way not only toward discovering but also actually using our spiritual gifts.[86]

Try to prophesy?

Would Paul have encouraged a potential prophet simply to try to prophesy, perhaps opening his mouth and speaking whatever came to mind? Because of the Old Testament background which defined false prophecy as something one did 'from his own heart' without having a revelation from God (Jer 23:16, 21–22; cf. Jn 11:51), I would expect Paul to be very cautious here. Unless someone thought he had a revelation (1 Cor 14:30), such a practice would no doubt have been discouraged as something that would just lead to prophesying when one had not received the gift of prophecy, and therefore just prophesying things the speaker had made up himself. This would totally nullify the feature that made prophecy unique and valuable among the gifts: the fact that it was based on a revelation from the Holy Spirit.

On the other hand, Paul would probably have encouraged a person who was timid and who thought he had received a revelation but was not quite sure. In such a case, the presence of mature, sound hearers in the congregation who would point out any false aspects of the prophecy (1 Cor 14:29; cf. 1 Thess

5:19–20) would be a sufficient safeguard for the welfare and stability of the congregation.

Summary

The word 'prophet' does not appear to describe a formally recognized office or position in the New Testament. Rather, it is a functional term: those who prophesy regularly are called 'prophets'. But even those who don't prophesy regularly may prophesy occasionally.

All believers have permission to prophesy (if they receive a revelation from the Holy Spirit), and all have a potential ability to prophesy. But only some are given an actual ability to prophesy, and no one can prophesy at will.

Although the Holy Spirit is sovereign in the distribution of spiritual gifts, there is normally an orderly and regular way in which he acts in this distribution of gifts. Specifically, prophecy appears to be a permanent or mostly permanent gift, even though no one can prophesy whenever he wants to. Prophetic abilities will vary greatly in degree, and Paul gives some indications of the way in which a believer can seek to increase his prophetic ability.

Application for today

The fact that the gift of prophecy can be given to any believer should greatly encourage all Christians today to be sensitive to such promptings of the Holy Spirit, for they may lead to a prophecy which would benefit the congregation. This availability of prophecy to all Christians should also encourage churches to have some corporate worship times (even if not on Sunday mornings, then on some other times) when any Christian could contribute, and when use of the gift of prophecy would be allowed, among other gifts. Even younger Christians should not be discouraged, so long as the safeguards in 1 Corinthians 14 are followed.

Yet the Holy Spirit distributes gifts 'as he wills', so no believer should be disappointed if the gift of prophecy, or even an occasional prophecy, is not given. Those who have prophesied in the past should not neglect that gift, but should presume that the gift was given permanently, and should expect to be able to continue to prophesy from time to time in the assembled congregation. Yet no one should begin to think that he controls the giving of revelations from the Holy Spirit so that he could prophesy whenever he decided or wanted to do so.

Since the gift of prophecy, like most spiritual gifts, can vary in strength, churches should be willing to be patient and encouraging towards those who are trying this gift for the first time (as they would with other gifts, such as teaching, evangelism, works of mercy, etc). Those who have the gift should expect that as it is used it may increase in strength or intensity—they may gain more ability to distinguish clearly what is a revelation and what is not, more evidence that the gift is edifying the church, more ability to report it in a helpful way to the church—and perhaps even more frequent and/or more extensive revelations will be received.

Those who wish to seek the gift of prophecy, as Paul commands the Corinthians to do, should ask:

1. Have I prayed and sincerely asked God for this gift?

2. Am I truly content with the gifts I presently have?

3. Am I growing towards Christian maturity?

4. Do I want this gift for the benefit of the church, and not for my own glory or status or prestige?

5. Am I using the gifts I presently have for the greatest benefit of the church?

If these things are done, then God may indeed give this gift. If so, then he should be praised and thanked.

11

Women and Prophecy:

Prophesying Encouraged, but Not the Judging of Prophecies

One specific question comes up with respect to the general matter of who could prophesy in the church: Does the statement in 1 Corinthians on women being 'silent' in the church (1 Cor 14:34) mean that women could not prophesy in church? And if the statement does not mean this, then what does it mean?

Before we examine 1 Corinthians 14:33b–35, it is important to note two other passages indicating that women could and did prophesy in New Testament churches.

Acts 21:9: Philip's daughters

When Paul and his companions came to Caesarea near the very end of Paul's third missionary journey, Luke wrote, 'And we entered the house of Philip the evangelist, who was one of the seven, and stayed with him. And he had four unmarried daughters, who prophesied' (Acts 21:8–9, RSV).

This must certainly be a record of women who prophesied in the assembly of a group of Christians, for the fact that Luke reports it strongly suggests that Paul and those with him were present while these women were prophesying. The verb used (a present participle) also suggests that the prophesying was a regular or continuing occurrence with these daughters: more literally, the text says, 'To this man [Philip] were four virgin daughters prophesying.' So here is one example of women (or girls—there is no indication of their age) who seem to have

215

used the gift of prophecy freely in the church.

1 Corinthians 11:5: Women who prophesy with a head covering

While instructing the Corinthians about worship in 1 Corinthians 11, Paul writes:

> Any man who prays or prophesies with his head covered dishonours his head, but any woman who prays or prophesies with her head unveiled dishonours her head—it is the same as if her head were shaven (1 Cor 11:4–5, RSV).

In this passage it is clear that public worship is in view. We have already seen that the New Testament views prophecy as a gift for public use (chapter 7, above), and surely the instruction about prayer could not apply to private prayer. Could a man never pray with his head covered, even when alone outdoors in cold weather? Could a woman never pray wth her head uncovered, even when alone in the privacy of her own home? Such restrictions would not occur in the New Testament, which encourages us to 'pray without ceasing' (1 Thess 5:17) and to 'pray at all times' (Eph 6:18, RSV).

Some have suggested that the prayer by women in 1 Corinthians 11 was inaudible prayer, unable to be heard by the congregation. But surely prophecy was audible—if it could not be heard (and understood) by others, it did not fulfil its purpose (see chapter 7, above). And if the prophecy was audible, there is no reason to doubt that the prayer was audible as well. Moreover, it is hard to imagine that Paul would tell the church to regulate *inaudible* speech, for how could they know when it was being done?

We must conclude that in 1 Corinthians 11:5 Paul gives instructions concerning the way in which women should pray and prophesy in public worship, and thereby implies that such praying and prophesying in the congregation is a legitimate activity for women.

It is not our purpose here to enter a detailed discussion of the question of head coverings in worship for women today, except to say that in 1 Corinthians 11 Paul affirms one temporary expression (head coverings) of an eternal, created difference (role differences between men and women). He sees head coverings as outward expressions of the differences between men and women, outward expressions which were commonly recognized in that society at that time. But there is no good reason for us to think that such an outward expression as style of head coverings (or styles of clothing generally) was intended to be a rule for all societies at all times. If the differences between men and women are not shown by head coverings in other societies and other cultures (such as ours today), then of course such temporary expressions as Paul mentions are not appropriate, and certainly not required for us today. But what is abiding is the eternal relationship between men and women which Paul depends on to support his teaching on the head coverings, the temporary expression.

1 Corinthians 14:33b–35: In what way should women be 'silent' in the churches?

After several verses given to a discussion of prophecy and the regulation of prophecy (1 Cor 14:29–33a), Paul continues with some directions about women in the congregation:

> As in all the churches of the saints, the women should keep silence in the churches. For they are not permitted to speak, but should be subordinate, as even the law says. If there is anything they desire to know, let them ask their husbands at home. For it is shameful for a woman to speak in church. Or did the word of God come forth from you, or are you the only ones it has reached? (1 Cor 14:33b–36).

This passage has long seemed baffling to commentators, but close attention to the structure of the larger context should enable us to understand its meaning. Before proposing a solution to this passage, however, I would like to examine two views which, upon inspection, turn out to be unpersuasive.

Does the passage forbid speech by noisy women?

Some explain this passage by saying that noisy or disorderly women were disrupting the worship service at Corinth, perhaps rudely shouting questions to their husbands seated across the room, or perhaps giving loud shouts characteristic of near-ecstatic worship. Advocates of this interpretation would say that Paul wanted to stop these disruptions and restore order to the service.

However, we must remember first that there simply is *no evidence* in verses 33b-35, or in the rest of the letter, or in any writing inside or outside the Bible, which indicates that disorder among women was a problem specifically in the Corinthian church. Some people *assume* there were noisy women in the church, but no clear evidence has turned up to prove this, and it must remain merely an assumption.

Of course, we *can* find evidence of wild behaviour by women in pagan religious rites at the time. But there is also evidence of wild behaviour by men. Therefore, it is illegitimate to use such evidence one-sidedly to claim that noisy women were a special problem at Corinth. This interpretation lacks solid historical support.

Some have tried to support this view from the Greek word *laleō*, here translated 'to speak'. The argument is that this word means 'to babble in disorderly utterance', and what Paul is forbidding is for women to babble incoherently.

However, this argument is not persuasive because *laleō* is simply a very common word (used sixty times by Paul; 298 times in the New Testament) meaning 'to speak', and Paul uses it frequently to refer to ordinary, intelligible speech: 'To the mature we *speak* wisdom' (1 Cor 2:6); 'He who prophesies *speaks* to men for their upbuilding' (1 Cor 14:3, RSV); 'Let two or three prophets *speak*' (1 Cor 14:29, RSV); 'To your shame I *am speaking*' (1 Cor 15:34), etc.

Of course Paul does use this word in reference to 'speaking in tongues' in 1 Corinthians 14—it was the most ordinary word available to him to refer to any act of 'speaking'—but that does not mean that *laleō* itself *meant* 'to speak in tongues' any more than the fact that the English word 'speak' is used in the phrase 'speaking in tongues' implies that the English word 'speak', when used by itself, *means* 'to speak in tongues'. Such an argument is just over-generalization from one specific use without paying attention to the range of meanings the word takes in other contexts.

So this suggestion, that Paul was forbidding speech by noisy or disorderly women, lacks both historical evidence and evidence in the words of the text itself. This interpretation also fails to explain verse 33b, which makes Paul's rule of silence applicable to all churches in Paul's time, not just the church at Corinth. The apostle says, 'As in *all the churches of the saints*, the women should keep silence...' (1 Cor 14:33b–34a). But surely the problem of 'disorderly women' was not one in all the churches of the saints at that time![87]

This is very significant. It means that any explanation of this passage which limits its application to the particular situation at Corinth is unconvincing. But that is just what this 'noisy Corinthian women' interpretation would have us believe—that noisy women *at Corinth* prompted Paul's directives. By contrast, Paul explicitly tells the Corinthians that in all the congregations of Christians in the first century (both Jewish and Gentile in origin) the women maintain the type of silence here commanded. He directs the Corinthians to conform to a practice which was universal in the early church.[88]

This 'noisy women' view is unpersuasive for another reason. It is inconsistent with Paul's solution. Where there are problems of disorder, the apostle simply prescribes order (as with tongues or prophecy in 1 Corinthians 14:27, 29, 31, and as with the Lord's supper in 1 Corinthians 11:33–34). If noise had been the problem in Corinth, he would have explicitly forbidden disorderly speech, not all speech.

Then, too, this view would force us to see Paul's remedy as inequitable, for he would be punishing *all* women for the deeds of some. He does not say, 'The *disorderly* women should keep silence.' It is unlike Paul, or any other New Testament writer, to make unfair rules of this sort.

In short, this first view is unpersuasive and should not be accepted.

Does this passage forbid women to speak in tongues?

Another position which has gained some support in recent years is the view that 1 Corinthians 14:33b–35 forbids women to speak in tongues in the church service. The primary argument in favour of this position is the claim that the main subject of chapters 12–14 (or at least chapter 14) is speaking in tongues.

However, Paul has finished discussing tongues in verse 28 and has gone on to the subject of prophecy. He has been discussing prophecy for the last four or five verses. No reader in Corinth would think that Paul had gone back to the subject of tongues, unless he had reintroduced this subject in verse 33b.

Moreover, prophecy is every bit as much Paul's concern as tongues in these chapters. In chapters 12–14, Paul mentions prophecy in eighteen verses and tongue-speaking also in eighteen. In chapter 14 alone the count is twelve verses having to do with prophecy and thirteen having to do with tongues. Furthermore, the closest contextual material to the verses about women being silent, verses 29–33a, does not refer to tongues, but it does contain a discussion of prophecy (vv. 29–33a).

So this second interpretation is inconsistent with the context and must also be rejected.

Does this passage forbid women to judge prophecies in the church service?

There is another interpretation which avoids these objections by seeing this passage not as relating to the first half of 1 Cor 14:29 (RSV) ('Let two or three prophets speak') but as relating to the second half of 1 Cor 14:29 (RSV) ('And let the others weigh what is said'). On this view, Paul would be saying, 'Let the others [that is, the rest of the congregation] weigh what is said [by the prophets...but] the women should keep silence in the churches.'[89]

In other words women could not give *spoken* criticisms of the prophecies which were made during a church service. This rule would not prevent them from silently evaluating the prophecies in their own minds (in fact, verse 29 implies that they should do so), but it would mean that they would not voice those evaluations in the assembled congregation.

Structurally this is in fact the most attractive solution available. It means that Paul followed a very logical procedure. First he gave a general statement: 'Let two or three prophets speak, and let the others weigh what is said' (1 Cor 14:29, RSV). Then he gave additional instructions about the first half of the verse (vv. 30–33a), and then he gave additional instructions about the second half of the verse (vv. 33b–35). This can be clearly seen in the following diagram.

29: *Let two or three prophets speak*	*and let the others weigh what is said*
30: one at a time	33b: As in every church,
31: you *can* do this, and	34: women shouldn't speak out and judge
32: the Holy Spirit won't force you	these prophecies; they should be subordinate
	35: They shouldn't even question the prophet:
33a: for God promotes not confusion but peace.	they can ask a question at home.

This structure for the passage is not clear at first glance because the comments in verses 30–33a grew quite long as Paul wrote. But the comments on verse 29a are a unified whole, no part of which can be removed. So there was no earlier opportunity for Paul to have introduced this section about women. If this interpretation is correct, then 'the women should keep silence' meant to Paul and his readers, 'Let them be silent when you are evaluating a prophecy.'

In addition to the way this interpretation gives an orderly and reasonable structure to the passage, two other facts about the text support this view.

First, this interpretation is consistent with the strong contrast in verse 34, 'For they are not permitted to speak, *but* should be subordinate...' (1 Cor 14:34, RSV). 'But' represents the Greek *alla*, indicating a strong contrast between speaking and being subordinate. Thus, the kind of speaking Paul has in mind is specifically speaking which involves insubordination. Not every type of speech would fit this description, but evaluating prophecies aloud certainly would. It would involve assuming the possession of superior authority in matters of doctrinal or ethical instruction, especially when it included criticism of the prophecy.

If this is the correct meaning of verse 34, then verse 35 is understandable. Suppose that some women in Corinth had wanted to evade the force of Paul's directive. The easy way to do this would be to say, 'We'll do just as Paul says. We won't speak up and criticize prophecies. But surely no one would mind if we asked a few questions! We just want to learn more about what these prophets are saying.' Then such questioning could be used as a platform for expressing in none-too-veiled form the very criticisms Paul forbids. Paul anticipates this possible evasion and writes, 'If there is anything they desire to know, let them ask their husbands at home. For it is shameful for a woman to speak [that is, question prophecies] in church' (1 Cor 14:35, RSV).

Of course, some women were unmarried, and would not have had a husband to ask. But there would have been other men within their family circles, or within the fellowship of the church, with whom they could discuss the content of the prophecies. Paul's general guideline is clear, even though he did not make pedantic qualifications to deal with every specific case.

Second, this interpretation is consistent with Paul's appeal to the Old Testament. Paul adds, in verse 34, 'As even the law says' (1 Cor 14:34, RSV). The probable source (for this is not a direct quotation from any Old Testament passage) is Genesis 2, where Adam is the 'firstborn' (with the concomitant headship in the family which that status implied), where he also has the authority from God to name Eve, and where Eve is made as a helper suitable for Adam.

In objection to this, some have denied that Paul is quoting the Old Testament here and have suggested that Paul is quoting a first-century Rabbinic law, or some Roman law, in this verse. But this suggestion is unconvincing, because Paul uses the word 'law' (Greek *nomos*) 119 times, and never once does it unambiguously refer to Rabbinic law or Roman law. When Paul uses 'the law' to support an argument, he generally refers to the Old Testament (as, for example, in 1 Corinthians 14:21, a few verses before our text).

Paul elsewhere appeals to the Old Testament to establish the idea of male headship and female submission to male leadership (see 1 Cor 11:8–9 and 1 Tim 2:13), and it is certainly possible, therefore, to see him as appealing to the Old Testament to support a distinction in authority in judging prophecies as well. But it would be difficult to derive from the Old Testament any prohibition against noisy women in church or against women speaking in tongues.

But in spite of the substantial considerations in favour of this interpretation, one final objection may be raised: Why didn't Paul make himself more clear and say, 'Let the women be silent *during the judging of prophecies*,' if that is what he meant?

The answer is that the New Testament writers often talk about silence in general, unrestricted terms while expecting the readers to know *from the context* which kind of silence is in view. 1 Corinthians 14:28, just a few verses away, is a good example: Paul says of the tongues-speaker: 'But if there is no one to interpret, *let each of them keep silence in church* and speak to himself and to God' (1 Cor 14:28, RSV). Now this does not mean the tongues-speaker had to maintain *total silence* throughout the worship service. He could no doubt participate in the singing, in praying, in reading Scripture, and in discussing concerns for prayer and thanksgiving. The command to be silent just meant to be silent *with respect to the particular type of speech under discussion*, namely, speaking in tongues.

There are several other examples showing that when the New Testament authors speak of 'silence' they often assume that the kind of silence intended is made clear by the larger context.[90]

So in 1 Corinthians 14:33b–35, once we see that the matter under discussion is prophecy and, more specifically, the evaluation of prophecies in church, it is natural to understand that 'the women should keep silence' means 'the women should keep silence *during the evaluation of prophecies*'.[91]

Is this passage then consistent with the rest of the New Testament teaching on men and women? It appears to be so. In this passage, though it has specific application to the judging of prophecies in the church service, Paul is arguing from a larger conviction about an abiding distinction between the roles appropriate to males and those appropriate to females in the Christian church. As in 1 Timothy 2:11–15, this distinction comes to focus in the prohibition of women from exercising doctrinal and ethical governance, even from time to time, over the congregation. Therefore, 1 Corinthians 14:33b–35 fits well with a consistent Pauline advocacy of women's participation without governing authority in the assembled church.

Summary

The New Testament clearly encourages women to participate fully in giving prophecies in the assembled church (Acts 21:9; 1 Cor 11:5). In connection with a discussion of prophecy, Paul does specify that the Corinthians should follow the practice of all the churches at that time, whereby 'the women should keep silence in the churches' (1 Cor 14:34, RSV). However, this does not imply a total silence, but only a silence with respect to the spoken evaluation of prophecies, the topic which Paul has just mentioned in the previous context (1 Cor 14:29).

Application for today

Outside of Pentecostal or charismatic churches today, one great problem is often 'spectator Christianity'—the lack of active participation by many of the members of the church. Another problem in many cases has been the failure to involve women adequately in the life and ministry of the church, and often there has been the feeling that many women have gifts—which are not being used in the church—to the detriment of everyone, women and men alike.

But if churches today will recognize that women—and men—can participate fully in the use of the gift of prophecy, then a large part of both of these problems will be overcome. There would be a significant increase in the use of this gift, which Paul considers the most valuable gift for the church, by both men and women, many of whom perhaps had not contributed much to the meetings of the assembled congregation before. From this increased use of prophecy, we would no doubt find that 'all may learn and all be encouraged' (1 Cor 14:31, RSV).

Moreover, if churches will recognize that along with full participation by women in worship, the New Testament also requires that governing authority over the congregation, even in the case of the evaluation of occasional prophecies, is reserved for men, then churches will gain the additional benefit of regularly modelling or picturing in their worship services the abiding and essential differences between biblical manhood and biblical womanhood, differences which are much in need of clear reaffirmation today.

12

The Duration of Prophecy:

How Long Will Prophecy Be Used in the Church?

Introduction

Many people reading this study have never seen the gift of prophecy functioning in their local church. In fact, outside of the charismatic movement and certain traditionally Pentecostal denominations, this gift is not now used and has not been used in recent history—for many churches, it has not been used in the history of their denominations.

Why not?

Is the non-use of this gift part of God's plan for the church? Was this gift only to be used during the New Testament time, then to fade away? Or is this gift still valid for use today, still valuable for the church—and perhaps even necessary if the church is to function the way God intends it to function?

This is the question of the *duration* of prophecy. Can we solve this question by examining the New Testament? In the New Testament itself, are there indications of how long God expected prophecy to function in the church?

On the one side of this question are charismatic and Pentecostal Christians who continue to use this gift, and who say it is valid for the entire church age.

On the other side are some Reformed and dispensational Christians who say that prophecy was one of the special gifts

227

associated with the foundation of the church at the time of the apostles, and that it was expected to cease functioning at a very early date, either around the time of the deaths of the last apostles, or at the time that the writing of the books of New Testament Scripture was complete. Their view is commonly called the cessationist view.

Probably in the middle are most contemporary evangelicals —neither charismatics nor cessationists, but still undecided about this question, and wondering if it can be decided clearly.

The discussion of this question turns on two main points: (1) the meaning of 1 Corinthians 13:8–13, and (2) the theological question of the relationship between the gift of prophecy and the written Scriptures of the New Testament. We shall examine these two points in order.

The interpretation of 1 Corinthians 13:8–13

This passage is important to the discussion because in it Paul mentions the gift of prophecy as something that is 'imperfect', and then says that what is 'imperfect' will 'pass away' (1 Cor 13:10). He even says when this will happen. It will happen 'when the perfect comes'. But when is that? And even if we can determine when it is, does that mean that Paul had in mind something that would answer this 'cessation' question for the church today?

We can begin by reading the passage again in full:

[8] Love never ends; as for prophecies, they will pass away; as for tongues, they will cease; as for knowledge, it will pass away. [9] For our knowledge is imperfect and our prophecy is imperfect; [10] but when the perfect comes, the imperfect will pass away. [11] When I was a child, I spoke like a child, I thought like a child, I reasoned like a child; when I became a man, I gave up childish ways. [12] For now we see in a mirror dimly, but then face to face. Now I know in part; then I shall understand fully, even as I have been fully understood. [13] So faith, hope, love abide, these three; but the greatest of these is love (1 Cor 13:8–13, RSV).

The purpose of 1 Corinthians 13:8–13

Our earlier analysis of the structure of 1 Corinthians 12–14 showed that Paul interrupts his discussion of spiritual gifts with chapter 13 of 1 Corinthians, in which he intends to put the entire discussion of gifts in proper perspective. It is not enough simply to 'seek the greater gifts' (1 Cor 12:31a). One must also 'seek after love' (1 Cor 14:1), thus coupling proper goals with proper motives. Without love, the gifts are without value (1 Cor 13:1–3). In fact, Paul argues, love is superior to all the gifts and therefore it is more important to act in love than to have any of the gifts.

In order to show the superiority of love, Paul argues that it lasts for ever, whereas the gifts are all temporary (1 Cor 13:8). Verses 9–12 further explain why the gifts are temporary. Our present knowledge and prophesying are partial and imperfect (v. 9), but someday something perfect will come to replace them (v. 10). This is explained by the analogy of a child who gives up childish thought and speech for the thought and speech of an adult (v. 11). Paul then elaborates further on verses 9–10 by explaining that our present perception and knowledge are indirect and imperfect, but that someday they will be direct and perfect (v. 12).

In this argument Paul connects the function of prophecy with the time of its cessation. It fills a certain need now, but does so only imperfectly. When 'the perfect' comes, that function will be better fulfilled by something else, and prophecy will cease because it will be made obsolete or useless (this is the probable nuance of the Greek term used here, *katargeō*, 'pass away' in verses 8 and 10).

So the overall function of 1 Corinthians 13:8–13 is to show that love is superior to gifts like prophecy because those gifts will pass away but love will not pass away.

1 Corinthians 13:10: The cessation of prophecy when Christ returns

Paul writes in verse 10, 'But when the perfect comes, the imper-

fect will pass away' (1 Cor 13:10, RSV). The phrase 'the imperfect (Greek *ek merous*, 'partial, imperfect') refers most clearly
to knowing and prophesying, the two activities which are said
to be done partially, imperfectly in verse 9 (also using in both
cases the same Greek phrase, *ek merous*). To bring out this
connection, we could translate,

> [8] Love never fails. Whether there be prophecies, they will *pass
> away*; whether there be tongues, they will cease; whether there be
> knowledge, it will *pass away*.
> [9] This is because we know *imperfectly* and we prophesy *imper-
> fectly*—[10] but when the perfect comes, the *imperfect* will *pass
> away*.

Thus, the strong links between the statements are made clear
by the repetition of two key terms, 'pass away' and 'imperfect'.

No doubt Paul also intended tongues to be included in the
sense of verse 9 as among those activities which are 'imperfect',
but omitted overly pedantic repetition for stylistic reasons. Yet
tongues must be understood as part of the sense of verse 9, for
verse 9 is the reason for verse 8, as the word 'for' (Greek *gar*)
shows. Thus verse 9 must give the reason why tongues, as well
as knowledge and prophecy, will cease. In fact, the repeated
'whether...whether...whether' in verse 8 suggests that Paul
could have listed more gifts here (wisdom, healing, interpretation?) if he had wished. But for our purposes it is sufficient that
'the imperfect' in verse 10 clearly includes the gift of prophecy.

(As we saw in chapter 5, Paul considers prophecy to be
imperfect [*ek merous*] because it gives only partial knowledge
of the subjects it treats, because the revelation which a prophet
receives is indirect and limited, and because the revelation is
often difficult to understand or interpret.)

So 1 Corinthians 13:10 means, 'When the perfect is come,
prophecy will pass away.' The only remaining problem is to
determine what time is meant by the word 'when'. Several factors in the context argue that the time of the Lord's return is the
time Paul has in mind.

(a) First, the word 'then' (Greek *tote*) in verse 12 refers to the time 'when the perfect is come' in verse 10. This is evident from looking at the verse: 'For now we see in a mirror dimly, but then face to face. Now I know in part; *then* I shall know even as I have been known' (1 Cor 13:12).

When shall we see 'face to face'? When shall we know 'even as we have been fully known'? These events can only happen when the Lord returns.

The phrase 'see face to face' is used several times in the Old Testament to refer to seeing God personally: see, for example, Genesis 32:30 and Judges 6:22 (exactly the same Greek wording as 1 Corinthians 13:12); Deuteronomy 5:4; 34:10; Ezekiel 20:35 (very similar wording); Exodus 33:11 (same concept, and same wording as some of the preceding passages in Hebrew, but different wording this time in Greek translation of the Septuagint). So the phrase 'face to face' is used in the Old Testament to speak of seeing God personally—not fully or exhaustively, for no finite creature can ever do that, but personally and truly nonetheless. So when Paul says, 'But then [we shall see] face to face,' he clearly means, 'Then we shall see God face to face.' Indeed, that will be the greatest blessing of heaven and our greatest joy for all eternity (Rev 22:4, RSV: 'They shall see his face').

The second half of 1 Corinthians 13:12 says, 'Now I know in part; then I shall know even as I have been known.' The second and third word for 'know'—the one for 'then I shall *know* even as I have been *known*'—is a somewhat stronger word for knowing (Greek *epiginōskō*), but certainly does not imply infinite knowledge or omniscience. Paul does not expect to know all things, and he does not say, 'Then I shall know all things,' which would have been easy in Greek.[92] Rather, he means that when the Lord returns he expects to be freed from the misconceptions and inabilities to understand (especially to understand God and his work) which are part of this present life. His knowledge will resemble God's present knowledge of him because it will contain no false impressions and will not be limited to what is able to be perceived in this age. But such knowledge will only occur when the Lord returns.

In conclusion, Paul says in verse 12, in effect,

> For now we see in a mirror dimly, but *then*, when Christ returns, we shall see God face to face; now I know in part, but *then*, when Christ returns, I shall know even as I have been known.

His word 'then' has to refer back to something in the previous verses which he has been explaining. We look first to verse 11, but see that nothing in verse 11 can be a future time Paul refers to as 'then': 'When I was a child, I spoke like a child, I thought like a child, I reasoned like a child; when I became a man, I gave up childish ways'(1 Cor 13:11, RSV). All of this refers to the past, not the future. It speaks of past events in Paul's life by way of providing a natural human illustration of what he has said in verse 10. But nothing in the verse speaks of a future time when something *will* happen.

So we look back to verse 10: 'But when the perfect comes, the imperfect will pass away' (1 Cor 13:10, RSV). Here is a statement about the future. At some point in the future, Paul says 'the perfect' *will* come, and 'the imperfect' *will* pass away, *will* be 'made useless'.

When will this happen? This is what is explained by verse 12. *Then*, at the time the perfect comes, we shall see 'face to face' and know 'even as we are known'.

This means that the time when 'the perfect' comes must be the time of Christ's return.[93]

Therefore, we can paraphrase verse 10: 'But *when Christ returns*, the imperfect will pass away.'[94]

Or, to use our conclusion above that 'the imperfect' certainly included prophecy, we can paraphrase, 'But *when Christ returns*, prophecy will pass away.'

Here then we find a definite statement about the time of the cessation of imperfect gifts like prophecy. They will 'be made useless' or 'pass away' *when Christ returns*. And this would imply that they will continue to exist and be useful for the church, all through the church age, including today, and right up to the day when Christ returns.

(b) Another reason why the time when 'the perfect' comes is the time when Christ returns is also evident from the purpose of the passage. Paul is attempting to prove the greatness of love, and in so doing he wants to establish that 'love never ends' (1 Cor 13:8, RSV). To do so, he argues that it will last beyond the time when the Lord returns, unlike present spiritual gifts. This makes a convincing argument: love is so fundamental to God's plans for the universe that it will last beyond the transition from this age to the age to come—it will continue for eternity.

(c) A third reason why this passage refers to the time of the Lord's return can be found in a more general statement from Paul about the purpose of spiritual gifts in the New Testament age. In 1 Corinthians 1:7 Paul ties the possession of spiritual gifts (Greek *charismata*) to the activity of waiting for the Lord's return: 'You are not lacking in any spiritual gift as you await the revelation of our Lord Jesus Christ.'

This suggests that Paul saw the gifts as a temporary provision made to equip believers for ministry *until the Lord returned*. So this verse provides a close parallel to the thought of 1 Corinthians 13:8–13, where prophecy and knowledge (and no doubt tongues) are seen, similarly, as necessary until Christ's return but unnecessary beyond that time.

1 Corinthians 13:10, therefore, refers to the time of Christ's return and says that prophecy will last among believers until that time. This means that we have a clear biblical statement that Paul expected the gift of prophecy to continue through the entire church age and to function for the benefit of the church until the Lord returns.

Objections

Various objections to this conclusion have been raised, usually by those who hold that the gift of prophecy has ceased in the church and should no longer be used. In this section, we shall examine those objections one at a time. Some of them deal with 1 Corinthians 13:8–13 specifically, and others deal with broader concerns.

1. *This passage does not specify when the gifts will cease*

The first objection to our conclusion above comes from Richard Gaffin's thoughtful study, *Perspectives on Pentecost*. While Dr Gaffin agrees that 'when the perfect comes' refers to the time of Christ's return, he does not think that this verse specifies the time of the cessation of certain gifts. He thinks, rather, that Paul is just viewing 'the entire period until Christ's return, without regard to whether or not discontinuities may intervene during the course of this period.'[95]

In fact, Gaffin argues, Paul's overall purpose is to emphasize the enduring qualities of faith, hope and love, especially love, and not to specify the time in which certain gifts will cease. He says:

> Paul is not intending to specify the time when any particular mode will cease. What he does affirm is the termination of the believer's present, fragmentary knowledge...when 'the perfect' comes. The time of the cessation of prophecy and tongues is an open question so far as this passage is concerned and will have to be decided on the basis of other passages and considerations.[96]

He then adds that, in addition to prophecy, tongues, and knowledge, Paul might just as well have added 'inscripturation' too—and if he had done this, the list would then have included an element which ceased long before Christ's return. (Inscripturation is the process of writing Scripture.) So, Gaffin concludes, it might be true of some of the others in the list as well.

In response to this objection it must be said that it does not do justice to the actual words of the text. Evangelicals have rightly insisted (and I know that Dr Gaffin agrees with this) that passages of Scripture are true not only in the main point of each passage, but also in the minor details that are affirmed as well. The main point of the passage may well be that love lasts for ever, but another point, and certainly an important one as well, is that verse 10 affirms, not just that these imperfect gifts will cease sometime, but that they will cease '*when* the perfect comes'. Paul specifies a certain time: '*When the perfect comes, the imperfect will pass away*' (1 Cor 13:10, RSV). But Dr Gaffin seems to claim that Paul is not actually saying this. Yet the force of the words cannot be avoided by affirming the overall theme of the larger context instead.

In addition, Dr Gaffin's suggestion does not seem to fit with the logic of the passage. Paul's argument is that it is specifically the coming of 'the perfect' which does away with prophecy, tongues and knowledge, because then there is a new, far superior way of learning and knowing things 'even as I have been known'. But *until* that time, the new and superior way of knowing has not come, and therefore these imperfect gifts are still valid and useful—the thing which will render them obsolete (the state of affairs at Christ's return) has not yet come.

Finally, it is precarious to put much weight on something we think Paul might have said but in fact did not say. To say that Paul might have included 'inscripturation' in this list means that Paul might have written, 'When Christ returns, inscripturation will cease.' But I cannot believe at all that Paul could have written such a statement, for it would have been false—indeed, a 'false prophecy' in the words of Scripture. For 'inscripturation' ceased long ago, when the book of Revelation was written by the Apostle John.

So Dr. Gaffin's objections do not seem to dislodge the force of our conclusions on 1 Corinthians 13:10. If 'the perfect' refers to the time of Christ's return, then Paul says that gifts such as prophecy and tongues will cease at that time, and implies therefore that they continue through the church age.

2. *The suggestion that prophecy was to cease when the New Testament was complete*

Those who make this second objection argue that 'when the

perfect comes' means one of several different things, such as 'when the church is mature' or 'when Scripture is complete' or 'when the Gentiles are included in the church'.

Probably the most careful statement of this view is found in the book by Robert L. Reymond, *What About Continuing Revelations and Miracles in the Presbyterian Church Today?*,[97] but another clear statement of a similar position is found in Walter Chantry's book, *Signs of the Apostles*.[98]

Chantry's argument depends on the fact that elsewhere in the New Testament the word here translated 'perfect' is used to refer to human maturity (1 Cor 14:20) or to maturity in the Christian life (as in 1 Cor 2:6). Yet here again we must note that a word does not have to be used to refer to the same thing every time it is used in Scripture—in some cases it may refer to 'mature' or 'perfect' manhood, in other cases some other kind of 'completeness' or 'perfection'. It is used in Hebrews 9:11, for example, to refer to the 'more perfect tent'—yet we would not therefore conclude that 'perfect' in 1 Corinthians 13:10 must refer to a perfect tent (or tabernacle). The precise reference of the word must be determined by the individual context, and there, as we have seen, the context indicates that 'when the perfect comes' refers to the time of Christ's return.

Dr Reymond's argument is somewhat different. He reasons as follows (p. 34):

(a) 'The imperfect' things mentioned in verses 9–10, prophecy, tongues and knowledge, are incomplete means of revelation, 'all relating to God's making his will known to his church'.

(b) 'The perfect' in this context must refer to something in the same category as the 'imperfect' things.

(c) Therefore 'the perfect' in this context must refer to a means of revelation, but a completed one. And this completed means of God's making his will known to his church is Scripture.

(d) Conclusion: 'When the perfect comes' refers to the time when the canon of Scripture will be complete.

Reymond notes that he is not saying that 'the perfect' refers exactly to the canon of Scripture, but rather to 'the completed revelatory process' which resulted in Scripture (p. 32). And in response to the objection that 'then I shall see face to face' in verse 12 refers to seeing God face to face, he answers that it may not mean this, but may simply mean seeing 'plainly' as opposed to 'obscurely' (p. 32).

In response, it may be said that this argument, while careful and consistent in itself, still depends on one prior assumption which is really the point at issue in this whole discussion: the authority of New Testament prophecy and related gifts. Once Dr Reymond assumes that prophecy (and tongues and the kind of 'knowledge' mentioned here) are Scripture-quality revelation, the whole argument falls into place. The argument could be recast as follows:

(a) Prophecy and tongues are Scripture-quality revelation.

(b) Therefore this whole passage is about Scripture-quality revelation.

(c) Therefore 'the perfect' refers to the perfection or completion of Scripture-quality revelation, or the completion of Scripture.

Yet in such an argument the first assumption determines the conclusion. Before this assumption can be made, it would have to be demonstrated from an inductive analysis of the New Testament texts on prophecy, such as I have attempted to do in this book. Yet, to my knowledge, no such inductive demonstration of the Scripture-quality authority of New Testament congregational prophecy has been made.

Moreover, there are some other factors in the text of 1 Corinthians 13:8–13 which are hard to reconcile with this position. The regular Old Testament usage of seeing 'face to face' as an expression not just for seeing clearly but for *personally* seeing God (see above) remains unexplained. And the fact that Paul includes himself in the expressions 'then I shall see face to face' and 'then I shall know as I have been known' make it difficult to view these as references to the time of the completion of Scripture. Does Paul really think that when the other apostles finally finish their contributions to the New Testament he will suddenly gain such a remarkable change in his knowledge that he will know as he has been known, and will go from seeing in a mirror dimly to seeing face to face?

In addition to the views of Reymond and Chantry, there have been other attempts to see 'when the perfect comes' as some time before Christ's return, but we will not treat them in detail here. Such views all seem to break down at 1 Corinthians 13:12, where Paul implies that believers will see God 'face to face' 'when the perfect is come'. This cannot be said about the time suggested in any of these other proposals.

The proposal about the completion of the 'canon' of New Testament Scripture (the group of writings which came to be included in the New Testament) also fails to fit Paul's purpose in the context. If we take A.D. 90 as the approximate date of the writing of Revelation, the last New Testament book written, then the end of the writing of Scripture came about thirty-five years after Paul wrote 1 Corinthians (about A.D. 55).

But would it be persuasive to argue as follows: 'We can be sure that love will never end, for we know that it will last more than thirty-five years!'? This would hardly be a convincing argument. The context requires rather that Paul be contrasting this age with the age to come, and saying that love will endure into eternity.[99]

In fact, we see a similar procedure elsewhere in 1 Corinthians. When Paul wants to demonstrate the eternal value of something, he does this by arguing that it will last beyond the day of the Lord's return (cf. 1 Cor 3:13–15; 15:51–58). By contrast, prophecy and other gifts will not last beyond that day.

Finally, these proposals fail to find any support in the immediate context. Whereas Christ's return is mentioned clearly in 1 Corinthians 13:12, no verse in this section mentions anything about the completion of Scripture or a collection of the books of the New Testament or the inclusion of the Gentiles in the church or the 'maturity' of the church (whatever that means—is the church really mature even today?). All of these suggestions bring in new elements not found in the context to replace one element—Christ's return—which clearly is right there in the context already.

So Richard Gaffin, who himself holds that the gift of prophecy is not valid for today, nevertheless says that the 'perfect' in 1 Corinthians 13:10 and the 'then' in verse 12 'no doubt refer to the time of Christ's return. The view that they describe the point at which the New Testament canon is completed cannot be made credible exegetically.'[100]

It should perhaps be said again that these alternative explanations of 1 Corinthians 13:10 often seem to be prompted by a prior conviction that New Testament prophecy consists of words equal to Scripture in authority. Now I have no objection to bringing to bear on one passage of Scripture what is clearly taught in other passages of Scripture, because I am convinced that all Scripture is God-breathed and therefore consistent with itself. But when the view that New Testament congregational prophecy was equal to Scripture in authority *is itself open to considerable doubt* (see chapters 2, 3 and 4, above), then it is appropriate to be very hesitant to use it as an explicit or even implicit factor influencing us to adopt a very doubtful interpretation of 1 Corinthians 13:10 as well. *Clear* teachings of Scripture elsewhere should rightly influence our interpretation of any one text of Scripture, but *doubtful or tentative* conclusions about teachings of Scripture elsewhere should have only very slight, if any, influence on the interpretation of any one text.

Dr D. Martyn Lloyd-Jones observes that the view which makes 'when the perfect comes' equal the time of the completion of the New Testament encounters another difficulty:

> It means that you and I, who have the Scriptures open before us, know much more than the apostle Paul of God's truth....It means that we are altogether superior...even to the apostles themselves, including the apostle Paul! It means that we are now in a position in which... 'we know, even as also we are known' by God....indeed, there is only one word to describe such a view, it is nonsense.'[101]

John Calvin, referring to 1 Corinthians 13:8–13, says, 'It is stupid of people to make the whole of this discussion apply to the intervening time.'[102]

3. *1 Corinthians 13 refers only to prophecies contained in Scripture.*[103]

This third objection also ignores the context of 1 Corinthians 13. Paul is talking about spiritual gifts and is showing how love is superior to them. In 1 Corinthians 'prophecy' certainly does not refer to 'written Scripture' but to a gift of prophecy which was not divinely authoritative. That is what Paul is telling the Corinthians how to use.

4. *Prophecy is a miraculous sign-gift associated with the apostles, and therefore ceased when the apostles died*

There is no doubt that miraculous gifts were closely associated with the apostles, and that miracles did confirm the truth of the apostles' message. In fact, most of the remarkable miracles in Acts were done by or through the apostles.

However, several other facts must be kept in mind:

(a) Almost everything in Acts (including evangelism and the founding of churches, for instance) is closely connected with the apostles. This tells us nothing about whether miracles could occur in relation to *other* Christians to confirm the truth of the gospel they were proclaiming or to serve some other purpose (edification of believers, ministries of mercy to those who were sick, etc), all through the history of the church. The fact that miracles were done mostly through the apostles does *not* tell us that they couldn't be done through others as well.

(b) Clearly not all miracles in the New Testament church were done by the apostles. James 5:14–15 indicates that James expected some instances of healing to occur through 'the elders of the church', not through the apostles. Galatians 3:5 implies that Christ was the one who presently, in the absence of the Apostle Paul, 'works miracles' among the Galatian churches.

And Philip and Stephen, both non-apostles, had miracles done by or through them as well: Acts 6:8, 15; 7:55–56; 8:7, 13, 39.

(c) Whatever we may think about the restriction of some 'miraculous' gifts or 'sign' gifts to the apostles, the gift of prophecy simply cannot be put in that category. The New Testament gives us evidence that the gift of prophecy was *clearly* not restricted to the apostles, but was used by ordinary believers in Corinth (1 Cor 12–14), in Antioch (Acts 11:28; 13:1; 15:32), in Tyre (Acts 21:4); in Caesarea (Acts 21:9, 10–11); in Jerusalem (Acts 11:28; 21:10); in Thessalonica (1 Thess 5:19–21); probably in Ephesus (see Acts 19:6; Eph 4:11); and probably in many other cities as well (Acts 20:23; and note that Eph 4:11 and Acts 2:17–18 speak not of any local church but of the church in general).

So *prophecy* was not restricted to or limited to the apostles, and should not be thought of as some kind of unique 'sign gift' which would only be used by the apostles. It was given for the use and benefit of the whole church.

5. *It is a historical fact that prophecy did cease early in the history of the church*

(a) First, we must object that the premise just stated is very doubtful on historical grounds.[104] There were people claiming to be prophets or to prophesy throughout the history of the early church—the problem was that too often they misunderstood their gift, or others misunderstood it, so that their utterances were (mistakenly) treated like actual words of God. Sometimes they would be tolerated, sometimes they were too much of a threat to the established leadership of the churches and they would begin splinter groups with several followers—tragically, no longer under the restraining and evaluating authority of the established church.

Then, too, others may have had 'revelations' given to them which they then did not express, or simply included without comment or attribution to the Holy Spirit in a prayer, or a sermon or word of exhortation, or in the writing of a hymn or some devotional literature.

On this first point, one additional comment is in order. If we assume that this study is correct in seeing New Testament congregational prophecy as based on a 'revelation' from the Holy Spirit yet not possessing the authority of God's own words, it must still be admitted that such a careful understanding of prophecy is one which might easily be blurred or forgotten.

It would eventually be very easy, then, for more and more Christian prophets, whether for good or ill motives, to begin to claim not only that they had received a 'revelation' from God or Christ, but also that they spoke with absolute divine authority in their words. This was in fact apparently what happened, at least in Montanism and probably in many other cases as well. Of course, if these prophets began to promote heretical ideas, the reaction of the rest of the church would eventually be to drive them out altogether. Someone who claims absolute divine authority would eventually be accepted or rejected; he could not be merely tolerated.

But along with this rejection of prophets who misunderstood their status there was perhaps also a rejection of the gift of prophecy altogether, so that a failure on the part of the church itself to understand the nature of the gift of prophecy might have been the cause of a fairly complete suppression of at least the public expression of the gift of prophecy in the church. This explanation is only a suggestion, and I am not offering it here as the result of investigation into the historical evidence which would be necessary to confirm or deny it.

(b) Second, it should be clear that I am not suggesting here that Paul was expressing in 1 Corinthians 13 an opinion on the relative frequency of prophesying in the history of the church. That would be subject to much variation depending on the spiritual maturity and vitality of the church in various periods, the degree to which prophecy was sought as a blessing or rejected as a heresy, the frequency with which public worship normally made provision for the exercise of this gift, and the degree to which the nature of New Testament prophecy was correctly understood.

What Paul is speaking about, however, is the total and final abolition of prophecy which is to be brought about by divine initiative at the return of Christ. And he is saying that he thinks that until the time of the return of Christ the gift of prophecy will at least to some extent remain available for use, and God will continue to give people the revelations which make prophecy possible.

With particular reference to prophecy, Calvin (*Commentary on 1 Corinthians*, p. 305) notes the abundance of spiritual gifts in Paul's day and comments (on 1 Cor 14:32):

> Today we see our own slender resources, our poverty in fact; but this is undoubtedly the punishment we deserve, as the reward for our ingratitude. For God's riches are not exhausted, nor has His liberality grown less; but we are not worthy of His largess, or capable of receiving all that He generously gives.

The relationship between the gift of prophecy and Scripture

In addition to the interpretation of 1 Corinthians 13:8–13, there is one other area of concern to the question of whether prophecy should continue being used in the church today. That area is the relationship between New Testament congregational prophecy and Scripture.

Does the continuation of prophecy challenge the sufficiency of Scripture or the closed canon?

Those who take a cessationist view of prophecy argue that once the last New Testament book was written (probably the book of Revelation around A.D. 90), then there were to be no more 'words of God' spoken or written in the church. *Scripture* was the complete and sufficient source of God's words for his people, and to add any more words from continuing prophetic utterances would be, in effect, either to add to Scripture or to compete with Scripture. In both cases, the sufficiency of Scripture itself would be challenged, and, in practice, its unique authority in our lives.

Now *if* New Testament congregational prophecy was like Old Testament prophecy and New Testament apostolic words in its authority, then this cessationist objection would indeed be true. *If* New Testament prophets today, for example, spoke words which we knew were the very words of God, then these words *would be* equal to Scripture in authority, and we *would be* obligated to write them down and add them to our Bibles whenever we heard them. But if we are convinced that God stopped causing Scripture to be written when the book of Revelation was completed, then we have to say that *this* kind of speech, uttering the very words of God, cannot happen today. And any claims to have new Scripture, new words of God, must be rejected as false.

This question is very important, because the claim that New Testament prophecy had authority equal to Scripture is the basis of perhaps every cessationist argument written today. Yet it must be noted that charismatics themselves do not seem to view prophecy that way. Mallone writes, 'To my knowledge no noncessationist in the mainstream of Christianity claims that revelation today is equal with Scripture.'[105] Perhaps it would be good for those arguing against continuing prophecy today to give a more sympathetic hearing to the most responsible charismatic spokesmen, simply for the purpose of being able to respond to something that charismatics *actually believe* (even if not always expressed in theologically precise form), instead of responding to something that cessationists say that charismatics believe or say that charismatics should believe.

Furthermore, aside from the question of current practice or belief, we have seen in chapters 3 and 4 (above) that ordinary congregational prophecy in New Testament churches did *not* have the authority of Scripture. It was not spoken in words which were the very words of God, but rather in merely human words. And because it has this character, there is no reason to think that it would not continue in the church right up until Christ returns. It does not threaten or compete with Scripture in authority but is subject to Scripture, as well as to the mature judgement of the congregation.

Moreover, the functions of apostolic teaching and congregational prophecy were different. The cessationist view depends on the supposition that the function of prophecy was to provide the church with divinely authoritative guidance until such guidance could be derived from a collection of apostolic writings. But in the examples of New Testament prophecy which we have looked at in chapters 5–8, above, it was evident that the function of congregational prophecy was often to provide very specific, localized information which was needed for the edification of the church and which could only be acquired through a revelation from the Holy Spirit. Access to the major doctrinal teachings contained in the apostolic writings would not make this sort of prophecy obsolete or useless.

The question of guidance

Yet one more concern comes up. It can be argued that even if those who use the gift of prophecy today *say* that it does not equal Scripture in authority, *in fact* it functions in their lives to compete with or even replace Scripture in giving guidance concerning God's will. Thus, prophecy today, it is said, challenges the doctrine of the sufficiency of Scripture for guidance in our lives.

Here it must be admitted that many mistakes have been made in the history of the church. John Macarthur points to the way in which the idea of further revelations has given rise to many heretical movements in the church.[106]

But here the question must be: Are abuses *necessary* to the functioning of the gift of prophecy? If we are to argue that mistakes and abuses of a gift or function make the gift or function itself invalid, then we would have to reject Bible teaching too (for many Bible teachers have taught error and started cults), and church administration and offices (for many church officers have led people astray, or have abused the privileges of their office), etc. The *abuse* of a gift does not mean that we must prohibit the *proper use* of the gift unless it can be shown that there cannot be proper use—that all use has to be abuse.

Moreover, specifically with respect to guidance, it is good to note how cautious many in the charismatic movement are about the use of prophecy to give specific guidance. Several quotations will illustrate this point.

Don Basham:

> Personally, I feel most comfortable with prophecies which do not predict or offer direction since I'm aware of the tremendous dangers inherent in such messages....I believe God is very sparing in His use of them. My personal experience has been that I've heard eight or ten times as many erroneous prediction prophecies as valid ones....
>
> What should our response be when someone prophesies over us? If the prophecy contains predictions or direction we should neither accept it nor reject it. We should rather place it in our 'pending file' and pray and trust the Lord to confirm it out of the mouths of at least two other witnesses if it is of Him. We should *never* act hastily on the basis of an unconfirmed predictive or directive prophecy, regardless of how inspired it may sound.[107]

Michael Harper:

> Prophecies which tell other people what they are to do—are to be regarded with great suspicion.[108]

Dennis and Rita Bennett:

> We should also be careful of personal, directive prophecy, especially outside the ministry of a mature and submitted man of God. Unrestrained 'personal prophecy' did much to undermine the movement of the Holy Spirit which began at the turn of the century....Christians are certainly given words for one another 'in the Lord'...and such words can be most refreshing and helpful, but there must be a witness of the Spirit on the part of the person receiving the words, and extreme caution should be used in receiving any alleged directive or predictive prophecy. Never undertake

any project simply because you were told to by presumed prophetic utterance or interpretation of tongues, or by a presumed word of wisdom, or knowledge. Never do something just because a friend comes to you and says: 'The Lord told me to tell you to do thus and thus.' If the Lord has instructions for you, He will give you a witness in your own heart, in which case the words coming from a friend...will be a confirmation to what God *has already been* showing you. Your guidance must also agree with Scripture....[109]

Donald Gee:

[There are] grave problems raised by the habit of giving and receiving personal 'messages' of guidance through the gifts of the Spirit....The Bible gives a place for such direction from the Holy Spirit....But it must be kept in proportion. An examination of the Scriptures will show us that as a matter of fact the early Christians did *not* continually receive such voices from heaven. In most cases they made their decisions by the use of what we often call 'sanctified common-sense' and lived quite normal lives. Many of our errors where spiritual gifts are concerned arise when we want the extraordinary and exceptional to be made the frequent and habitual. Let all who develop excessive desire for 'messages' through the gifts take warning from the wreckage of past generations as well as of contemporaries....The Holy Scriptures are a lamp unto our feet and a light unto our path.[110]

Donald Bridge:

'Illuminism' is a centuries-old phrase to describe something which is not at all new....It is the claim to direct personal revelations from God which transcend the 'ordinary' experiences of disciplined prayer and Bible-study....The illuminist constantly finds that 'God tells him' to do things....Illuminists are often very sincere, very dedicated, and possessed of a commitment to obey God that shames more cautious Christians. Nevertheless they are treading a dangerous path. Their ancestors have trodden it before, and always with disastrous results in the long run. Inner feelings and special promptings are by their very nature subjective. The Bible provides our objective guide.[111]

Donald Bridge and David Phypers:

> Any attempt to give highly specific instructions to the group, or to
> individuals in it, under the guise of prophecy should be strenuously
> discouraged by the leaders of the meeting because of problems
> which will almost invariably arise as a result....In our experience,
> while prophecies have sometimes spoken very directly to individu-
> als' needs, the Christians giving the prophecies have always been
> personally unaware of those needs, and each prophecy has always
> been couched in general terms perfectly acceptable to the whole
> gathering. Only later has the specific usefulness of the prophecy
> been realized when the Christian particularly spoken to has tes-
> tified to its helpfulness.[112]

These quotations illustrate a cautious and hesitant view
towards receiving guidance through prophecy. They indicate
an awareness among many in the charismatic movement that
the primary function of prophecy is not guidance or prediction
but 'upbuilding, encouragement, and comfort' (1 Cor 14:13)
(see chapter 7, above) as the Holy Spirit brings to mind things
which by themselves may seem quite ordinary and hardly
unusual or dramatic, but which are meeting specific needs of
the moment in the congregation, and are being 'quickened' or
made unusually effective in the hearts of God's people by the
same Holy Spirit.

On the other hand, even among very 'Reformed' cessationists, there is a willingness to admit some kind of continuing 'illumination' by the Holy Spirit in believers' lives:

For example, Richard Gaffin says:

> Often, too, what is seen as prophecy is actually a spontaneous,
> Spirit-worked application of Scripture, a more or less sudden grasp
> of the bearing that biblical teaching has on a particular situation or
> problem. All Christians need to be open to these more spontane-
> ous workings of the Spirit.[113]

And Robert Reymond defines 'illumination' as 'the Holy Spirit's enabling of Christians generally to understand, to recall to mind, and to apply the Scriptures they have studied.'[114]

But if these writers will allow for the present activity of the Holy Spirit enabling Christians to understand, or recall to mind, or apply, or grasp the teachings of Scripture, then there does not seem to be such a great difference in principle between what they are saying and what many in the charismatic movement are doing (even though there will probably be some remaining differences over the precise way guidance functions—yet this is not so much a difference about prophecy as about guidance generally, and particularly the way guidance from Scripture relates to guidance from advice, counsel, conscience, circumstances, sermons, etc). The larger point is that what Gaffin and Reymond here call 'illumination' it seems the New Testament would call a 'revelation', and what they would call a spoken report of such illumination it seems the New Testament would call a 'prophecy'.

So I wonder if there may be room for more joint theological reflection on this area. Charismatics would have to realize that cessationists are sceptical about the scope and frequency of such 'illumination', whether it is right to call it New Testament prophecy, whether it really does have value for the church, and whether we are right to seek it. And cessationists would have to realize that their own highly developed and carefully formulated doctrine of the sufficiency of Scripture in guidance is not usually shared or even understood by much of evangelicalism, including those in the charismatic movement. Nevertheless, perhaps the Reformed idea of 'illumination' is not far from what is happening in prophecy today, and may provide a category in which it would not be seen to challenge the sufficiency of Scripture.

As another model for comparison, it is helpful to hear the conclusion of Donald Bridge:

What authority does prophecy carry? The same authority as that of any other Christian activity in the church, like leadership, counselling, teaching....If it is true, it will prove to be true. Spiritual people will respond warmly to it. Wise and proven leaders will approve and confirm it. The enlightened conscience will embrace it.[115]

When this perspective on guidance in prophecy is coupled with the many biblical evidences we have seen concerning the non-divinely authoritative nature of prophecy in the New Testament, there seems to be no reason to object to its continuing use today.

So in the larger area of the relationship between the gift of prophecy and Scripture, we see no reason to think that prophecy would cease. Just as it functioned simultaneously with the actual presence of living apostles in the churches and did not compete with or pose a challenge to the unique ruling authority of the apostles, so today prophecy can exist and function simultaneously with the presence of the completed, written Scripture in our churches without challenging or competing with the unique ruling authority which Scripture and Scripture alone has in our lives.

Spiritual gifts as characteristic of the New Covenant age

One further consideration is appropriate here. The New Testament many times indicates that one distinctive characteristic of the New Covenant age (the period between Pentecost and Christ's return, also called the 'church age') is the possession of spiritual gifts by all God's people.

Therefore, once the New Covenant age is inaugurated at Pentecost, the Holy Spirit is poured out in power on the church, and one result is that God's people are given gifts like prophecy, speaking in tongues, and seeing visions (Acts 2:1-21). Another result is special power for gospel proclamation (Acts 1:8; cf. 2:37, 47; 4:4, etc).

Spiritual gifts also characterize the receipt of the Holy Spirit by others in the New Testament, such as the household of Cornelius (Acts 10:46), or the disciples in Ephesus (Acts 19:6). The

Corinthians experienced the characteristically 'New Covenant' experience of the Holy Spirit when they believed the gospel and then in 'every way' they were 'enriched in Christ in all speech and all knowledge' (1 Cor 1:5), with the result that Paul could say, 'You are not lacking in any spiritual gift, as you wait for the revealing of our Lord Jesus Christ' (1 Cor 1:7, RSV). In fact, what Paul says about Christians corporately being the 'body of Christ', all with differing gifts, given for the common good (1 Cor 12:12–31), we rightly understand to be true not just of the church at Corinth, but of all churches and all Christians today: to be a New Covenant Christian is to be a spiritually gifted Christian.

Paul affirms the same truth in Ephesians when he says that Christ, in ascending to heaven, 'gave gifts to men' (Eph 4:8, RSV)—gifts that would enable the whole body to work together, so that 'when each part is working properly', the church itself 'makes bodily growth and upbuilds itself in love' (Eph 4:16, RSV). Once again, the possession of various spiritual gifts for the benefit of the whole church is *characteristic* of the New Testament age.

Now if the apostles were the foundation of the church, and if they had a unique authority to write Scripture for the church for all time, then it is understandable that the office of apostle would not continue beyond the first century, when the last apostle died. In fact, Paul suggests that he is the last one who will ever be appointed as an apostle (see 1 Cor 15:8 in a context of resurrection appearances to apostles). So we may say *either* that the office of apostle is no longer present in the church, *or* (perhaps more correctly) that the office of apostle has now been replaced by the presence of *the writings of the apostles* (=the New Testament) in the church.

But we have no reason to expect that any other gifts have been replaced in this way. In fact, if spiritual gifts are *characteristic* of the New Covenant age, then our expectation would be that a normally functioning New Covenant church would have the continuing experience of all the gifts mentioned in the

New Testament, and that these gifts, characteristic as they are of the church age, would continue in the church up until the time of the Lord's return. Where the Holy Spirit is at work in New Covenant power, should we not rightly expect to see all the gifts of the Holy Spirit present and functioning in the church?

Summary

In 1 Corinthians 13:8–13 Paul tells the Corinthians that prophecy will continue until but not beyond the time when Christ returns. Thus, it is acceptable to paraphrase 1 Corinthians 13:10, 'When Christ returns, the gift of prophecy will cease.' This text, together with the nature of prophecy as not equal to Scripture in authority but valuable for the edification of the church, leads us to conclude that the gift of prophecy will continue to be valid and available for Christians to use right up until the time when the Lord returns.

Application for today

Once we are aware that prophecy is a gift appropriate for the entire church age (from Pentecost until Christ's return), it should encourage us to think about how we might encourage its use in our own lives and churches today. If indeed it is God's intention that this gift continue to be used in the church, then our failure to allow or encourage its use can only result in our spiritual detriment, and we can expect, if we follow scriptural guidelines and avoid abuses, that its renewed use will bring added spiritual blessing and vitality to our churches.

13

Encouraging and Regulating Prophecy in the Local Church

If this study on the gift of prophecy has been persuasive to some who have read it, and if there has been an agreement that, in general, the conclusions of this study are indeed what the Bible itself teaches about the gift of prophecy, then the question naturally arises: What shall we do about it? Are there appropriate ways to go about encouraging the use of the gift of prophecy in our local churches? And if this gift is encouraged, how can we regulate it so as to avoid possible abuses of the gift?

This question can be answered differently for two different groups: (1) those Christians in churches where the gift of prophecy is not used but where the pastor and perhaps other church leaders would like to encourage its use; and (2) those Christians in churches where the gift of prophecy is already being used.

For churches which do not use the gift of prophecy but would like to

Here I have listed several suggestions of my own—suggestions which churches may find helpful.

(a) *Pray*. Pray seriously for God's guidance and wisdom on how and when to approach this subject in the church. As with any new proposals or suggestions which come to a church, the matter of being sensitive to the Lord's timing, and having his blessing on what is done, is of utmost importance. If the timing is right, and if it is preceded by prayer, then God will already have been preparing other people's hearts in the church to see a need in this area as well.

(b) *Teach.* The pastor and/or other church leaders can teach on this subject in the regular Bible teaching times which the church provides. This may be on Sunday mornings, Sunday evenings, at a mid-week Bible study and prayer meeting, or perhaps in an adult Bible class. The teaching, of course, should be thoroughly grounded in Scripture, and 'pure ... peaceable, gentle, open to reason, full of mercy and good fruits, without uncertainty or insincerity' (Jas 3:17, RSV).

Ordinarily it would be good then, after this period of teaching has ended, to wait for several weeks or perhaps months while the teaching 'soaks in' and there is opportunity to see if it finds consent in the hearts of many or most of the Lord's people in the congregation. (If the teaching is faithful to Scripture, then it should find consent—perhaps not unanimous, but certainly significant, especially in those who are mature in the Word.)

(c) *Go slowly and be patient.* Peter says that elders in the church should not be 'domineering' (1 Pet 5:3), a directive which reminds church leaders not to be pushy or to try to force their way on the church through political or psychological pressure, or by forcefulness of personality. And Jesus tells us, 'Blessed are the meek, for they shall inherit the earth' (Mt 5:5, RSV), a teaching which again reminds us not to be pushy or to try to force our way apart from the work of the Holy Spirit in people's hearts.

In this issue, which is admittedly new for many people, a gentle, patient, truly pastoral approach will in the end bring about the results the Lord desires, for it will not frighten away or alienate people unnecessarily.

(d) *Use the gift of prophecy in ways it has already been functioning in the church.* I give this suggestion both to the pastoral staff and church officers, and to all Christians who are concerned about the gift of prophecy. It may sound like a strange suggestion, but I think it can be a very helpful one.

It is probably true that the gift of prophecy has already been functioning in partial and provisional ways in the ordinary life of a vital, active church. Sometimes in church prayer meetings, for example, someone may have felt unusually 'led' or 'prompted' by the Holy Spirit to pray for a particular matter—perhaps one that had not recently been on his or her mind, at least not this extensively. And perhaps that prayer has brought an unusual response in the hearts of many others present. I would not hesitate to say that this seems to be the result of a 'revelation' from the Holy Spirit by which the topic to pray for, and perhaps several specific aspects of how to pray, were brought to mind by the Holy Spirit just before or during the time the person was praying. And perhaps that same matter was 'revealed' by the Holy Spirit to several others, who also felt deeply the need to pray in such a way. It seems that we would be right to say that this was already an instance of the gift of prophecy functioning in our church, without our calling it that or really being aware of exactly what was happening.

Therefore, if people want to encourage the use of the gift of prophecy more, one way in which that could be done is to be sensitive to any promptings of the Holy Spirit which might come during times of corporate prayer, and then expressing those promptings in the form of a prayer (or a 'prophetic prayer') to the Lord.

Another example might be found in the direction of meetings of the church which are not planned in a formal way in advance. Recently, when praying with a group of Christians with whom I had not previously met for prayer, I kept thinking about a particular Scripture song which I wanted to sing. But before I said something, one of the women in the group started that song, and we all joined in. Afterwards, another man in the group mentioned that that song had been on his mind at just the same time. We had come from different situations and I at least had not heard the song recently—I simply understood this as a prompting from the Holy Spirit in the direction of our praise.

This can happen when Christians gather more informally, perhaps on Sunday evenings or at other times, for the singing of hymns, the reading of Scripture, and expressions of prayer and praise to the Lord. It may be that there have already been times in our recent memories when the Holy Spirit would bring to the minds of several different people exactly the same hymn to choose, or readings of Scripture from various passages, all of which were on the same theme, or even a common sense of the tone or direction of worship which the Holy Spirit was giving to the meeting—perhaps sometimes an attitude of reverence and silence before the Lord, sometimes one of brokenness and repentance for sin, sometimes one of heartfelt intercession for a particular need, sometimes one of overwhelming joy and thanksgiving and praise. It was this kind of sensitivity to the leading of the Holy Spirit which has often given great vitality to the unstructured worship services of the Plymouth Brethren, for example, with everyone present sensing that the Holy Spirit was working among his people in a perceptible way.

Once again, those who wish to see an increase in the gift of prophecy in a local church could encourage people simply to be open to and sensitive to any prompting from the Holy Spirit in the direction of unstructured times of worship. Even if responding to such promptings from the Holy Spirit is not called 'prophecy', the result in benefit to the church could nonetheless be a very similar and very positive one.

Another example of ways in which the gift of prophecy has probably already been functioning in many churches would be during Sunday morning sermons. If there are times when the pastor has departed from his prepared outline and spent a few minutes of the sermon on something that he thought the Lord was strongly impressing on his mind just before or during the time he was speaking, then, once again, it seems that the Apostle Paul would have been happy to call that a 'revelation' from the Holy Spirit, and even though the pastor did not think of it as prophecy or call it by that name, it actually was the functioning of the gift of prophecy in the assembled meeting of the church. Many pastors for whom this has happened can testify that such spontaneous additions to their planned messages have at times been exactly the thing which spoke to a definite need, often a previously unknown need, in the congregation.

A pastor who was concerned to see the gift of prophecy functioning more effectively in his church could make a habit of cultivating an attitude of prayerfulness and a conscious dependence on the Lord before and during the time he is preaching (which would of course be a good thing anyway!), and, if the Holy Spirit from time to time brings to mind something which is doctrinally consistent with Scripture, and which, as far as he can tell, will bring edification to the congregation, then he can go ahead and add that material to what he is saying.

Yet there is a danger here. What a pastor is normally supposed to do on Sunday morning is not to *prophesy* (for we cannot predict when the Holy Spirit will reveal something), but to *teach*. It is the expectation of the congregation that he will *teach*, and the New Testament understands such teaching to be *teaching from Scripture*. Now the process of teaching Scripture is almost always done in a better and more effective way when there is *preparation*. Not to prepare for a time of Bible teaching (when one has opportunity to prepare, or could make opportunity to prepare) is not being more spiritual, it is simply being lazy. It is to subject the congregation to poorly organized, rambling thoughts which could have been communicated in half the time and with twice the effect if the pastor had taken the time to prepare.

So if a pastor does not prepare for a Bible teaching, but says he is 'trusting the Lord' to bring something to mind, then he is, in my opinion, trying to *force* the Lord to reveal something to him when he speaks. But that is just another example of 'forcing a test on the Lord your God', something Jesus clearly forbids in Luke 4:12: 'You shall not force a test on the Lord your God' (New American Standard Bible). If you are on the pinnacle of the temple, taking the steps down is to use the ordinary means God has provided. Jumping and hoping God will perform a miracle to save you is 'forcing a test on the Lord'. Similarly, if a pastor is to give a Bible teaching, taking the time to prepare is using the ordinary *means* which God has provided. But stepping into the pulpit without preparing is like jumping off the pinnacle of the temple. It involves refusing to use the ordinary means God has made available and demanding that he provide some kind of extraordinary revelation to rescue you from your dilemma!

So although it is right to be sensitive to such promptings from the Lord if they do come, they should never be allowed to take the place of adequate preparation for the solemn responsibility of the teaching of Scripture to the assembled congregation.

A fourth way in which the gift of prophecy can be used without actually calling it 'prophecy' can be in occasional times of personal conversation or counselling, when it seems that the Lord is bringing something to mind in a clear or strong way. Once again, *if* such an apparent revelation is consistent with Scripture, and if it seems appropriate in the conversation, then it can be incorporated into the ordinary conversation as it is going on, and, if this really was from the Lord, he will use it in a way that he deems appropriate.

(e) Finally, *if* the four preceding steps have been followed and have been accepted by the church, and *if* the congregation and its leadership will accept it, *make provision for the use of prophecy in the less formal worship gatherings of the church*.

In order for the gift of prophecy to be used as Paul directs in 1 Corinthians 14, it requires a time when the congregation is gathered in a less formally structured meeting than what usually occurs on Sunday mornings. Most Sunday morning worship services do not give opportunity for spontaneous, individual contributions of any kind. Therefore, it would not seem appropriate to try to inject the gift of prophecy in these settings (unless the church decides to change the entire format of Sunday morning worship services). It may well be that the church will decide to keep a more formal Sunday morning service, where visitors can come and find a rather predictable format, with predictable times of beginning and ending the service. I think the decision on that is best left up to the individual congregation, and can vary according to the size of the congregation and the cultural setting in which the church finds itself.

Yet there are other times when Christians in the congregation gather for worship in a less formal way. This may be on Sunday evenings, or at mid-week prayer meetings, or in smaller house groups. In these situations, if the preceding steps have been followed and there has already been some clear teaching on the use of the gift of prophecy in the church, then those in leadership in these meetings may think it appropriate to give some opportunity for the use of the gift of prophecy in these worship services.

If so, then it would be helpful to give a brief word of explanation at the beginning of the worship time. The leader would want to say that the time of worship will allow opportunity for spontaneous, individual contributions, perhaps the reading of Scripture, a request for the singing of a hymn, a prayer request or a word of testimony. One of these kinds of contributions may be a 'prophecy', that is, reporting something the Lord brings to mind spontaneously during the worship service. If the Holy Spirit should work in anyone present to give such a prompting or 'revelation', then it is certainly acceptable to say it to the group, for the edification of all present.

Of course, whoever is in charge of the worship time will want to be sure that everything is done in an orderly way, and in an edifying way, and that if any prophecies are given, that they are subject to the evaluation of the rest of the congregation. In fact, the leader would want to encourage everyone present to *evaluate or 'weigh what is said'* (1 Cor 14:29, RSV), to 'test everything; hold fast what is good' (1 Thess 5:21, RSV). And if among the men in the congregation there are those who wish to make a spoken evaluation of any prophecy, they should feel free to do so after it has been spoken.

In every case the leader should try to avoid any unnecessary sense of tension, stiffness, or formality which would make this appear strange or unusual. It should be seen as simply the normal, usual way in which the Lord works among his people when they gather in his presence to worship him!

Those who speak such prophecies in the church should be encouraged not to be overly dramatic (and thus attract excessive attention to themselves rather than to the Lord), and on the other hand not to be flippant or frivolous (and thus 'despise prophesying': 1 Thess 5:20, RSV). They should be told beforehand that it is not appropriate to think of prophecy after the analogy of Old Testament prophets, and therefore it would not be right to preface what they say with the declaration, 'Thus says the Lord.'

Rather, they might begin with something like, 'I think the Lord is putting on my mind that...' or, 'It seems that the Lord is showing us...' or something equivalent to that. If this is indeed a revelation from the Lord, even with a mild preface such as this, it will certainly find confirmation in the hearts of the Lord's people and will bring about the results that the Lord wants.

Above all, it is important that whoever speaks a prophecy keep in mind an attitude of love which seeks the good of those listening, not the fame or reputation or prestige of the one speaking. Therefore, the speaker will be sure to speak so others can understand, and to keep in mind that the goal is the edification of those who hear (1 Cor 14:26 [RSV]: 'Let all things be done for edification').

Those in leadership at such worship services should also continue to remind themselves of the provisions which Paul makes in 1 Corinthians 14 regulating the worship service of the church, especially:

(a) They should keep asking themselves: Is this *edifying* the church? (See 1 Cor 14:26.)

(b) They should not let any one gift or person dominate the worship service. There should not be too many prophecies and they should not take too long. This directive comes from the fact that Paul says that those speaking in tongues should be limited to 'only two or at most three' (1 Cor 14:27, RSV), and also that those prophesying should be limited: 'Let two or three prophets speak' (1 Cor 14:29, RSV). Different people come with different things to contribute (1 Cor 14:26), and this should be allowed, even if some people who receive revelations are not allowed to speak. Paul doesn't seem worried about this (see 1 Corinthians 14:29, which limits the prophets to two or three, and 1 Corinthians 14:30, which says that the first prophet should stop if someone else receives a revelation).

(c) They should maintain an atmosphere of orderliness (1 Cor 14:32–33, 40), along with courtesy towards all, and one which allows spontaneous contributions, and yet is also content to allow times of silence when people individually wait on the Lord and pray to him.

Finally, with regard to many practical questions concerning the gift of prophecy, it would be helpful for people to gain from the practical experience and wisdom of years that can come from those who have been in the charismatic or Pentecostal movements a long time. Sometimes we who have been more or less outside the charismatic movement think we see quite plainly the dangers and abuses that can come with the use of gifts like prophecy, but I think most non-charismatics would be surprised to find that those *within* the charismatic movement often see the problems with equal or greater clarity, and talk about them in a helpful way in their writings.

Three books that might be mentioned with regard to practical discussions about the use of prophecy in general are Michael Harper, *Prophecy: A Gift for the Body of Christ* (Logos 1964), Bruce Yocum, *Prophecy* (Word of Life 1976), and Donald Gee, *Spiritual Gifts in the Work of Ministry Today* (Gospel Publishing House 1963) (pp. 40-62 on the gift of prophecy).

With regard to the specific area of evaluating prophecy, there are valuable sections in George Mallone, ed., *Those Controversial Gifts* (IVP 1983), pp. 41–47, Bruce Yocum, *Prophecy* (Word of Life 1976), pp. 103-121, and Don Basham,

A Handbook on Tongues, Interpretation and Prophecy (Whitaker Books 1971), pp. 111-116.

Now I do not agree with everything these writers say. For example, I realize that some of these writers will *define* prophecy as 'the word of God for the present situation'—and so will be in disagreement with the definition of prophecy which I have argued for in this book. Yet *in practice*, especially among the more mature and responsible segments of the charismatic movement, prophecy has been *treated* not exactly as 'the word of God' but very much as I am suggesting here: the report of something God spontaneously brings to mind. And because prophecy has been treated that way in practice, these writers can provide many helpful suggestions in the practical realm.

For churches which already use the gift of prophecy.

Much of what has already been said will apply to these churches as well, but some additional reminders and suggestions are also appropriate.

(a) Remember that what is spoken in any prophecy today is not the word of God, but is simply a human being reporting in merely human words something which God has brought to mind. Therefore do not encourage people to think that prophecy is actually the word of God, or there will be, at least implicitly, a misunderstanding and a confusion between the authority of Scripture and the authority of prophecy. Gently teach people and encourage them not to say, 'Thus says the Lord,' before they report a prophecy to the church, or to speak for the Lord in the first person in a way that gives the impression that the words have God's absolute authority.

(b) Be sure to test prophecies, to *evaluate* them by Scripture and by what else you know to be true. No matter how mature one is in the Christian life, no matter how frequently or with what powerful results one has used the gift of prophecy, it can never be free from evaluation by God's assembled people. During early 1987 the embarrassing publicity which Oral

Roberts received could have been avoided, it seems to me, if this principle had been followed. He was, I think, convinced that God had revealed to him that he would take his life if a certain sum of money was not raised by the end of March 1987. If he had subjected his impression of this 'revelation' to a mature group of advisors, no doubt many of them would have seen it to be an idea contrary to the way God encourages us to give money 'not under compulsion' (2 Cor 9:7), and contrary to the way in which God in Scripture is never seen to act to hold one man's life hostage only to be redeemed by the voluntary (or rather, non-voluntary) gifts of others. Evaluation would have prevented that mistake, and can prevent many others.

(c) Be sure you emphasize *Scripture* as the place where people can always go to hear the voice of the living God. It is in Scripture that God speaks to us, even today, and all through our lives. Rather than hoping at every worship service that the highlight would be some prophecy from God himself, those who use the gift of prophecy most need to be encouraged once again to find our focus of excitement, our joy, our expectation, our delight in Scripture itself. There we have a treasure of infinite worth: our Creator speaking to us in words we can understand.

In churches where the gift of prophecy is functioning, and especially there, the emphasis must continually be on the fact that it is in Scripture that we are to find guidance for our lives. In Scripture is our source of direction, our focus when seeking God's will, our sufficient and completely reliable standard. It is God's words in Scripture of which we can with confidence say, 'Your word is a lamp to my feet and a light to my path' (Ps 119:105).

14

Why Do We Need the Gift of Prophecy Today?

Is this whole discussion really important? Will we lose anything if we go on as we have before, largely neglecting the gift of prophecy in our churches?

In order to answer this question, we should first remember what Scripture itself says about the importance of this gift. The Apostle Paul valued this gift so highly that he told the Corinthians, 'Make love your aim, and earnestly desire the spiritual gifts *especially that you may prophesy*' (1 Cor 14:1, RSV). Then at the end of his discussion of spiritual gifts he said again, 'So, my brethen, *earnestly desire to prophesy*' (1 Cor 14:39, RSV). And he said, 'He who prophesies *edifies the church*' (1 Cor 14:4, RSV).

Now we must ask ourselves a hard question today: If Paul was eager for the gift of prophecy to function at Corinth, troubled as the church was by immaturity, selfishness, divisions and other problems, then should we not also be eager for this gift to function once again in our churches today? If we are Christians, and especially evangelical Christians who profess to believe and obey *all* that Scripture says, should we not also believe and obey these statements on the gift of prophecy?

But in addition to these direct statements from Scripture, might we also see, from the overall teaching of Scripture on the nature of prophecy, some specific benefits that would come to our churches if we were to allow this gift to function? I think there are such benefits.

First, if the argument presented here is correct, to neglect prophecy is to be disobedient to Scripture. That is reason enough to know that there will be negative consequences in our churches, and at least the lack of the full blessing that would be ours if we obeyed.

Second, if this gift is allowed to function and is encouraged in our lives, it would undoubtedly add an element of closeness to God and sensitivity to his promptings in our daily walk. Now some may object that this is just 'too subjective' an emphasis— and they may claim that we need to be 'more objective' than this in living our Christian lives. Such added emphasis on subjectivity, they may say, will simply open us up to doctrinal error, mistaken ethical guidance, and a wrongful neglect of guidance from Scripture in our lives.

But it is probably true that those who make this objection are exactly the Christians who need this subjective process most in their own Christian lives! They are the ones who have the *least* likelihood of being led into error, for they already place great emphasis on solid grounding in the word of God. Yet they especially need this gift, for at times their lives can become too exclusively intellectual and too narrowly doctrinal in focus. But this gift cannot be forced to happen by intellectual arguments or doctrinal investigations. Rather, it requires a different kind of activity—it requires waiting on the Lord, listening for him, hearing his prompting in our hearts.

In other words, for those who are completely evangelical, theologically orthodox, doctrinally mature, intellectually well-informed, biblically literate Christians, probably what is most needed is a strong balancing influence of a more vital 'subjective' relationship with the Lord in their daily lives. I have to say that personally, as I am working with Scripture from an academic perspective day after day, I often sense that need in my own life.

Third, I am convinced that if the gift of prophecy were allowed to function, at least in some gatherings in the life of the church, it would add a rich new measure of vitality in worship, a sense of awe that comes from seeing God at work at this very moment and in this very place, the overwhelming sense of wonder that causes us to exclaim 'truly God is in this place'.

These then are the benefits that would come to the church. There are possibilities of error or abuse—as with any gift (think of teaching, or administration, for example). But the possibilities of abuse can be guarded against through careful teaching and through regulating the gift according to the principles taught in Scripture. And the potential for benefit to the church—and to our own spiritual lives—is very significant.

APPENDIX A

The Office of Apostle

The discussion in chapter 2 dealt with the authority of the apostles. It concluded that the apostles spoke and wrote words with absolute divine authority—'words of the Lord'. Because the written words of the apostles were words of God, many of them became part of the New Testament which we have today.

But just who were the apostles? How many apostles were there? What were the requirements for being an apostle? And are there apostles today?

At the outset it must be made clear that the answers to these questions depend on what one means by the word 'apostle'. Today some people use the word 'apostle' in a very broad sense, to refer to an effective church planter, or to a significant pioneer in missionary work ('William Carey was an apostle to India,' for example). If we use the word 'apostle' in that broad sense, of course everyone would agree that there are still apostles today—for there are certainly effective missionaries and church planters today.[116]

But there is another sense for the word 'apostle'. Usually in the New Testament the word refers to a special office, 'apostle of Jesus Christ'. In this narrow sense of the term, there are no more apostles today, and we are to expect no more. This is because of what the New Testament says about the qualifications for being an apostle and about who the apostles were.

Qualifications of an apostle

The two qualifications for being an apostle were (1) having seen Jesus after his resurrection with one's own eyes (thus, being an 'eyewitness of the resurrection'), and (2) having been specifically commissioned by Christ as his apostle.[117]

The fact that an apostle had to have seen the risen Lord with his own eyes is indicated by Acts 1:22, where Peter said that the person to replace Judas 'must become with us *a witness to his resurrection*' (RSV). Moreover, it was 'to the apostles whom he had chosen' that 'he presented himself alive after his passion by many proofs, appearing to them during forty days' (Acts 1:2–3, RSV; cf. Acts 4:33).

Paul makes much of the fact that he *did* meet this qualification, even though it was in an unusual way (Christ appeared to him in a vision on the road to Damascus and appointed him as an apostle: Acts 9:5–6; 26:15–18). So when he is defending his apostleship he says, 'Am I not an apostle? Have I not *seen* Jesus our Lord?' (1 Cor 9:1, RSV). And when recounting the people to whom Christ appeared after his resurrection, Paul says, 'Then he appeared to James, then to all the apostles. Last of all, as to one untimely born, he appeared also to me. For I am the least of the apostles, unfit to be called an apostle' (1 Cor 15:7–9, RSV).

These verses combine to indicate that unless someone had seen Jesus after the resurrection with his own eyes, he could not be an apostle.

The second qualification, being specifically appointed by Christ as an apostle, is also evident from several verses. First, though the term 'apostle' is not common in the gospels, the twelve disciples are called 'apostles' specifically in the context where Jesus is commissioning them, 'sending them out' to preach in his name:

And he called to him his twelve disciples and gave them authority over unclean spirits, to cast them out, and to heal every disease and

every infirmity. The names of the twelve *apostles* are these....
These twelve Jesus sent out, charging them, '....And preach as you
go, saying, "The kingdom of heaven is at hand..."' (Mt. 10:1-7,
RSV).

Similarly, Jesus commissions his apostles in a special sense to
be his 'witnesses ... to the end of the earth' (Acts 1:8, RSV). And
in choosing another apostle to replace Judas, the eleven apostles did not take the responsibility on themselves, but prayed
and asked Christ to make the appointment:

> 'Lord, who knows the hearts of all men, show which one of these
> two you have chosen to take the place in this ministry and
> apostleship from which Judas turned aside'....And they cast lots
> for them, and the lot fell on Matthias; and he was enrolled with the
> eleven apostles (Acts 1:24–26).

Paul himself insists that Christ personally appointed him as an
apostle. He tells how, on the Damascus Road, Jesus told him
that he was appointing him as an apostle to the Gentiles: 'I have
appeared to you for this purpose, to appoint you to serve and
bear witness...delivering you from the people and from the
Gentiles—to whom I send you' (Acts 26:16–17, RSV).

He later affirms that he was specifically appointed by Christ
as an apostle (see Rom 1:1; Gal 1:1; 1 Tim 1:12; 2:7; 2 Tim
1:11).

Who were apostles?

The initial group of apostles numbered twelve—the eleven
original disciples who remained after Judas died, plus Matthias,
who replaced Judas: 'And they cast lots for them, and the lot
fell on Matthias; and he was enrolled with the eleven apostles'
(Acts 1:26, RSV). So important was this original group of twelve
apostles, the 'charter members' of the office of apostle, that we
read that their names are inscribed on the foundations of the
heavenly city, the New Jerusalem: 'And the wall of the city had

twelve foundations, and on them the twelve names of the twelve apostles of the Lamb' (Rev 21:14, RSV).

We might at first think that such a group could never be expanded, that no one could be added to it. But then Paul clearly claims that he, also, is an apostle. And Acts 14:14 calls both Barnabas and Paul apostles: 'When the apostles Barnabas and Paul heard of it...' (RSV). So with Paul and Barnabas there are fourteen 'apostles of Jesus Christ'.

Then James the brother of Jesus (who was not one of the twelve original disciples) seems to be called an apostle in Galatians 1:19: Paul tells how, when he went to Jerusalem, 'I saw none of the other apostles except James the Lord's brother' (RSV).[118] Then in Galatians 2:9 James is classified with Peter and John as 'pillars' of the Jerusalem church. And in Acts 15:13–21 James, along with Peter, exercises a significant leadership function in the Jerusalem Council, a function which would be appropriate to the office of apostle. Furthermore, when Paul is listing the resurrection appearances of Jesus he once again seems so readily to classify James with the apostles:

> Then he appeared to James, then to all the apostles. Last of all, as to one untimely born, he appeared also to me. For I am the least of the apostles, unfit to be called an apostle, because I persecuted the church of God...(1 Cor 15:7–9, RSV).

Finally, the fact that James could write the New Testament epistle which bears his name would also be entirely consistent with his having the authority which belonged to the office of apostle, the authority to write words which were the words of God. All these considerations combine to indicate that James the Lord's brother was also commissioned by Christ as an apostle. That would bring the number to fifteen 'apostles of Jesus Christ' (the twelve plus Paul, plus Barnabas, plus James).

Were there more than these fifteen? There may possibly have been a few more, though we know little if anything about them, and it is not certain that there were any more. Others of course had seen Jesus after his resurrection ('Then he appeared to more than five hundred brethren at one time...' 1 Cor 15:6, RSV). From this large group it is possible that Christ appointed some others as apostles—but it is also very possible that he did not. The evidence is insufficient.

Romans 16:7 says, 'Greet Andronicus and Junias, my kinsmen and my fellow prisoners; they are men of note among the apostles, and they were in Christ before me' (RSV).

There are several translation problems in the verse, so no clear conclusions can be reached. 'Men of note' may be also translated 'men noted by' (the apostles). 'Junias' (a man's name) may also be translated 'Junia' (a woman's name).[119] 'Apostles' here may not mean the office 'apostles of Jesus Christ', but may just mean 'messengers' (the word is used in this broad sense in Philippians 2:25; 2 Corinthians 8:23; John 13:16).[120] The verse has too little clear information to allow us to draw a conclusion.

Others have been suggested as apostles. Silas (Silvanus) and sometimes Timothy are mentioned because of 1 Thessalonians 2:6: 'Though we might have made demands as apostles of Christ' (RSV). Does Paul include Silas and Timothy here, since the letter begins, 'Paul, Silvanus, and Timothy' (1 Thess 1:1, RSV)?

It is not likely that Paul is including Timothy in this statement, for two reasons. (1) He says just four verses earlier, 'We had already suffered and been shamefully treated at Philippi, as you know' (1 Thess 2:2, RSV), but this seems to refer to the beating and imprisonment which happened just to Paul and Silas, not to Timothy (Acts 16:19). So the 'we' in verse 6 does not seem to include all of the people (Paul, Silvanus, Timothy) mentioned in the first verse. The letter *in general* is from Paul, Silas and Timothy, but Paul knows that the readers will naturally understand the appropriate members of the 'we' when he does not mean to include all three of them in certain sections of the letter. He does not specify 'we—*that is, Silas and I*—had suffered and been shamefully treated at Philippi, as you know,' because the Thessalonians will know who the 'we' are that he is talking about.

(2) This is also seen in 1 Thessalonians 3:1–2, where the 'we' certainly cannot include Timothy:

> Therefore when we could bear it no longer, we were willing to be left behind at Athens alone, and we sent Timothy, our brother and God's servant in the gospel of Christ, to establish you in your faith and to exhort you (1 Thess 3:1–2, RSV).

In this case, the 'we' refers either to Paul and Silas, or else just to Paul alone (see Acts 17:14–15; 18:5). Apparently Silas and Timothy had come to Paul in Athens 'as soon as possible' (Acts 17:15, RSV)—though Luke does not mention their arrival in Athens—and Paul had sent them back to Thessalonica again to help the church there. Then he himself went to Corinth, and they later joined him there (Acts 18:5).

It is most likely that 'we were willing to be left behind at Athens alone' (1 Thess 3:1, RSV) refers to Paul alone, both because he picks up the argument again in verse 5 with the singular 'I' ('when I could bear it no longer, I sent that I might know your faith' [1 Thess 3:5, RSV]), and because the point of extreme loneliness in Athens would not be made if Silas had stayed with him.[121] In fact, in the previous paragraph, Paul seems to explain that by 'we' in these statements he generally means 'I', for he says, 'We wanted to come to you—I, Paul, again and again—but Satan hindered us' (1 Thess 2:18, RSV). Apparently he is using 'we' more frequently in this epistle as a courteous way of including Silas and Timothy, who had spent so much time in the Thessalonian church, in the letter to that church. But the Thessalonians would have had little doubt who was really in charge of this great mission to the Gentiles, and on whose apostolic authority the letter primarily (or exclusively) depended.

So it is just possible that Silas was himself an apostle, and that 1 Thessalonians 2:6 hints at that. He was of course a leading member of the Jerusalem church (Acts 15:22), and could well have seen Jesus after his resurrection, and then been appointed as an apostle. But we cannot be very certain.

The situation with Timothy is different, however. Just as he is excluded from the 'we' of 1 Thessalonians 2:2 (and 3:1–2), so he seems to be excluded from the 'we' of 1 Thessalonians 2:6. Moreover, as a native of Lystra (Acts 16:1–3) who had learned of Christ from his grandmother and mother (2 Tim 1:5), it seems impossible that he would have been in Jerusalem before Pentecost and would there have seen the risen Lord and come to believe in him and then suddenly have been appointed as an apostle. Moreover, Paul's pattern of address in his letters always jealously guards the title 'apostle' for himself, never allowing it to be applied to Timothy or others of his travelling companions (note 2 Cor 1:1; Col 1:1: 'Paul, an apostle of Christ Jesus...and Timothy our brother' [RSV]; and then Phil 1:1, 'Paul and Timothy, *servants* of Christ Jesus' [RSV]). So Timothy, as important a role as he had, should not rightly be considered one of the apostles.

This gives us a limited but somewhat imprecisely numbered group who had the office 'apostles of Jesus Christ'. There seem to have been at least fifteen, perhaps sixteen or even a few more who are not recorded in the New Testament.

Yet it seems quite certain that there were none appointed after Paul. When Paul lists the resurrection appearances of Christ, he emphasizes the unusual way in which Christ appeared to him, and connects that with the statement that this was the 'last' appearance of all, and that he himself is indeed 'the least of all the apostles, unfit to be called an apostle'.

He appeared to Cephas [Peter], then to *the twelve*. Then he appeared to more than five hundred brethren at one time, most of whom are still alive, though some have fallen asleep. Then he appeared to *James*, then to *all the apostles. Last of all*, as to one untimely born, he appeared also to me. For I am the least of the apostles, unfit to be called an apostle... (1 Cor 15:5–9, RSV).

Summary

The word 'apostle' can be used in a broad or narrow sense. In a broad sense, it just means 'messenger' or 'pioneer missionary'. But in a narrow sense, the most common sense in the New Testament, it refers to a specific office, 'apostle of Jesus Christ'. These apostles had unique authority to found and govern the early church, and they could speak and write words of God. Many of their written words became the New Testament Scriptures.

In order to qualify as an apostle, someone (1) had to have seen Christ with his own eyes after he rose from the dead, and (2) had to have been specifically appointed by Christ as an apostle. There was a limited number of apostles, perhaps fifteen or sixteen or a few more—the New Testament is not explicit on the number. The twelve original apostles (the eleven plus Matthias) were joined by Barnabas and Paul, very probably James, perhaps Silas, and maybe even Andronicus and Junias or a few unnamed others. It seems that no apostles were appointed after Paul, and certainly, since no one today can meet the qualification of having seen the risen Christ with his own eyes, there are no apostles today. In place of living apostles present in the church to teach and govern it, we have instead the writings of the apostles in the books of the New Testament. Those New Testament Scriptures fulfil for the church today the absolutely authoritative teaching and governing functions which were fulfilled by the apostles themselves during the early years of the church.

APPENDIX B

The Canon of Scripture

It is crucial for us to know and believe the words of God spoken to us in Scripture. Before we can do this, however, we must know which writings belong in the Bible and which do not. This is the question of the *canon* of Scripture, which may be defined as follows: 'The *canon* of Scripture is the list of all the books that belong in the Bible.'

We must not underestimate the importance of this question. The words of Scripture are the words by which we nourish our spiritual lives. Thus we can affirm the comment of Moses to the people of Israel in reference to the words of God's law: 'For it is no trifle for you, but *it is your life*, and thereby you shall live long in the land which you are going over the Jordan to possess' (Deut 32:47, RSV).

To add to or subtract from God's words would be to prevent God's people from obeying him fully, for commands that were subtracted would not be known to the people, and words that were added might require things of the people which God had not commanded. Thus, Moses warned the people of Israel, 'You shall not *add to* the word which I command you, nor *take from* it; *that you may keep* the commandments of the Lord your God which I command you' (Deut 4:2, RSV).

The precise determination of the extent of the canon of Scripture is thus of utmost importance for believers. If we are to trust and obey God absolutely we must have a collection of words which we are certain are God's own words to us. If there

are any sections of Scripture about which we have doubts
whether they are God's words or not, we will not consider them
to have absolute divine authority and we will not trust them as
much as we would trust God himself.

The Old Testament canon

Scripture itself shows us several aspects in the historical
development of the canon. The earliest collection of written
words of God was the Ten Commandments. These were two
tablets of stone on which God himself wrote the words which he
commanded his people: 'And he gave to Moses, when he had
made an end of speaking with him upon Mount Sinai, the two
tables of the testimony, tables of stone, written with the finger
of God' (Ex 31:18, RSV). Again we read, 'And the tables were
the work of God, and the writing was the writing of God, gra-
ven upon the tables' (Ex 32:16, RSV; cf. Deut 4:13; 10:4). These
stone tablets were deposited in the ark of the covenant (Deut
10:5) and constituted the terms of the covenant between God
and his people.[122]

This collection of absolutely authoritative words from God
grew in size throughout the time of Israel's history. Moses himself wrote additional words to be deposited in the ark of the
covenant:

> When Moses had finished writing the words of this law in a book,
> to the very end, Moses commanded the Levites who carried the ark
> of the covenant of the Lord, 'Take this book of the law, and put it
> by the side of the ark of the covenant of the Lord your God, that it
> may be there for a witness against you' (Deut 31:24–26, RSV).

The immediate reference of the verse is apparently to the book
of Deuteronomy, but other references to writing by Moses
indicate that the first four books of the Old Testament were
written by him as well (see Ex 17:14; 24:4; 34:27; Num 33:2;
Deut 31:22).

After the death of Moses, Joshua also added to the collection of written words of God: 'Joshua wrote these words in the book of the law of God' (Josh 24:26, RSV). This is especially surprising in light of the command not to add to or take away from the words which God gave the people through Moses: 'You shall not add to the word which I command you, nor take from it...' (Deut 4:2, RSV; cf. 12:32). In order to have disobeyed such a specific command, Joshua must have been convinced that God himself had authorized such additional writing.

Later, others in Israel, usually those who fulfilled the office of prophet, wrote additional words from God.

1 Samuel 10:25, RSV—'Then Samuel told the people the rights and duties of the kingship; and he wrote them in a book and laid it up before the Lord.'

1 Chronicles 29:29, RSV—'Now the acts of King David, from first to last, are written in the Chronicles of Samuel the seer, and in the Chronicles of Nathan the prophet, and in the Chronicles of Gad the seer.'

2 Chronicles 20:34, RSV—'Now the rest of the acts of Jehoshaphat, from first to last, are written in the Chronicles of Jehu the son of Hanani, which are recorded in the Book of the Kings of Israel' (cf. 1 Kings 16:7 where Jehu the son of Hanani is called a prophet).

2 Chronicles 26:22, RSV—'Now the rest of the acts of Uzziah, from first to last, Isaiah the prophet the son of Amoz wrote.'

2 Chronicles 32:32, RSV—'Now the rest of the acts of Hezekiah, and his good deeds, behold, they are written in the vision of Isaiah the prophet the son of Amoz, in the Book of the Kings of Judah and Israel.'

Jeremiah 30:2, RSV—'Thus says the Lord, the God of Israel: Write in a book all the words that I have spoken to you.'

Other passages could be cited (cf. 2 Chron 9:29; 12:15; 13:22; Is 30:8; Jer 29:1; 36:1-32; 45:1; 51:60; Ezek 43:11; Hab 2:2; Dan 7:1), but the process of growth in the collection of written words from God should be clear. The Old Testament does not specify all the details of every book, but it does record for us several examples of the way in which this growth occurred, usually through the agency of a prophet chosen by God to be his spokesman.

This process of growth in the Old Testament canon continued until the time of the end of the writing process. If we date Haggai in 520 B.C., Zechariah in 520 to 518 B.C. (with perhaps more material added after 480 B.C.), and Malachi around 435 B.C., we have an idea of the approximate dates of the last Old Testament prophets. Roughly coinciding with this period are the books of Ezra and Nehemiah: Ezra went to Jerusalem in 458 B.C. and Nehemiah was in Jerusalem from 445 to 433 B.C..[123] Esther was written sometime after the death of Xerxes I (= Ahasuerus) in 465 B.C., and a date during the reign of Artaxerxes I (464–423 B.C.) is probable.

Thus, after approximately 430 B.C., no more writings were added to the Old Testament canon. The subsequent history of the Jewish people was recorded in other writings, such as the books of the Maccabees, but these writings were not thought worthy to be included with the collections of God's words from earlier years.

The belief that divinely authoritative words from God had ceased is quite clearly attested in several strands of extra-biblical Jewish literature. In 1 Maccabees (about 100 B.C.) the author writes of the defiled altar, 'So they tore down the altar, and stored the stones in a convenient place on the temple hill until there should come a prophet to tell what to do with them' (1 Macc 4:45–46, RSV). They apparently knew of no one who could speak with the authority of God as the Old Testament prophets had done. The memory of an authoritative prophet among the people was one that belonged to the distant past, for the author could speak of a great distress 'such as had not been since the time that prophets ceased to appear among them' (1 Macc 9:27; cf. 14:41, RSV).

Josephus (born A.D. 37/38) explained, 'From Artaxerxes to our own times a complete history has been written, but has not been deemed worthy of equal credit with the earlier record, because of the failure of the exact succession of the prophets'

(*Against Apion* 1.41). This statement by the greatest Jewish historian of the first century A.D. shows that he knew of the writings now considered part of the 'Apocrypha', but that he (and the very common Jewish viewpoint which he represents) considered these other writings 'not...worthy of equal credit' with what we now know as the Old Testament Scriptures. There were, in Josephus' viewpoint, no more 'words of God' added to Scripture after about 430 B.C.

Rabbinic literature reflects a similar conviction in its repeated statement that the Holy Spirit (in the Spirit's function of inspiring prophecy) departed from Israel. 'After the latter prophets Haggai, Zechariah, and Malachi had died, the Holy Spirit departed from Israel, but they still availed themselves of the *bath qol*' (*Babylonian Talmud, Yomah* 9b, repeated in *Sota* 48b, *Sanhedrin* 11a, and *Midrash Rabbah* on Song of Songs, 8.9.3).[124]

The Qumran community (the Jewish sect which left behind the Dead Sea Scrolls) also awaited a prophet whose words would have authority to supersede any existing regulations (see 1QS 9.11), and other similar statements are found elsewhere in ancient Jewish literature (see 2 Baruch 85.3 and Prayer of Azariah 15).

Thus, writings subsequent to about 430 B.C. were not accepted by the Jewish people generally as having equal authority with the rest of Scripture.

In the New Testament, we have no record of any dispute between Jesus and the Jews over the extent of the canon. Apparently, there was full agreement between Jesus and his disciples on the one hand, and the Jewish leaders or Jewish people on the other hand, that additions to the Old Testament canon had ceased after the time of Ezra, Nehemiah, Esther, Haggai, Zechariah, and Malachi. This fact is confirmed by the quotations of Jesus and the New Testament authors from the Old Testament. According to one count, Jesus and the New Testament authors quote various parts of the Old Testament Scriptures as divinely authoritative over 295 times,[125] but not once do they cite any statement from the books of the Apocrypha or any other writings as having divine authority.[126] The absence of any such reference to other literature as divinely authoritative, and the extremely frequent reference to hundreds of places of the Old Testament as divinely authoritative, gives strong confirmation to the fact that the New Testament authors agreed that the established Old Testament canon, no more and no less, was to be taken as God's very words.

What then shall be said about the Apocrypha, the collection of books included in the canon by the Roman Catholic church but excluded from the canon by Protestantism?[127] These books were never accepted by the Jews as Scripture, but throughout the early history of the church there was a divided opinion on whether they should be part of Scripture or not.[128] The fact that they were included by Jerome in his Latin Vulgate translation of the Bible (completed in A.D. 404) gave support to their inclusion, even though Jerome himself said they were not 'books of the canon' but merely 'books of the church' which were helpful and useful for believers. The wide use of the Latin Vulgate in subsequent centuries guaranteed their continued accessibility, but the fact that they had no Hebrew original behind them, and their exclusion from the Jewish canon, as well as the lack of their citation in the New Testament, led many to view them with suspicion or to reject them as authoritative.

It was not until 1548, at the Council of Trent, that the Roman Catholic church officially declared the Apocrypha to be part of the canon (with the exception of 1 and 2 Esdras and the Prayer of Manasses). At this point, Roman Catholics would hold that the church has the authority to constitute a literary work as 'Scripture', while Protestants have held that the church cannot *make* something to be Scripture, but can only *recognize* what God has already caused to be written as his own words.

Thus the writings of the Apocrypha should not be regarded as part of Scripture: (1) They do not claim for themselves the same kind of authority as the Old Testament writings; (2) they were not regarded as God's words by the Jewish people from whom they originated; and (3) they were not considered to be Scripture by Jesus or the New Testament authors. We must conclude that they are merely human words, not God-breathed words like the words of Scripture. They do have value for historical and linguistic research, but they have never been part of the Old Testament canon, and they should not be thought of as part of the Bible. Therefore, they have no binding authority for the thought or life of Christians today.

In conclusion, with regard to the canon of the Old Testament, Christians today should have no doubt that anything needed has been left out, or that anything which is not God's words has been put in.

The New Testament canon

The development of the New Testament canon begins with the writings of the apostles. It should be remembered that the writing of Scripture primarily occurs in connection with God's great acts in redemptive history. The Old Testament records and interprets for us the calling of Abraham and the lives of his descendants, the Exodus from Egypt and wilderness wanderings, the establishment of God's people in the land of Canaan, the establishment of the monarchy, and the exile and return from captivity. Each of these great acts of God in history is interpreted for us in God's own words in Scripture. The Old Testament closes with the expectation of the Messiah to come (Mal 3:1–4; 4:1–6). The next stage in redemptive history is the coming of the Messiah, and it is not surprising that no further Scripture would be written until this next and last great event in the history of redemption occurred.

This is why the New Testament consists of the writings of the apostles. It is primarily the apostles who are given the ability from the Holy Spirit to recall accurately the words and deeds of Jesus and to interpret them rightly for subsequent generations.

Jesus promised this empowering to his disciples (who were

called apostles after the resurrection) in John 14:26 (RSV): 'But the Counsellor, the Holy Spirit, whom the Father will send in my name, he will teach you all things, and bring to your remembrance all that I have said to you.' Similarly, Jesus promised further revelation of truth from the Holy Spirit when he told his disciples:

> When the Spirit of truth comes, he will guide you into all the truth; for he will not speak on his own authority, but whatever he hears he will speak, and he will declare to you the things that are to come. He will glorify me, for he will take what is mine and declare it to you (Jn 16:13–14, RSV).

Thus, the disciples are promised amazing gifts to enable them to write Scripture: the Holy Spirit would teach them 'all things', would cause them to remember 'all' that Jesus had said, and would guide them into 'all the truth'.

Furthermore, those who have the office of apostle in the early church are seen to claim an authority equal to that of the Old Testament prophets, an authority to speak and write words which are God's very words. Peter encourages his readers to remember 'the commandment of the Lord and Saviour through your apostles' (2 Pet 3:2, RSV). To lie to the apostles (Acts 5:2) is equivalent to lying to the Holy Spirit (Acts 5:3) and lying to God (Acts 5:4).

This claim to be able to speak words which were the words of God himself is especially frequent in the writings of the Apostle Paul. He claims not only that the Holy Spirit has revealed to him 'what no eye has seen, nor ear heard, nor the heart of man conceived' (1 Cor 2:9, RSV), but also that when he declares this revelation, he speaks it 'in words not taught by human wisdom but taught by God's Spirit, interpreting spiritual things in spiritual words' (1 Cor 2:13).[129]

Similarly, Paul tells the Corinthians, 'If any one thinks that he is a prophet, or spiritual, he should acknowledge that what I am writing to you is a command of the Lord' (1 Cor 14:37, RSV). The word translated 'what' in this verse is a plural relative pronoun in Greek (*ha*) and more literally could be translated, 'The things that I am writing to you.' Thus, Paul claims that his directives to the church at Corinth are not merely his own but a command of the Lord. In defending his apostolic office, Paul says that he will give the Corinthians 'proof that Christ is speaking in me' (2 Cor 13:3, RSV). Other similar verses could be mentioned (for example, Rom 2:16; Gal 1:8-9; 1 Thess 2:13; 4:8,15; 5:27; 2 Thess 3:6, 14).

The apostles, then, have authority to write words which are God's own words, equal in truth status and authority to the words of the Old Testament Scriptures. They do this in order to record, interpret, and apply to the lives of believers the great truths about the life, death and resurrection of Christ.

It would not be surprising therefore to find some of the New Testament writings being placed with the Old Testament Scriptures as part of the canon of Scripture. In fact, this is what we find in at least two instances. In 2 Peter 3:16 (RSV), speaking of Paul's letters, Peter says, 'There are some things in them hard to understand, which the ignorant and unstable twist to their own destruction, as they do the other scriptures.' The word translated 'Scriptures' here is *graphē*, a word which occurs fifty times in the New Testament and which refers to the Old Testament Scriptures in every one of those fifty occurrences. Thus, the word 'Scripture' was a technical term for the New Testament authors and it was used only of those writings which were thought to be God's words, or were thought to be part of the canon of Scripture. But in this verse, Peter classifies Paul's writings with the 'other scriptures' (meaning the Old Testament Scriptures). Paul's writings are therefore considered by Peter also to be worthy of the title 'Scripture' and thus worthy of inclusion in the canon.

A second instance is found in 1 Timothy 5:17–18. Paul says, 'Let the elders who rule well be considered worthy of double honour, especially those who labour in preaching and teaching; *for the scripture says*, 'You shall not muzzle an ox when it is treading out the grain,' and, 'The labourer deserves his wages'

(1 Tim 5:17–18, RSV). The first quotation from Scripture is found in Deuteronomy 25:4, but the second quotation, 'The labourer deserves his wages,' is found nowhere in the Old Testament. It does occur, however, in Luke 10:7 (with exactly the same words in the Greek text). So here we have Paul apparently quoting a portion of Luke's gospel and calling it 'Scripture', that is, something which is to be considered part of the canon.[130]

Thus, the New Testament began to grow and its writings began to be accepted as part of the canon by the early church.

Because the apostles by virtue of their apostolic office had authority to write words of Scripture, any authentic writing of the apostles was accepted by the early church as part of the canon of Scripture. If we accept the arguments for the traditional views of authorship of the New Testament writings,[131] then we have most of the New Testament in the canon because of direct authorship by the apostles. This would include Matthew, John, Romans to Philemon (all of the Pauline epistles), James,[132] 1 and 2 Peter, 1, 2, and 3 John and Revelation.

This leaves five books: Mark, Luke, Acts, Hebrews and Jude, which were not written by apostles. The details of the historical process by which these books came to be counted as part of Scripture by the early church are scarce, but Mark, Luke and Acts were commonly acknowledged very early, probably because of the close association of Mark with the apostle Peter, and of Luke (the author of Luke-Acts) with the Apostle Paul. Similarly, Jude apparently was accepted by virtue of the author's connection with James (see Jude 1) and the fact that he was the brother of Jesus.[133]

The acceptance of Hebrews as canonical was urged by many in the church on the basis of an assumed Pauline authorship. But from very early times there were others who rejected Pauline authorship in favour of one or another of several different suggestions. Origen, who died about A.D. 254, mentions various theories of authorship and concludes, 'But who actually wrote the epistle, only God knows.'[134] Thus, the acceptance of Hebrews as canonical was not entirely due to a belief in Pauline authorship. Rather, the intrinsic qualities of the book itself must have finally convinced early readers, as they continue to convince believers today, that whoever its human author may have been, its ultimate divine author can only have been God himself. The majestic glory of Christ shines forth from the pages of the epistle to the Hebrews so brightly that no believer who reads it seriously should ever want to question its place in the canon.

This brings us to the heart of the question of canonicity. The final criterion for deciding whether a writing belongs in the canon or not is divine authorship. If the words of the book are God's words (through human authors), then the book belongs in the canon. If the words of the book are not God's words, it does not belong in the canon. The question of authorship by an apostle is important because it was primarily the apostles to whom Christ gave the ability to write words with absolute divine authority. If a writing can be shown to be by an apostle, then its absolute divine authority is automatically established. Thus, the early church automatically accepted the writings of the apostles as part of the canon.

But the existence of some New Testament writings which were not authored directly by apostles shows that there were others in the early church to whom Christ also gave the ability, through the work of the Holy Spirit, to write words which were God's own words and also therefore part of the canon. In these cases, the early church had the task of *recognizing* which writings had the characteristic of being God's own words (through human authors).

For some books (at least Mark, Luke and Acts, and perhaps Hebrews and Jude as well), the church had, at least in some areas, the personal testimony of some living apostles to affirm the absolute divine authority of these books. In other cases, and in some geographical areas, the church simply had to decide whether it heard the voice of God himself speaking in the words of these writings. In these cases, the words of these books would have been *self-attesting*, that is, the words would have borne witness to their own divine authorship as Christians read them. Especially with the book of Hebrews, this seems to have been the case.

Yet it should not be surprising that the church would ultimately be able to make such a decision quite well, for Jesus had said, 'My sheep hear my voice, and I know them, and they follow me' (Jn 10:27, RSV). It is in fact true that God's people hear the voice of God speaking in the words of Scripture as they hear them in no other writings. It should not be thought impossible or unlikely, therefore, that the early church would be able to use a combination of factors, including apostolic endorsement, consistency with the rest of Scripture, and the perception of a writing as 'God-breathed' on the part of an overwhelming majority of believers, to decide that a writing was in fact God's words (through a human author) and therefore worthy of inclusion in the canon. Nor should it be thought unlikely that the church would be able to use this process over a period of time— as writings were circulated to various parts of the early church—and finally to come to a completely correct decision, without excluding any writings that were in fact 'God-breathed', and without including any that were not.

In A.D. 367, the thirty-ninth Paschal Letter of Athanasius contained an exact list of the twenty-seven New Testament books we have today. This was the list of books accepted by the churches in the eastern part of the Mediterranean world. Thirty years later, in A.D. 397, the Council of Carthage, representing the church in the western part of the Mediterranean world, agreed with the East on the same list. These are the earliest final lists of our present-day canon.

Should we expect any more writings to be added to the canon? The first two verses of the Epistle to the Hebrews put this question in the proper historical perspective, the perspective of the history of redemption:

In many parts and in various ways God spoke of old to the fathers by the prophets, but in these last days he has spoken to us by a Son, whom he appointed the heir of all things, through whom also he created the world (Heb 1:1–2).

The contrast here is between two ways of God's speaking to mankind. On the one hand, there are God's words in the Old Testament which came 'in many parts and in various ways'. The implied contrast with 'many parts and various ways' is speaking by God in *one part* and in *one way*, namely, 'by a Son'. The contrast between the former speaking 'of old' and the recent speaking 'in these last days' suggests that God's speech to us by his Son is the culmination of his speaking to mankind, and is his greatest and final revelation to mankind in this period of redemptive history. The exceptional greatness of the revelation which comes through the Son, far exceeding any revelation in the Old Covenant, is emphasized again and again throughout chapters 1 and 2 of Hebrews. These facts all indicate that there is a finality to the revelation of God in Christ and that once this revelation has been completed, no more is to be expected.

But where do we learn about this revelation through Christ? The New Testament writings contain the final, authoritative and sufficient interpretation of Christ's work of redemption. The apostles and their close companions report Christ's words and deeds and interpret them with absolute divine authority. When they have finished their writing, there is no more to be added with the same absolute divine authority. Thus, once the writings of the New Testament apostles and their authorized companions are completed, we have in written form the final record of everything that God wants us to know about the life, death and resurrection of Christ, and its meaning for the lives of believers for all time. Since this is God's greatest revelation for mankind, no more is to be expected once this is complete. In this way, then, Hebrews 1:1–2 shows us why no more writings can be added to the Bible after the time of the New Testament. The canon is now closed.

Of course, it is not Hebrews 1:1–2 alone that proves the finality of the New Testament revelation that we now have, but rather the truth about the history of redemption which is represented in this passage, and which comes to such clear expression in these two verses.

A similar kind of consideration might be drawn from Revelation 22:18–19:

> I warn every one who hears the words of the prophecy of this book: if any one adds to them, God will add to him the plagues described in this book, and if any one takes away from the words of the book of this prophecy, God will take away his share in the tree of life and in the holy city, which are described in this book (Rev 22:18–19, RSV).

The primary reference of these verses is clearly to the book of Revelation itself, for John refers to his writing as 'the words of the prophecy of this book' in verses 7 and 10 of this chapter (and the entire book is called a prophecy in Revelation 1:3). Furthermore, the reference to 'the tree of life and ... the holy city, which are described in this book' indicates that the book of Revelation itself is intended.

But if we believe in God's providential care in the writing of Scripture, we will not view it as accidental that this statement comes at the end of the last chapter of Revelation, and that Revelation is the last book in the New Testament. In fact, Revelation has to be placed last in the canon. For many books, their placement in the assembling of the canon is of little consequence. But just as Genesis must be placed first (for it tells us of creation), so Revelation must be placed last (for its focus is to tell us of the future). The events described in Revelation are historically subsequent to the events described in the rest of the New Testament and require that Revelation be placed where it is. Thus, it is not inappropriate for us to understand this exceptionally strong warning at the end of Revelation as applying in a secondary way to the whole of Scripture. Placed here, where it must be placed, the warning forms an appropriate conclusion to the entire canon of Scripture. Along with Hebrews 1:1–2 and the history-of-redemption perspective implicit in those verses, this passage also indicates to us that we should expect no more Scripture to be added beyond what we already have, at least not until a new stage of redemptive history is inaugurated by the Lord's return.

How do we know, then, that we have the right books in the canon of Scripture which we now possess? The question can be answered in two different ways. First, if we are asking *what we should base our confidence on*, the answer must ultimately be that our confidence is based on the faithfulness of God. We know that God loves his people, and it is supremely important that God's people have his own words, for they are our life (Deut 32:47; Mt 4:4). They are more precious, more important to us, than anything else in this world. We also know that God our Father is in control of all history, and he is not the kind of Father who will trick us or fail to be faithful to us or keep from us something we absolutely need.

The severity of the punishments in Revelation 22:18–19 which come to those who add to or take from God's words also confirms the importance for God's people of having a correct canon. If one adds to the words of the prophecy 'God will add to him the plagues described in this book', and if one takes away from the words of this prophecy, 'God will take away his share in the tree of life and in the holy city' (Rev 22:18–19, RSV). There could be no greater punishments than these, for they are the punishments of eternal judgement. This shows that God himself places supreme value on our having a correct collection of God-breathed writings, no more and no less. In light of this fact, could it be right for us to believe that God our Father, who controls all history, would allow all of his church for almost 2,000 years to be deprived of something which he himself values so highly, and which is so necessary for our spiritual lives?[135]

The preservation and correct assembling of the canon of Scripture should ultimately be seen by believers, then, not as part of church history subsequent to God's great central acts of redemption for his people, but as an integral part of the history of redemption itself. Just as God was at work in creation, in the calling of his people Israel, in the life, death and resurrection of Christ, and in the early work and writings of the apostles, so God was at work in the preservation and assembling of the books of Scripture for the benefit of his people for the entire church age. Ultimately, then, we base our confidence in the correctness of our present canon on the faithfulness of God.

But the question of how we know that we have the right books can be answered in a somewhat different way as well. We might wish to focus on *the process by which we become persuaded* that the books we have now in the canon are the right ones. In this process two factors are at work: the activity of the Holy Spirit convincing us as we read Scripture for ourselves, and the historical data which we have available for our consideration.

Regarding the work of the Holy Spirit, we can say that the Holy Spirit works *as we read Scripture* to convince us that the books we have in Scripture are all from God and are his words to us. Jesus said, 'My sheep hear my voice, and I know them, and they follow me' (Jn 10:27, RSV), and as Christians read Scripture they hear the voice of their Saviour and their God speaking to them in these words. It has been the testimony of Christians throughout the ages that as they read the books of the Bible, and then as they read other books, they realize that the words of Scripture speak to their heart as no other books do. Day after day, year after year, Christians find that the words of the Bible are indeed the words of God speaking to them with an authority, a power and a persuasiveness that no other writings possess. Truly the word of God is 'living and active, sharper than any two-edged sword, piercing to the division of soul and spirit, of joints and marrow, and discerning the thoughts and intentions of the heart' (Heb 4:12, RSV).

Yet the process by which we become persuaded that the present canon is right is also helped by historical data. Of course, if indeed the assembling of the canon is one part of God's central acts in the history of redemption (as was stated above), then Christians today should not presume to take it upon themselves to attempt to add to or subtract from the books of the canon. Nevertheless, a thorough investigation of the historical circumstances surrounding the assembling of the canon is helpful in confirming our conviction that the decisions made by the early church were correct decisions. Some of this historical data has been mentioned in the preceding pages. Other, more detailed, data is available for those who wish to pursue more specialized investigations.[136]

Yet one further historical fact should be mentioned: there are in existence today no strong candidates for addition to the canon and there are no strong objections to any book presently in the canon. Of those writings which early in the church were thought by some to be appropriate for inclusion in the canon, it is safe to say that there are none which present-day evangelicals would ever want to include. Some of the very early writers distinguished themselves quite clearly from the apostles, and their writings from the writings of the apostles. Ignatius, for example, says, 'I do not order you as did Peter and Paul; they were apostles, I am a convict; they were free, I am even until now a slave' (Ignatius, *To the Romans*, 4.3; compare the attitude towards the apostles in 1 Clement 42:1,2; 44:1–2; Ignatius, *To the Magnesians*, 7:1; 13:1–2, *et al*).

In other writings, even those that were for a time thought by some to be worthy of inclusion in the canon, there are doctrinal teachings which are contradictory to the rest of Scripture. 'The Shepherd' of Hermas, for example, teaches 'the necessity of penance' and

> the possibility of the forgiveness of sins at least once after baptism.... The author seems to identify the Holy Spirit with the Son of God before the Incarnation, and to hold that the Trinity came into existence only after the humanity of Christ had been taken up into heaven (*Oxford Dictionary of the Christian Church*, p. 641).

The Gospel of Thomas, which for a time was held by some to belong to the canon, ends with the following statement (par. 114):

Simon Peter said to them: Let Mary go away from us, for women are not worthy of life. Jesus said: Lo, I shall lead her, so that I may make her a male, that she too may become a living spirit, resembling you males. For every woman who makes herself a male will enter the kingdom of heaven.

All other existing documents which in the early church had any possibility of inclusion in the canon are similar to these in that they either contain explicit disclaimers of canonical status or include some doctrinal aberrations which clearly make them unworthy of inclusion in the Bible.

On the other hand, there are no strong objections to any book currently in the canon. In the case of several New Testament books which were slow to gain approval by the whole church (books such as 2 Peter or 2 and 3 John), much of the early hesitancy over their inclusion can be attributed to the fact that they were not initially circulated very widely, and that full knowledge of the contents of all the New Testament writings spread through the church rather slowly. (Martin Luther's hesitancies concerning James are somewhat understandable in light of the doctrinal controversy in which he was engaged, but such hesitancy was certainly not necessary. The apparent doctrinal difficulties are easily resolved once it is recognized that James is using three key terms: justification, faith, and works in senses different from those in which Paul used them.)[137]

There is therefore historical confirmation for the correctness of the current canon. Yet it must be remembered in connection with any historical investigation that the work of the early church was not to *bestow divine authority* or even ecclesiastical authority upon some merely human writings, but rather to *recognize* the divinely authored characteristic of writings that already had such a quality. This is because the ultimate criterion of canonicity is divine authorship, not human or ecclesiastical approval.[138]

At this point someone may ask a hypothetical question about what we should do if another one of Paul's epistles were dis-

covered, for example. Would we add it to Scripture? The answer should probably be that if a great majority of believers
were convinced that this was indeed an authentic Pauline epistle, written in the course of Paul's fulfilment of his apostolic
office, then the nature of Paul's apostolic authority would
require that this epistle would also be God's own words, and
that therefore it should be added to Scripture. Its divine
authorship would also guarantee that its teachings would be
consistent with the rest of Scripture. But it must immediately
be said that such a hypothetical question is just that: hypothetical. It is exceptionally difficult to imagine what kind of historical data might be discovered that could convincingly
demonstrate to the church as a whole that a letter lost for over
1,900 years was genuinely authored by Paul, and it is more
difficult still to understand how our sovereign God could have
faithfully cared for his people for over 1,900 years and still
allowed them to be continually deprived of something which he
intended them to have as part of his final revelation of himself
in Jesus Christ. These considerations make it so highly improb-
able that any such manuscript would be discovered at some
time in the future, that such a hypothetical question really does
not merit further serious consideration. It is mere speculation
and devoid of present value for the church.

In conclusion, are there any books in our present canon
which should not be there? No. We can rest our confidence in
this fact in the faithfulness of God our Father, who would not
lead all his people for nearly 2,000 years to trust as his word
something that is not. And we find our confidence repeatedly
confirmed both by historical investigation and by the work of
the Holy Spirit in enabling us to hear God's voice in a unique
way as we read from every one of the sixty-six books in our present canon of Scripture.

But are there any missing books; books which should have
been included in Scripture but were not? The answer must be
no. In all known literature there are no candidates that even
come close to Scripture when consideration is given both to

their doctrinal consistency with the rest of Scripture and to the type of authority which they claim for themselves (as well as the way those claims of authority have been received by other believers). Once again, God's faithfulness to his people convinces us that there is nothing missing from Scripture that God thinks we need to know for obeying him and trusting him fully. The canon of Scripture today is exactly what God wanted it to be, and it will stay that way until Christ returns.

Some study questions for personal application

Why is it important to your Christian life to know which writings are God's words and which are not? How would your relationship with God be different if you had to look for his words which were scattered among all the writings of Christians throughout church history? How would your Christian life be different if God's words were contained not only in the Bible but also in the official declarations of the church throughout history?

Have you had doubts or questions about the canonicity of any of the books of the Bible? What caused those questions? What should someone do to resolve them?

From time to time one hears of the publication of a book containing 'the unknown sayings of Jesus' or 'the lost books of the Bible' or 'the Scriptures which the early church suppressed' or 'the story of Jesus' boyhood'. Sometimes these are hoaxes, but usually they are legitimate English translations of quite ancient documents, some of them dating from the first or second century A.D. For what reason might these writings be valuable? What are the dangers in publicizing them with titles such as those mentioned above? With what attitude should a Christian read them? Would you like to read some of these writings? Why? Would it make any difference to your Christian life if you never read these non-canonical writings?

Mormons, Jehovah's Witnesses and members of other cults have claimed present-day revelations from God which they count equal to the Bible in authority. What reasons can you give to indicate the falsity of those claims? In practice, do these people treat the Bible as an authority equal to these other 'revelations'?

Those who wish to examine the Old Testament Apocrypha can read it in modern English translation.[139] Compare the effect which these writings have on you with the effect Scripture has on you. Some may want to make a similar comparison with some writings from a collection of books called the *New Testament Apocrypha*.[140] Is the spiritual effect of these writings on your life positive or negative? How does it compare with the spiritual effect which the Bible has on your life? (My personal experience has been that after reading some of this literature, returning to the Bible itself has been like a breath of fresh air. In contrast with these writings the Bible has an evident majesty, dignity and God-breathed quality which none of them share. Many other Christians have told me of similar impressions: in the Bible they hear the voice of their Creator speaking to their hearts as in no other writings. Because this is so, I think that an examination of these other writings will generally strengthen, not weaken a Christian's confidence in the unique divine authority of the Bible.)

This appendix has been taken from the author's forthcoming book *Systematic Theology: An Introductory Course* and is printed here by permission of Inter-Varsity Press (United Kingdom).

APPENDIX C

The Sufficiency of Scripture

Explanation and scriptural basis

Are we to look for other words from God in addition to what we have in Scripture? The doctrine of the *sufficiency of Scripture* addresses that question.

We can define the sufficiency of Scripture as follows:

> The *sufficiency of Scripture* means that Scripture contains all the words of God which he intends his people to have at each stage of redemptive history, and that it contains everything we need God to tell us for salvation, for trusting him perfectly and for obeying him perfectly.

This definition emphasizes the fact that it is in Scripture alone that we are to search for God's words to us. It also reminds us that God considers what he has told us in the Bible to be enough for us, and that we should rejoice in the great revelation that he has given us and be content with it.

Significant scriptural support and explanation of this doctrine is found in 2 Timothy, where Paul tells Timothy, 'From childhood you have known the sacred writings which are able to make you wise unto salvation through faith in Jesus Christ' (2 Tim 3:15). The context shows that 'sacred writings' here means the written words of Scripture (2 Tim 3:16). This is an indication that the words of God which we have in Scripture are all the words of God we need in order to be saved: these words are able to make us wise 'unto salvation'. This is confirmed by other passages which talk about the words of Scripture as the means God uses to bring us to salvation (Jas 1:18; 1 Pet 1:23).

Other passages indicate that the Bible is sufficient to equip us for living the Christian life. Once again Paul writes to Timothy:

> All Scripture is God-breathed and profitable for teaching, for reproof, for correction, and for training in righteousness, in order that the man of God may be complete, equipped for every good work (2 Tim 3:16–17).

Here Paul indicates that one purpose for which God caused Scripture to be written was to train us that we might be 'equipped for *every good work*'. If there is any 'good work' which God wants a Christian to do, this passage indicates that God has made provision in his word for training the Christian in it. Thus, there is *no* 'good work' which God wants us to do other than those that are taught somewhere in Scripture. It can equip us for *every* good work.

A similar teaching is found in Psalm 119: 'Blessed are those whose way is blameless, who walk in the law of the Lord!' (v.1, RSV). This verse shows an equivalence between being 'blameless' and 'walking in the law of the Lord': those who are blameless *are* those who walk in the law of the Lord. Here again is an indication that *all* that God requires of us is recorded in his written word. Simply to do all that the Bible commands us is to be blameless in God's sight.

In order to be morally perfect in God's sight, then, what must we do in addition to what God commands us in Scripture? Nothing! Nothing at all! If we simply keep the words of Scripture we will be 'blameless' and we will be doing 'every good work' which God expects of us.

Now we realize that we will never perfectly obey all of Scripture in this life (see 1 Jn 1:8–10; Jas 3:2). Thus, it may not at first seem very significant to say that all we have to do is what God commands us in the Bible, since we will never obey it all in this life anyway.

But this truth is of great significance to our Christian lives, for it enables us to *focus* our search for God's words to us on the Bible alone and saves us from the endless task of searching through all the writings of Christians throughout history, or through all the teachings of the church, or through all the subjective feelings and impressions that come to our minds from day to day,[141] in order to find what God requires of us. In a very practical sense, it means that we are *able* to come to clear conclusions on many teachings of Scripture.

It does require some work, but it is *possible* to find all the biblical passages that are directly relevant to the matters of marriage and divorce, for example, or the responsibilities of parents to children, or the relationship between a Christian and civil government, or our responsibility for truthfulness in speech. It means, moreover, that it is possible to collect all the passages that directly relate to doctrinal issues such as the atonement, or the person of Christ, or the work of the Holy Spirit in the believer's life today. In these and hundreds of other moral and doctrinal questions, the biblical teaching about the *sufficiency* of Scripture gives us confidence that we *will* be able to find what God requires us to think or to do in these areas. In many of these areas we can attain confidence that we, together with the vast majority of the church throughout history, *have* found and correctly formulated what God wants us to think or to do. Simply stated, this doctrine of the sufficiency of Scripture enables us to study systematic theology and ethics and find answers to our questions.

At this point we differ from Roman Catholic theologians, who would say that we have not found all that God says to us about any particular subject until we have listened also to the official teaching of the church throughout its history. We would respond that although the history of the church may help us to *understand* what God says to us in the Bible, never in church history has God added to the content of Scripture, or added any words addressed to mankind which are equal to Scripture in authority. Nowhere in church history outside of Scripture has

God added any additional things which he requires us to believe or to do. Scripture is sufficient to equip us for 'every good work', and to walk in its ways is to be 'blameless' in God's sight.

At this point we also differ from non-evangelical theologians who are not convinced that the Bible is God's word in any unique or absolutely authoritative sense, and who would therefore search not only the Bible but also many other early Christian writings in an attempt to find not so much what God said to mankind but rather what many early Christians experienced in their relationship with God, or with Christ. They would attempt to find, therefore, not a single, unified conclusion about what God wants us to think or do with regard to any particular question, but a diversity of opinions and viewpoints collected around some major unifying ideas. All of these viewpoints held by early Christians in any of the early churches would then be potentially valid viewpoints for Christians to hold today as well. To this we would reply that our search for answers to theological and ethical questions is not a search to find what various believers have thought in the history of the church, but is a search to find and understand what God himself says to us in his own words, and that these words are found in Scripture and only in Scripture.

It must be stated that the doctrine of the sufficiency of Scripture does not imply that *God* cannot add any more words to those he has already spoken to his people. It rather implies that *man* cannot add on his own initiative any words to those that God has already spoken. Furthermore, it implies that in fact God *has not* spoken to mankind any more words which he expects us to believe or obey other than those which we have now in the Bible.

This point is important for it helps us to understand how God could tell his people that his words to them were sufficient at many different points in the history of redemption, and how he could nevertheless add to those words at later points in the history of redemption. For example, in Deuteronomy 29:29 (RSV)

Moses says, 'The secret things belong to the Lord our God; but the things that are revealed belong to us and to our children for ever, that we may do all the words of this law.'

This verse reminds us that God has always taken the initiative in revealing things to us. He has decided what to reveal and what not to reveal. At each stage in redemptive history, the things that God had revealed were for his people for that time, and they were to study, believe, and obey those things. With further progress in the history of redemption, more of God's words were added, recording and interpreting that history (see appendix B above regarding the development of the canon). Thus, at the time of the death of Moses, the first five books of our Old Testament were sufficient for God's people *at that time*. But God directed later authors to add more so that Scripture would be sufficient for believers in those subsequent times. For Christians today, the words from God which we have in the Old and New Testaments together are sufficient for us *during the church age*. After the death, resurrection and ascension of Christ, and the founding of the early church as recorded in the New Testament, no further central redemptive acts of God in history (acts which have direct relevance for all God's people for all subsequent time) have occurred, and thus no further words of God have been given to record and interpret those acts for us.

This means that we can cite Scripture texts from throughout the canon to show that the principle of the sufficiency of God's revelation to his people at each particular time has remained the same. In this sense, these verses which talk about the sufficiency of Scripture in earlier periods are directly applicable to us as well, even though the extent of the Bible to which they refer in our situation is greater than the extent of the Scripture to which they referred in their original setting. The following texts from Scripture thus apply to us also in that sense:

Deuteronomy 4:2: (RSV)—'You shall not add to the word which I command you, nor take from it; that you may keep the commandments of the Lord your God which I command you.'

Deuteronomy 12:32: (RSV)— 'Everything that I command you you shall be careful to do; you shall not add to it or take from it.'

Proverbs 30:5-6: (RSV)—'Every word of God proves true; he is a shield to those who take refuge in him. Do not add to his words, lest he rebuke you, and you be found a liar.'

Revelation 22:18-19: (RSV)—'I warn every one who hears the words of the prophecy of this book: if any one adds to them, God will add to him the plagues described in this book, and if any one takes away from the words of the book of this prophecy, God will take away his share in the tree of life and in the holy city, which are described in this book.'[142]

From this doctrine of the sufficiency of Scripture we can derive several practical applications for our Christian lives. The following list is intended to be helpful but not exhaustive in that regard.

1. The sufficiency of Scripture should encourage us whenever we are trying to discover what God would have us to think (regarding some particular doctrinal issue of concern to us) or to do (regarding a particular situation which has come into our lives). We should be encouraged that everything God wants to tell us about that question is to be found in Scripture. This does not mean that the Bible has unlimited answers to all the questions that might be thought up by our idle curiosity, for 'the secret things belong to the Lord our God' (Deut 29:29, RSV). But it does mean that when we are facing a problem of genuine importance to our Christian life, we should approach Scripture with the confidence that from it God will provide us with guidance for that problem.

There will of course be some times when the answer we find is that Scripture does not speak directly to our question. (This would be the case, for example, if we tried to find from Scripture what 'order of worship' to follow on Sunday mornings, or whether it is better to kneel or perhaps to stand when we pray, or at what time we should eat our meals during the day. In those cases, we may conclude that God has not required us to think or to act in any certain way with regard to that question (except, perhaps, in terms of more general principles regarding our attitudes and goals). But in many other cases we will find direct and clear guidance from the Lord to equip us for 'every good work' (2 Tim 3:17, RSV).

As we go through life, frequent practise in searching Scripture for guidance will result in greater and greater ability to find accurate, carefully formulated answers to our problems and questions. Lifelong growth in understanding Scripture will thus include growth in the skill of rightly understanding and applying the Bible's teachings to specific questions.

2. The sufficiency of Scripture reminds us that we are to add nothing to Scripture, and that we are to consider no other writings of equal value to Scripture. This implication is violated by almost all cults and sects. Mormons claim to believe the Bible, for example, but also claim divine authority for the *Book of Mormon*. Christian Scientists similarly claim to believe the Bible but in practice hold the book, *Science and Health with a Key to the Scriptures*, by Mary Baker Eddy, on a par with Scripture or above it in authority. These practices violate God's commands not to add to his words, and we should not think that any additional words from God to us would be found in these writings.

3. The sufficiency of Scripture also tells us that God does not require us to believe anything about himself or his redemptive work which is not found in Scripture. Among the collections of writings from the time of the early church are some collections of alleged sayings of Jesus which were not preserved in the gospels. It is likely that at least some of the 'sayings of Jesus' found in these writings are rather accurate records of things Jesus actually said (though it is now impossible for us to determine with any high degree of probability which sayings those are). But it does not really matter at all for our Christian lives if we ever read any of those sayings, for God has caused to be recorded in Scripture everything that we need to know about Jesus' words and deeds in order to trust and obey him perfectly.

What more could we want? These collections of sayings do have some limited value in linguistic research and perhaps in the study of the history of the church, but they are of no direct value whatever for us in learning what we should believe about the life and teachings of Christ, or in formulating our doctrinal or ethical convictions.

4. The sufficiency of Scripture shows us that no modern revelations from God are to be placed on a level equal to Scripture in authority. At various times throughout the history of the church, and particularly in the modern charismatic movement, people have claimed that God gave revelations through them for the benefit of the church. However we may evaluate such claims, we must be careful never to allow (in theory or in practice) the placing of such revelations on a level equal to Scripture. (In fact, the more responsible spokesmen for the modern charismatic movement seem generally to agree with this caution.) We must insist that God does not require us to believe anything about himself or his work in the world which is contained in these revelations but not in Scripture. And we must insist that God does not require us to obey any moral directives which come to us through such means but are not confirmed by Scripture. The Bible contains everything we need God to tell us for trusting and obeying him perfectly.[143]

It should also be noted at this point that whenever challenges to the sufficiency of Scripture have come in the form of other documents to be placed alongside Scripture (whether from extra-biblical Christian literature of the first century, or from the accumulated teachings of the Roman Catholic church, or from the books of various cults such as the *Book of Mormon*), the result has always been (i) to de-emphasize the teachings of the Bible itself; and (ii) to begin to teach some things which are contrary to Scripture. This is a danger of which the church must constantly be aware.

5. With regard to living the Christian life, the sufficiency of Scripture reminds us that nothing is sin which is not forbidden by Scripture (either explicitly or by implication). To walk in the

law of the Lord *is* to be 'blameless' (Ps 119:1). Therefore we are not to add prohibitions beyond those already stated in Scripture. From time to time there may be situations in which it would be wrong, for example, to drink coffee or Coca-cola, to go to the cinema, or to eat meat offered to idols (see 1 Cor 8–10), but unless some specific teaching or some general principle of Scripture can be shown to prohibit these (or any other activities) for all believers for all time, we must insist that these activities are not *in themselves* sinful and they are not *in all situations* prohibited by God for his people.

This also is an important principle because there is always the tendency among believers to begin to neglect the regular daily searching of Scripture for guidance and to begin to live by a set of written or unwritten rules (or denominational traditions) concerning what one does or does not do in the Christian life.

Furthermore, whenever we add to the list of sins which are prohibited by Scripture itself, there will be harm to the church and to the lives of individual believers in other ways. The Holy Spirit will not empower obedience to rules which do not have God's approval from Scripture,[144] nor will believers generally find delight in obedience to commands which do not accord with the laws of God written on their hearts. In some cases, Christians may repeatedly and earnestly plead with God for 'victory' over supposed sins which are in fact no sins at all, so no 'victory' will be given because the attitude or action in question is in fact not displeasing to God. Great discouragement in prayer and frustration in the Christian life generally may be the outcome.

In other cases, continued or even increasing disobedience to these new 'sins' will result, together with a false sense of guilt and a resulting alienation from God which should never have occurred. There will often arise as well an increasingly uncompromising and legalistic insistence on these new rules by those who do follow them, and genuine fellowship among believers in the church will fade away. Evangelism will often be stifled, for the silent proclamation of the gospel which comes from the lives of believers will at least seem to include the additional requirement that one must fit this uniform pattern of life in order to become a member of this body of Christ.

One clear example of such an addition to the commands of Scripture is found in the opposition of the Roman Catholic Church to 'artificial' methods of birth control, a policy which finds no valid support in Scripture. Widespread disobedience, alienation and false guilt have been the result. Yet such is the propensity of human nature to make such rules that other examples can probably be found in the written or unwritten traditions of almost every denomination.

6. A parallel consideration to the preceding one is the fact that the sufficiency of Scripture tells us that nothing is required of us by God which is not commanded in Scripture (either explicitly or by implication). This reminds us that the focus of our search for God's will ought to be on Scripture, not primarily on seeking guidance through prayer for changed circumstances or altered feelings or direct guidance from the Holy Spirit apart from Scripture. It also means that if someone claims to have a message from God for us concerning what we ought to do, we need never think that it is sin to disobey such a message unless it can be confirmed by the application of Scripture itself to our situation.

The discovery of this great truth could bring tremendous joy and peace to the lives of thousands of Christians who spend countless hours seeking God's will outside of Scripture and continually being uncertain about whether they have found it. In fact, in the lives of many Christians today there is probably very little confidence in their ability to discover God's will with much or any certainty. Thus, there is little striving after God's will (for who can know it?), and little growth in holiness before God.

The opposite ought to be true. Christians who are convinced of the sufficiency of Scripture should begin eagerly to seek God's will *and to find it* in Scripture. They should be eagerly and regularly growing in obedience to God. This would result in great freedom and peace in the Christian life, and more and more we would be able to say with the Psalmist: 'I will keep thy law continually, for ever and ever; and I shall walk *at liberty*, for I have sought thy precepts.... Great peace have those who love thy law; nothing can make them stumble' (Ps 119:44–45,165, RSV).

7. The sufficiency of Scripture reminds us that in our doctrinal and ethical teaching we should emphasize what Scripture emphasizes and be content with what God has told us in Scripture. There are some subjects about which God has told us little or nothing in the Bible. We must remember that 'the secret things belong to the Lord our God' (Deut 29:29, RSV) and that God has revealed to us in Scripture exactly what he deemed right for us. We must not be discontent with this and think that Scripture is something less than it should be, or begin to wish that God had given us much more information about subjects on which there are very few scriptural references. Of course there will be some situations where we are confronted with a particular problem that requires a great deal of attention, far greater than the emphasis which it receives in the teaching of Scripture or of the New Testament as a whole. But those situations should be relatively infrequent and should not be representative of the general course of our lives or ministries.

It is characteristic of many cults that they will emphasize obscure portions or teachings of Scripture (one thinks again of the Mormon emphasis on baptism for the dead, a subject which is mentioned in only one verse in the Bible [1 Cor 15:29], in a phrase whose meaning is apparently impossible now to determine with certainty). But a similar error was made by an entire generation of liberal New Testament scholars in the earlier part of this century who devoted most of their scholarly lives to a search for the sources 'behind' our present gospel narratives, or to a search for the 'authentic' sayings of Jesus.

Unfortunately, a similar pattern has too often occurred among evangelicals within various denominations. The doctrinal matters that have divided evangelical Protestant denominations from one another have almost uniformly been matters on which the Bible places relatively little emphasis, and matters in which our conclusions must be drawn from skilful inference much more than from direct biblical statements. (For example, abiding denominational differences have occurred or been maintained over the 'proper' form of church government, the exact nature of Christ's presence in the Lord's Supper, the exact sequence of the events of the last days, the categories of persons who should be admitted to the Lord's Supper, the way in which God planned that the merits of Christ's death would be applied to believers and not applied to unbelievers, the correct subjects for baptism, the proper understanding of the 'baptism in the Holy Spirit', etc.)

We should not say that these issues are all *unimportant*, nor should we say that Scripture gives no solution to any of these questions (indeed, with respect to many of them I plan to defend a specific solution in a forthcoming book in Christian doctrine). But the point here is that all of these topics are ones that receive relatively little direct emphasis in Scripture, and it is ironic and tragic that denominational leaders will so often give vast portions of their lives to defending precisely the minor doctrinal points which make their denominations different from others. Is such effort really motivated by a desire to bring unity of understanding to the church; or by human pride, by a desire to retain power over others, and by an attempt at self-justification which is displeasing to God and ultimately unedifying to the church?

Some study questions for personal application

In the process of growing in the Christian life and deepening your relationship with God, approximately how much emphasis have you placed on reading the Bible itself and how much on reading other Christian books? In seeking to know God's will for your daily life, what is the relative emphasis which you have put on reading Scripture itself and on reading other Christian books? Do you think the doctrine of the sufficiency of Scripture will cause you to place more emphasis on reading Scripture itself?

What are some of the doctrinal or moral questions which you are wondering about right now? Has this discussion increased your confidence in the ability of Scripture to provide a clear answer for some of those questions?

Have you ever wished that the Bible would say more than it does about a certain subject? Or less? What do you think motivated that wish? After reading this Appendix, how would you approach someone who expressed such a wish today? How is God's wisdom shown in the fact that he chose not to make the Bible a great deal longer or a great deal shorter than it actually is?

How might the definition of what it is to be blessed in Psalm 119:1 change your view of what success is in your daily life? In your career?

Sometimes people make decisions based on all the information they have been able to obtain at the time of the decision, but then later learn new information that causes them to feel great regret. (Examples might be a businessman who misses a great investment opportunity, or a person who because of pressing circumstances misses his or her regular daily visit to an aged parent and then learns that the parent died that day.) Can you explain how the doctrine of the sufficiency of Scripture would save Christians from excessive regrets and false guilt in cases like these?

If the Bible contains everything we need God to tell us for obeying him perfectly, what is the role of the following in helping us to find God's will for ourselves: advice from others; sermons or Bible classes; our consciences; our feelings; the leading of the Holy Spirit as we sense him prompting our inward desires and subjective impressions; changes in circumstances; present day prophecy?

In the light of this discussion, how would you find God's perfect will for your life? Is it possible that there would be more than one perfect choice in many decisions which we make? (Consider Ps 1:3 and 1 Cor 7:39 in seeking an answer.)

Are there times when you have understood the principles of Scripture well enough with regard to a specific situation but have not known the facts of the situation well enough to know how to apply those scriptural principles correctly? In seeking to know God's will, can there be any other things we need to know except (a) the teaching of Scripture and (b) the facts of the situation in question, together with (c) skill in applying (a) to (b) correctly? What then is the role of prayer in seeking guidance? What should we pray for?

This appendix has been taken from the author's forthcoming book, *Systematic Theology: An Introductory Course,* and is printed here by permission of Inter-Varsity Press (United Kingdom).

Notes

1. I have argued this extensively elsewhere: see W. A. Grudem, 'Scripture's Self-Attestation and the Problem of Formulating a Doctrine of Scripture' in *Scripture and Truth*, edited by D. A. Carson and John Woodbridge (IVP 1983), pp. 19–59.

2. Thomas Edwards, *A Commentary on the First Epistle to the Corinthians* (Hodder & Stoughton 1903), p. 384.

3. G. W. H. Lampe, '"Grievous wolves" (Acts 20:29),' in *Christ and Spirit in the New Testament*, (Fs. C. F. D. Moule), ed. B. Linders and S. Smalley (Cambridge Univ. Press, 1973), p.258.

4. Erich Fascher, *PROPHĒTĒS: Eine sprach- und religionsgeschichtliche Untersuchung* (Töpelmann 1927).

With respect to the specific question of the Delphic Oracle, it should be noted that the role of the prophet at the oracle differs from that of the Old Testament prophets. The woman who receives the inspired utterance, the Pythia, may be called a *promantis* (with respect to her disclosure of the future) or a *prophētis* (with respect to her role as a mouthpiece of the god). But the *prophētēs*, the 'prophet', was one who heard her words and then interpreted and proclaimed them to the enquirers who were seated in another room. He himself was not inspired by the god in any way. So here the 'prophet' (*prophētēs*) word group is 'neutral in the question whether the person who bears the name is divinely inspired or not'. It may mean simply one who translated the Pythia's semi-coherent babbling into an intelligible response.

5. Christians living inside Palestine also spoke Aramaic, and for many of them it was their primary language, but even in Palestine most people were thoroughly bilingual—fluent in both Greek and

313

Aramaic. Compare A.W. Argyle, 'Greek among the Jews of Palestine in New Testament Times' *NTS* 20 (1974) especially pp. 87–89; J. N. Sevenster, *Do You Know Greek? How Much Greek could the First Jewish Christians Have Known?* NovTSupp 19 (Brill 1968).

6. There are some other instances where prophets are mentioned in Revelation, but little can be said about them. The two prophets in Revelation 11 appear to be special end-time figures who function in the period immediately prior to the Lord's return (note Revelation 11:14 and 15).

None of the other seven uses of the word 'prophet' in Revelation is very specific (Rev 10:7; 11:18; 16:6; 18:20, 24; 22:6). Sometimes Old Testament prophets seem to be in view, and sometimes New Testament prophets, but without further specification of their character or function.

In Revelation 19:10 (RSV) we read, 'For the testimony of Jesus is the spirit of prophecy.' The sentence is difficult to understand with certainty, but apparently 'spirit' here means something like 'essence', or 'central message', or 'main purpose'.

7. Richard B. Gaffin, *Perspectives on Pentecost* (Presbyterian and Reformed 1979), p. 96. Gaffin's discussion on pages 93–102 is the most careful statement of the position that Ephesians 2:20 applies to all prophets in the New Testament churches and shows that the gift of prophecy has ceased.

8. See Appendix B at the end of the book for discussion of the reasons why the New Testament is closed and we are to expect no further writings to be added to it.

9. Gaffin, *Perspectives*, pp. 94–95.

10. See Acts 13:50; 15:2; and in Paul's writings 2 Corinthians 6:7; 7:3; 13:11; Philippians 1:19, 25; 2 Thessalonians 1:4; 2:2. Somewhat ambiguous are Ephesians 1:1; 5:5; and 2 Thessalonians 1:12.

11. It seems that James is to be counted among the apostles, both because of his leadership role demonstrated here in the Jerusalem church and because of his apparent inclusion among the 'apostles' in Galatians 1:19 and 1 Corinthians 15:7. Moreover, he writes with apostolic authority in the epistle of James.

12. Such a picture of the foundational role of the apostles in the church would also be consistent with Jesus' statement to Peter: 'And I tell you, you are Peter, and on this rock I will build my church, and the gates of hell shall not prevail against it' (Mt 16:18), especially if

Peter is understood here as a representative of the apostolic leadership of the early church in his confession of Jesus as the Messiah and the Son of the living God.

13. As we shall see later in this investigation, while the term 'prophet' does emphasize the fact of receiving revelations from God, it in itself says nothing about the question of whether absolute divine authority attaches to the reporting of those revelations to other people. Thus, the word 'prophet' in itself did not imply that the apostles had absolute divine authority—it was their status as 'apostles' which gave them that authority. The word 'prophet' only emphasized one particular function, the function of receiving revelations from God at this particular point.

It should not be objected that adding 'who are also prophets' is redundant because the word 'apostles' already carried the idea of one who received revelations. It is a matter of emphasizing one particular function of the apostles for Paul's immediate purpose in this context. He does the same thing in 1 Timothy 2:7, for example, when he emphasizes his role as 'preacher' and 'teacher' even though those were of course functions that belonged to the office of apostle in itself.

14. Gaffin, *Perspectives,* pp. 93–94.

15. Gaffin, *Perspectives,* pp. 94–95.

16. Technically the word 'fellow-elder' in Greek is not exactly the same, because it has a prefix attached to it in Greek, but the root word is the same and the readers would have immediately seen the connection between the two terms.

17. Roy Clements, for example, suggests that Ephesians 2:20 refers to 'some verbally inspired but non-apostolic figures like Luke and Mark', and that the whole phrase may refer to 'the circle of apostolic witness from whom the New Testament canon derives': see Roy Clements, *Word and Spirit: The Bible and the Gift of Prophecy Today* (UCCF Booklets 1986), p. 21. Although I favour view 4, for reasons explained above, I can see the possibility of this interpretation and its consistency with the rest of what I am suggesting in this book about the gift of prophecy in ordinary New Testament congregations.

18. See Wayne Grudem, *The Gift of Prophecy in 1 Corinthians* (University Press of America 1982), pp. 3–5, 110–113, etc.

19. In 1 Corinthians 11:31 he uses it to mean 'evaluate'; in 11:29 to mean 'distinguish' (or 'evaluate'); in 6:5 to mean 'give a legal judgement'; and in 4:7, to mean 'distinguish'. In Romans 14:1 he apparently

means 'arguments' or 'disputes' by *diakriseis*.

20. I have treated this question of the possible relationship between 1 Corinthians 14:29 and 12:10, and the meaning of 'distinguishing between spirits', in a much more technical article: Wayne Grudem, 'A Response to Gerhard Dautzenberg on 1 Corinthians 12:10', *Biblische Zeitschrift* 22:2 (1978), pp. 253–270.

21. A. Bittlinger, *Gifts and Graces: A Commentary on 1 Corinthians 12–14*, trans. by H. Klassen (Hodder & Stoughton 1967), p. 46.

22. A. Robertson and A. Plummer, *A Critical and Exegetical Commentary on the First Epistle of St. Paul to the Corinthians,* ICC (Clark 1914), p. 267.

23. F. Godet, *Commentary on St. Paul's First Epistle to the Corinthians,* trans. by A. Cusin, 2 vols. (Clark 1898), vol. 2, p. 303.

24. So, for example, D. A. Carson, *Showing the Spirit: A Theological Exposition of 1 Corinthians 12–14* (Baker 1987), p. 120, with references to other literature.

25. This sense of *diakrinō* gains some confirmation also from the fact that in the middle voice it takes a distinctive sense, 'to doubt', a related idea which carries an intensified nuance of weighing closely competing ideas in one's mind.

26. Kenneth L. Gentry, Jr. *The Charismatic Gift of Prophecy: A Reformed Analysis* (Whitefield Seminary Press 1986), mentions the fact that Old Testament prophecies were 'judged', even though they were God's words, but Gentry indicates no awareness of the possibility of a different kind of judging or evaluating in 1 Corinthians, nor does he give consideration to the evidence discussed here suggesting that there was in fact such a difference.

27. Richard B. Gaffin, *Perspectives on Pentecost* (Presbyterian and Reformed 1979), pp. 97–99, affirms that there are not two kinds of revelation from God, one 'canonical' for the whole church, and the other 'private', for individual believers, but he gives no arguments or evidence in support of this statement, and does not show how it can be true in the light of the verses I examine in the immediately following paragraphs here, for example, or of 1 Corinthians 14:24–28. Moreover, the precise question is not really the *kind* of revelation but the authority attaching to the *report* of that revelation to others.

28. Gentry, *Reformed Analysis*, pp. 34–35 seems to suggest that all conversations at Philippi reporting such a revelation of sin would have absolute divine authority, but were limited to the age of the apostles

(and could perhaps have been spoken by prophets 'in all the churches'). But Paul's words suggest no such restriction: He is writing to the entire Philippian church, and talking about God's revealing *anything* in which they weren't acting with a Christ-like mind. It seems to me that Gentry's view requires an inordinately large number of prophets and prophecies at Philippi—and gives too restrictive a view of the way God convicts his people of sin in *anything* in which they are not Christ-like in their thinking (through revealing it to them in their individual consciences, not just through dozens or hundreds of private prophecies all with authority equal to Scripture).

29. Carson, *Showing the Spirit*, p. 163.

30. Gaffin, *Perspectives*, pp. 60–61, rightly concludes that prophecy in 1 Corinthians is connected with revelation, but does not analyse the various strands of evidence we have examined here indicating that prophecy at Corinth had lesser authority than the words of Scripture or the words of the apostles. His discussion of 1 Corinthians 14:29 is subsumed under a discussion of distinguishing between spirits in 1 Corinthians 12:10 (pp. 70–71). But it is doubtful that 'distinguishing between spirits' in 12:10 is, as he says, a 'companion gift' to prophecy, since it is only mentioned once in the New Testament, and the connection with prophecy is not clear there (see above, on 1 Corinthians 12:10).

31. See BAGD, p. 180, III.2.b.

32. BAGD, p. 747.

33. Note also the variant reading in texts $\mathbf{p}^{38}$ (apparently) and **D**, at Acts 19:1–2: 'While Paul was wanting according to his own will to go to Jerusalem, *the Spirit said to him* to return to Asia: And passing through the upper regions he came to Ephesus' (not prophecy).

34. Richard B. Gaffin, *Perspectives on Pentecost* (Presbyterian and Reformed 1979), p. 66.

35. It is sometimes alleged that a number of Old Testament predictions were not fulfilled exactly, but there are generally reasonable solutions for these passages. See, for example, Gleason Archer, *Encyclopedia of Bible Difficulties* (Zondervan 1982).

36. D. A. Carson, *Showing the Spirit: A Theological Exposition of 1 Corinthians 12–14* (Baker 1987), p. 98.

37. Gaffin, *Perspectives*, says it is 'overly pedantic' to see mistakes in Agabus' predictions (p. 66), and notes that 'predictive prophecy can of course be exact and detailed but is not necessarily so' (p. 66).

Yet the point is that the prophecy of Agabus *is* exact and detailed when it is made. The only question is whether the two main details are fulfilled. Gaffin shows no examples elsewhere in Scripture where similar non-fulfilment of details is seen to occur with divinely authoritative Old Testament prophecy—indeed, there would seem to be some difficulty with holding to biblical inerrancy if there were such examples.

38. This is also the position taken by Robert L. Reymond, *What About Continuing Revelations and Miracles in the Presbyterian Church Today?* (Presbyterian and Reformed 1977), p. 28.

39. The conjunction 'but' is not in some ancient manuscripts, but the weight of evidence favours seeing it as in Paul's original epistle. Even without it, however, the negative command (do not despise) followed by the positive command (test) seems to require this sense of contrast: do not reject outright (but) evaluate.

40. Gaffin, *Perspectives,* p. 71, notes that the same Greek word used here for 'test' (*dokimazō*) is also used of 'proving' Paul's apostolic words in Romans 12:2 and Ephesians 5:10, and concludes that the command to 'test' here does not imply lesser authority for New Testament prophecy. However, (1) in both the verses he mentions, it is not apostolic words which are to be 'tested' but patterns of conduct which the believers are to 'try' in practice, and (2) in 1 Thessalonians 5:21 (RSV) the following phrase, 'hold fast to what is good', implies that *some* of what is tested will *not* be good.

41. This argument is from Roy Clements, *Word and Spirit: The Bible and the Gift of Prophecy Today* (UCCF Booklets 1986), p. 24, and Carson, *Showing the Spirit,* p. 96.

42. On the history of prophecy in the early church after the period of the New Testament, note the following: Ronald A. Kydd, *Charismatic Gifts in the Early Church* (Hendriksen 1984) (a detailed recent study which sees wide evidence of 'charismatic' activity in the church up to about the middle of the third century); George Mallone (ed.), *Those Controversial Gifts* (Inter-Varsity 1983), pp. 23–25; Michael Green, *I Believe in the Holy Spirit* (Hodder & Stoughton 1975), pp. 172–174; Max Turner, 'Spiritual Gifts Then and Now', *Vox Evangelica* 15 (1985), pp. 41-43 (with notes to other literature).

43. Bruce Yocum, *Prophecy* (Word of Life 1976), p. 24.

44. Clements, *Word and Spirit*, p. 26.

45. If Acts 13:2 refers to prophecy, it would also fall in this category. But it is doubtful whether we should take it as referring to the gift

of prophecy at all (see discussion above).

46. Dennis and Rita Bennett, *The Holy Spirit and You* (Kingsway 1971), p. 146.

47. Donald Gee, *Spiritual Gifts in the Work of Ministry Today* (Gospel Publishing House 1963), pp. 48–49.

48. Bruce Yocum, *Prophecy* (Word of Life 1976), p. 79. A similar view is found in the popular charismatic writer Don Basham, *A Handbook on Tongues, Interpretation and Prophecy* (Whitaker Books 1971), pp. 111–116. Several other charismatic writers with similar views are quoted in Victor Budgen, *The Charismatics and the Word of God* (Evangelical Press, 1985), pp. 31–32. But Budgen differs, arguing repeatedly that since *some* prophecy (through OT prophets and NT apostles) had absolute authority, *all* prophecy must share such authority. Yet he does not prove this point, which is crucial to his whole book.

49. George Mallone (ed.), *Those Controversial Gifts* (Inter-Varsity 1983), pp. 39–40. Similar views on the non-divinely authoritative nature of New Testament prophecy are found in the non-charismatic writers Charles E. Hummel, *Fire in the Fireplace: Contemporary Charismatic Renewal* (Inter-Varsity 1978), p. 157, and Roy Clements, *Word and Spirit*, p. 25.

50. Gaffin, *Perspectives*, p. 72. See also John F. Macarthur, Jr., *The Charismatics: A Doctrinal Perspective* (Zondervan 1978), chapters 2 and 3, and Budgen, *Charismatics*, pp. 25–44.

51. Donald Bridge, *Signs and Wonders Today* (IVP 1985), pp. 202–204.

52. Timothy Pain, *Prophecy*, Ashburnham Insights Series (Kingsway 1986), p. 56. Bruce Yokum, *Prophecy*, p. 38, gives an example in support of a phrase like, 'I believe the Lord has shown me that...'

53. Gee, *Spiritual Gifts,* p. 48.

54. Bridge, *Signs and Wonders Today*, p. 203.

55. The New Testament authors, and especially Paul, generally use another verb, *gnōrizō*, to speak of human activity in making something known (1 Cor 12:3; 15:1; 2 Cor 8:1; Gal 1:11, etc).

56. If Paul only listed *miraculous* gifts in 1 Cor 12:8–11, it would not prove his point, because it would leave out those who had non-miraculous gifts. Therefore, in order to include *all* the Corinthians (and, by implication, all Christians), he has to have in the list some 'non-miraculous' gifts. And 'word of wisdom' and 'word of know-

ledge' are the only obvious candidates for that category.

Furthermore, the terms 'word of wisdom' and 'word of knowledge' include no special vocabulary that would apply to some kind of special or miraculous utterance, but are made up of simple, very common words for 'word' (Greek *logos*), 'wisdom' (Greek *sophia*), and 'knowledge' (Greek *gnōsis*), and no reader at Corinth would have taken these simple expressions to mean anything other than 'the ability to speak wisely' and 'the ability to speak with knowledge' unless there had been further clear signals to that effect in the context or the way Paul described the gifts.

What contemporary charismatics frequently call 'word of wisdom' and 'word of knowledge' would have been called simply 'prophecy' by the Apostle Paul.

57. For a defence of this 'interpretation of Scripture' function for New Testament prophets, see E. Earle Ellis, *Prophecy and Hermeneutic in Early Christianity: New Testament Essays* (Eerdmans 1978). Two persuasive responses to Ellis are found in David Hill, *New Testament Prophecy* (John Knox 1979), pp. 103–106, and David E. Aune, *Prophecy in Early Christianity and the Ancient Mediterranean World* (Eerdmans 1983), pp. 339–346. Regarding 'charismatic exegesis' of Scripture, Aune rightly concludes, 'There is virtually no evidence … that this activity was carried out by those who were labeled 'prophets' in early Christianity' (p. 345).

58. Michael Harper, *Prophecy: A Gift for the Body of Christ* (Logos 1964), p. 8.

59. Dennis and Rita Bennett, *The Holy Spirit and You* (Kingsway 1971), pp. 108–109.

60. Colossians 3:16 does speak of 'teaching (Greek *didaskō*) and admonishing one another in all wisdom, singing psalms, hymns, and spiritual songs with thanks in your hearts to the Lord', but this certainly does not mean that every Christian was expected to stand before the assembled congregation and function as a Bible teacher— there were many men as well as women who did not have a gift of teaching and who would not do that. Colossians 3:16 must rather be using the word 'teach' in a broader, more general sense than the sense in which it is used in 1 Timothy 2:12 and the many other passages mentioned above where it refers to biblical and/or doctrinal instruction given to the assembled church.

61. In chapter 11, below, I argue that 1 Corinthians 14:33b–35 is

best understood to fit this pattern also, assuming that women will participate in worship but forbidding them to exercise doctrinal control or authority in the congregation. It is therefore consistent with what we find in the rest of Paul's writings.

62. G. Stälin, TDNT 5, 821.

63. Bruce Yocum, *Prophecy* (Word of Life 1976), pp. 88–102.

64. John F. Macarthur, Jr., *The Charismatics: A Doctrinal Perspective* (Zondervan 1978), pp. 15, 19; also note p. 203 where he attributes to the charismatic movement a renewal of much effective music in the church today.

65. For a fuller statement of these and other objections see David Hill, 'On the Evidence for the Creative Role of Christian Prophets' (*NTS* 20 [1973–74], 262–274); also his *New Testament Prophecy* (Marshall, Morgan & Scott 1979), pp. 160–185.

66. Bruce Yocum, *Prophecy* (Word of Life 1976), p. 82.

67. Yokum, *Prophecy*, p. 83.

68. See several examples in W. Grudem, *The Gift of Prophecy in 1 Corinthians* (University Press of America 1982), p. 192, n. 23; compare BAGD, p. 230, 8.a.

69. Compare Numbers 14:11, Deuteronomy 29:3 [2] on the refusal of Israel to believe these positive signs (Note also Ex 7:3; Deut 34:11; Josh 24:5; Ps 78:43; 105:27; 135:9; Jer 32:20–21; Wisd 10:16; Sir 45:3; Bar 2:11.)

70. This is the interpretation of 1 Corinthians 14:20–25 adopted by D. A. Carson, *Showing the Spirit: A Theological Exposition of 1 Corinthians 12–14* (Baker 1987), pp. 108–117, where this whole passage receives a lengthy analysis with extensive references to other literature and views.

71. O. Palmer Robertson, 'Tongues: Sign of Covenantal Curse and Blessing', *WTJ* 38 (1975–76), 43–53.

72. Zane Hodges, 'The Purpose of Tongues,' *Bib Sac* 120 (1963), 226–33.

73. Robertson is followed at this point by Richard B. Gaffin, *Perspectives on Pentecost* (Presbyterian and Reformed 1979), pp. 106–109.

John F. Macarthur, Jr., *The Charismatics: A Doctrinal Perspective* (Zondervan 1978), sees tongues *both* as a judicial sign of judgement to Israel *and* as a sign of the transition to a period of gospel proclamation to all nations. But a fundamental flaw in this argument is that Macarthur also here overlooks the fact that in 1 Corinthians 14:20–25 Paul is talking about an *abuse* of tongues (speaking without interpretation), not a *proper* use of tongues (speaking with interpretation, vv. 27–28).

74. Carson, *Showing the Spirit,* p. 111, in response to Robertson and Gaffin.

75. However, the prophets and the congregation may or may not know to whom their words apply (cf. 1 Pet 1:11, Acts 2:30, 21:11).

76. For statements of this view see H. von Campenhausen, *Ecclesiastical Authority and Spiritual Power in the Church of the First Three Centuries,* trans. by J. A. Baker (Black 1969); E. Käsemann, 'Ministry and Community in the New Testament', in *Essays on New Testament Themes,* SBT 41, trans. by W. J. Montague (SCM 1969), pp. 63–94; also Käsemann's 'Sentences of Holy Law in the New Testament', in *New Testament Questions of Today,* trans. by W. J. Montague (SCM 1969), pp. 66–81. A similar position is taken by James D. G. Dunn, *Jesus and the Spirit: A Study of the Religious and Charismatic Experience of Jesus and the First Christians as Reflected in the New Testament* (SCM 1975), pp. 180–182; 285–300.

77. Richard B. Gaffin, *Perspectives on Pentecost* (Presbyterian and Reformed 1979), p. 51.

78. See J. Dunn, *Jesus and the Spirit,* p. 285.

79. Bruce Yocum, *Prophecy* (Word of Life 1976), p. 68.

80. Michael Harper, *Prophecy: A Gift for the Body of Christ* (Logos 1964), p. 28.

81. Donald Gee, *Spiritual Gifts in the Work of Ministry Today* (Gospel Publishing House 1963), pp. 43–44.

82. 1 Corinthians 14:33b–35 does not prohibit women from prophesying. See the discussion in chapter 11, below.

83. Romans 11:29 (RSV) says, 'For the gifts and the call of God are irrevocable.' However, this is not directly relevant to our enquiry about the use of spiritual gifts in the church, for in the context of Romans 11 Paul is talking about access to covenant blessings given to a particular nation, the Jews, and not about specific abilities for ministries given to individuals. Therefore, it is not a passage that contributes to our present investigation.

84. Richard B. Gaffin, *Perspectives on Pentecost* (Presbyterian and Reformed 1979), p. 54.

85. Romans 12:6 could also be translated to mean, 'If prophecy, in

agreement with the faith' (that is, in agreement with received Christian doctrine). But this takes 'faith' in a sense not clearly demonstrated for any of Paul's writings. (Jude 3 is the only clear example of this use in the New Testament: see BAGD, p. 664, 3 for other suggested examples, none of which is unambiguous.) Paul's expression for this would more likely have been 'according to sound teaching' or 'sound doctrine', or 'according to the traditions you have received'.

Moreover, prophesying should be done not just so it is consistent with sound doctrine, but also so it is consistent with the common facts of experience which are known to be true—so the test is incomplete. In addition to that, nowhere else does Paul tell the person prophesying to regulate its content or judge it. That is left up to the hearers (1 Cor 14:29; 1 Thess 5:19–21). And such a command would seem to put some kind of restriction on prophesying so that those who knew the doctrines of the faith could prophesy with much more confidence and authority than those who were new to Christianity. But these factors seem foreign to first-century prophecy as we find it in the New Testament. It is best to translate, therefore, 'Whoever prophesies, in proportion to (his) faith.'

86. Gaffin, *Perspectives,* p. 53.

87. Grammatically it is possible to make 'as in all the churches of the saints' (1 Cor 14:33b, RSV) modify the preceding clause, 'for God is not a God of confusion but of peace' (1 Cor 14:33a, RSV) (so KJV, following the Textus Receptus, and NASB). The option to do this arises because verse divisions are all the work of later editors and were not part of what Paul wrote.

However, this reading does not fit the sense of the passage. After saying something about the character of God, which is always the same, it would be pointless for Paul to add, 'As in all the churches of the saints,' as if the Corinthians would have imagined that God would be a God of peace in some churches but not in others. But if 'as in all the churches of the saints' modifies the following instructions about behaviour in worship, it makes very good sense. The Corinthians should not deviate from the standards for worship which are followed by all churches everywhere. This is the reading of the NIV, RSV, ASV, NEB and the modern scholarly Greek texts of both the United Bible Societies and the editors of the Nestle-Aland text.

It should not be thought that such a reading is awkward or inelegant

Greek. Paul opens a sentence with a similar clause beginning with 'as' in Ephesians 5:24 and Philippians 2:22.

88. D. A. Carson, *Showing the Spirit: A Theological Exposition of 1 Corinthians 12–14* (Baker 1987), p. 122, notes another significant factor: the word for 'churches' is plural in verse 34: 'Let the women keep silence in the *churches*.' This means that Paul is talking about a practice that goes beyond one local church to 'the churches' generally, no matter what one does with verse 33b.

We can add that this plural expression 'the churches' adds another strong reason why verse 33b should be joined to verse 34. If it weren't, the text would be unclear, for the readers would see a statement about 'the churches' without knowing which churches Paul was referring to. In other words, 'Let the women keep silence in *the churches*' almost requires a previous specification of which churches are meant, and assumes that the readers will know which churches they are. 'All the churches of the saints' provides such an explanation, if 33b is joined to verse 34, and the sense is clear.

89. This section follows James Hurley, *Man and Woman in Biblical Perspective* (Eerdmans 1981), pp. 188–194.

90. See, for example, Luke 9:36; 18:39; and, with other words for silence, Acts 11:18; 21:14; a very similar context provides a parallel also in 1 Timothy 2:12. These passages and others are discussed at more length in Wayne Grudem, *The Gift of Prophecy in 1 Corinthians* (University Press of America 1982), pp. 242–244.

91. This is also the position taken by Carson, *Showing the Spirit*, pp. 121–133, with a long analysis of various views and references to relevant literature.

92. Greek *epignōsomai ta panta* would say, 'I shall know all things.'

93. I have stated it this way because, more precisely, 'the perfect' in 1 Corinthians 13:10 is not Christ himself, but is a method of acquiring knowledge which is so superior to present knowledge and prophecy that it makes these two obsolete. For when this 'perfect' comes it renders the imperfect useless. But only the kind of knowledge Paul expected in the final consummation of all things could be so qualitatively different from present knowledge that it could provide this kind of contrast and be called 'the perfect' as opposed to 'the imperfect'.

94. D. A. Carson, *Showing the Spirit: A Theological Exposition of 1 Corinthians 12–14* (Baker 1987), pp. 70–72, gives several similar

reasons why the time 'when the perfect comes' must be the time of Christ's return (with references to other views, and to the literature).

Among 'cessationists' (those who hold that gifts such as prophecy have 'ceased' and are not valid for today), some, but not all, agree that the time 'when the perfect comes' must be the time of Christ's return: see John F. Macarthur, Jr., *The Charismatics: A Doctrinal Perspective* (Zondervan 1978), pp. 165–166, and Richard B. Gaffin, *Perspectives on Pentecost* (Presbyterian and Reformed 1979), p. 109.

95. Richard B. Gaffin, *Perspectives on Pentecost* (Presbyterian and Reformed 1979), pp. 109–110.

96. Gaffin, *Perspectives,* p. 111.

97. Robert L. Reymond, *What About Continuing Revelations and Miracles in the Presbyterian Church Today?* (Presbyterian and Reformed 1977), pp. 32–34. Kenneth L. Gentry, Jr., *The Charismatic Gift of Prophecy: A Reformed Analysis* (Whitefield Seminary Press 1986), pp. 31–33, lists both this view and the view of Dr Gaffin (see objection 1, above) as acceptable options.

98. Walter J. Chantry, *Signs of the Apostles: Observations on Pentecostalism Old and New* (Banner of Truth 1976), pp. 51–52.

99. Some argue that faith and hope will not endure in heaven, so 1 Corinthians 13:13 only means that faith and hope last until, not beyond, Christ's return. However, if faith is dependence on God and trust in him, and if hope is a confident expectation of future blessings to be received from God, then there is no reason to think that we will cease to have faith and hope in heaven. (See Carson's good discussion of faith, hope and love as 'eternally permanent virtues' in *Showing the Spirit*, pp. 74–75.)

100. Gaffin, *Perspectives,* p. 109; compare Max Turner, 'Spiritual Gifts Then and Now,' *Vox Evangelica* 15 (1985), p. 38.

101. D. Martyn Lloyd-Jones, *Prove All Things*, ed. by Christopher Catherwood (Kingsway 1985), pp. 32–33.

102. John Calvin, *The First Epistle of Paul the Apostle to the Corinthians,* trans. by J. W. Fraser, ed. by D. W. Torrance and T. F. Torrance (Eerdmans 1960), p. 281 (on 1 Cor 13:10).

103. This is the position of S. D. Toussaint, 'First Corinthians Thirteen and the Tongues Question', *Bib Sac* 120 (1963), pp. 311–316.

104. The view that miracles died out early in the history of the church was argued at length by Benjamin B. Warfield, *Miracles: Yesterday and Today, True and False* (formerly published as *Counterfeit*

Miracles, 1918) (Eerdmans 1953). It should be noted that Warfield's argument, though frequently quoted, is really a historical survey, not an analysis of biblical texts. Moreover, Warfield's purpose was not to refute any use of spiritual gifts among Christians like those in much of the charismatic movement today, whose doctrine (on all matters other than spiritual gifts) and whose church affiliation put them in the mainstream of evangelical Protestantism. Warfield rather was refuting the spurious claims to miracles which had come from some branches of Roman Catholocism at various periods in the history of the church, and from various heretical sects. It is open to question whether modern-day cessationists are right to claim Warfield's support when opposing something which is far different in doctrine and life from what Warfield himself opposed.

Warfield's position has come in for criticism from evangelical historians as well: see Max Turner, 'Spiritual Gifts Then and Now', *Vox Evangelica* 15 (1985), pp. 41–43, with notes to other literature; Donald Bridge, *Signs and Wonders Today* (IVP 1985), pp. 166–177; and Ronald A. Kydd, *Charismatic Gifts in the Early Church* (Hendriksen, 1984).

105. George Mallone, ed., *Those Controversial Gifts* (IVP 1983), p. 21.

106. John F. Macarthur, Jr., *The Charismatics: A Doctrinal Perspective* (Zondervan 1978), chapters 2–6; see especially pp. 27ff.

107. Don Basham, 'Questions and Answers', *New Wine* 9:1 (Jan. 1977), p. 29.

108. Michael Harper, *Prophecy: A Gift for the Body of Christ* (Logos 1964), p. 26.

109. Dennis and Rita Bennett, *The Holy Spirit and You* (Kingsway 1971), p. 107.

110. Donald Gee, *Spiritual Gifts in the Work of Ministry Today* (Gospel Publishing House 1963), pp. 51–52.

111. Donald Bridge, *Signs and Wonders Today* (IVP 1985), p. 183.

112. Donald Bridge and David Phypers, *Spiritual Gifts and the Church* (IVP 1973), p. 64.

113. Gaffin, *Perspectives,* p. 120. Gaffin also allows for the possibility of an unreliable spoken response to something that had been revealed by the Holy Spirit (at least at the time of the New Testament). (See page 66 on Acts 21:4.) But if someone could give an unreliable spoken response to a revelation in the time of the New Testa-

ment, could people not do that today as well? And could that not be
what is happening in prophecy?

114. Reymond, *'What About...?*, pp. 28–29.

115. Bridge, *Signs and Wonders,* p. 204.

116. There is also a general sense for the Greek word *apostolos*
('apostle') where it is used simply to mean 'messenger' or 'one who is
sent'. The Greek term is used in that general sense three times in the
New Testament: John 13:16; 2 Corinthians 8:23; Philippians 2:25. But
these passages are not discussing the office of 'Apostle of Jesus
Christ', which is much more narrowly understood in the New Testament.

117. These two qualifications are discussed in detail in the classic
essay by J. B. Lightfoot, 'The name and office of an Apostle', in his
commentary, *The Epistle of St. Paul to the Galatians* (first published
1865; reprinted Zondervan 1957), pp. 92–101; see also K. H.
Rengstorf, *'apostolos', TDNT* 1, 398–447.

118. It is not in a strict sense absolutely necessary to translate Galatians 1:19 this way, including James among the apostles. (The New
International Version reads, 'I saw none of the other apostles—only
James, the Lord's brother.') Yet the translation *'except* James the
Lord's brother' seems clearly preferable, because (1) the Greek
phrase is *ei mē*, which ordinarily means 'except' (BAGD, p. 22, 8a),
and in the great majority of New Testament uses designates something that is part of the previous group but is 'excepted' from it; and
(2) in the context of Galatians 1:18, it would not make much sense for
Paul to say that when he went to Jerusalem he saw Peter, and no other
people except James—or Peter, and no other *church leaders* except
James—for he stayed there 'fifteen days' (Gal 1:18). So he must mean
he saw Peter, and no other *apostles* except James. But this classifies
James with the apostles. See discussion in E. D. Burton, *The Epistle
to the Galatians*, ICC (T. & T. Clark 1920), p. 60. (Burton says, *'ei mē*
means here, as always before a noun, "except"' (*ibid*).)

119. See grammatical note with many other examples of names like
'Junias' in A. T. Robertson, *A Grammar of the Greek New Testament*
(Broadman 1934), pp. 172–73.

120. John Murray, *The Epistle to the Romans* (2 vols. in 1;
Eerdmans 1968), vol. 2, pp. 229–230, says that if it means that
Andronicus and Junias were apostles themselves, 'then the word
'apostles' would be used in a more general sense of messenger'.

121. See the discussion in Leon Morris, *The First and Second Epistles to the Thessalonians*, NIC (Eerdmans 1959), pp. 98–99. Morris says, 'The practice in this Epistle differs somewhat from that in the Pauline epistles generally. The plural is used almost throughout, whereas in most of his letters Paul prefers the singular' (p. 98; cf. pp. 46–47). Morris takes the plurals here to refer only to Paul himself.

122. See Meredith Kline, *The Structure of Biblical Authority* (Eerdmans 1972), especially pages 48–53 and 113–130.

123. See 'Chronology of the Old Testament' in *The New Bible Dictionary,* ed. J. D. Douglas (Eerdmans 1962), p. 221.

124. That 'the Holy Spirit' is primarily a reference to divinely authoritative prophecy is clear both from the fact that the *bath qol* (a voice from heaven) is seen as a substitute for it, and from the very frequent use of 'the Holy Spirit' to refer to prophecy elsewhere in Rabbinic literature.

125. See Roger Nicole, 'New Testament Use of the Old Testament,' in *Revelation and the Bible,* ed. Carl F. H. Henry (Tyndale Press 1959), pp. 137–141.

126. Jude 14–15 does cite 1 Enoch 60:8 and 1:9, and Paul at least twice quotes pagan Greek authors (see Acts 17:28; Titus 1:12), but these citations are more for purposes of illustration than proof. Never are the works introduced with a phrase like, 'God says,' or, 'Scripture says,' or, 'It is written;' phrases which imply the attribution of divine authority to the words cited. (It should be noted that neither 1 Enoch nor the authors cited by Paul are part of the Apocrypha.)

127. The Apocrypha includes the following writings: 1 and 2 Esdras, Tobit, Judith, the Rest of Esther, the Wisdom of Solomon, Ecclesiasticus, Baruch (including the Epistle of Jeremiah), the Song of the Three Holy Children, Susanna, Bel and the Dragon, the Prayer of Manasses, and 1 and 2 Maccabees. These writings are not found in the Hebrew Bible, but they were included with the Septuagint (the translation of the Old Testament into Greek which was used by many Greek-speaking Jews at the time of Christ). A good recent translation is *The Oxford Annotated Apocrypha* (Revised Standard Version) edited by Bruce M. Metzger (Oxford University Press 1965). Metzger includes brief introductions and helpful annotations to the books.

128. See G. Douglas Young, 'The Apocrypha' in *Revelation and the Bible,* ed. Carl F. H. Henry, pp. 169–185.

129. This is my own translation of the last phrase of 1 Corinthians

2:13; see Wayne A. Grudem, 'Scripture's Self-Attestation' in *Scripture and Truth,* ed. D. A. Carson and J. Woodbridge (Zondervan 1983), p. 365, note 61. But this translation is not crucial to the main point: namely, that Paul speaks words taught by the Holy Spirit, a point which is affirmed in the first part of the verse, no matter how the second half is translated.

130. Luke himself is not an apostle, but his gospel is here accorded authority apparently equal with that of the apostolic writings. Perhaps this was due to his very close association with the apostles, especially Paul.

131. The subject of authorship of individual writings of the New Testament belongs to the study of New Testament introduction. For a defence of traditional views of authorship of the New Testament writings, see Donald Guthrie, *New Testament Introduction,* (IVP 1970).

132. James seems to be considered an apostle in Galatians 1:19 and 1 Corinthians 15:7. He also fulfils functions appropriate to an apostle in Acts 12:17; 15:13; 21:18; Galatians 2:9, 12; and perhaps Jude 1.

133. The acceptance of Jude in the canon was slow, primarily because of doubts concerning his quotation of the non-canonical book of Enoch.

134. Origen's statement is quoted in Eusebius, *Ecclesiastical History,* 6.25.14.

135. This is of course not to affirm the impossible notion that God providentially preserves every word in every copy of every text, no matter how careless the copyist, or that he must miraculously provide every believer with a Bible instantly. Nevertheless, this consideration of God's faithful care of his children should certainly cause us to be thankful that in God's providence there is no significantly attested textual variant which would change any point of Christian doctrine or ethics, so faithfully has the text been transmitted and preserved. It should also cause us to be thankful that in the ongoing mission work of the church a translation of the Bible has frequently been the first and most widely printed book in many languages and cultures throughout the world. Furthermore, we must be thankful that all attempts to eradicate the Bible through violent persecution have always failed, and will always continue to fail, for God will not allow his church to be without his Word.

136. An excellent recent study is David G. Dunbar, 'The Biblical

Canon' in *Hermeneutics, Authority and Canon* ed. D. A. Carson and John Woodbridge (Zondervan 1986), pp. 259–360.

137. See R. V. G. Tasker, *The General Epistle of James,* TNTC (Tyndale Press 1956), pp. 67–71.

138. It is at this point that evangelical Protestants differ both with Roman Catholics (who would say that official church endorsement is a means of giving divine authority to a writing) and with some non-evangelical Protestants (who would not agree with the idea of a category of writings that have joint human and divine authorship and would therefore question the idea of a canon based on such a criterion).

139. A good recent translation is *The Oxford Annotated Apocrypha* (RSV) edited by Bruce M. Metzger (Oxford University Press 1965). The word 'apocrypha' means 'hidden' (or literally 'hidden things'), but it is not known how this term came to be attached to these writings. There is also a collection of non-biblical writings from the time of the New Testament called 'New Testament apocrypha' (see next note), but these are much less commonly read. When people speak of 'the apocrypha' without further specification, they are referring only to the Old Testament Apocrypha.

140. E. Hennecke, *New Testament Apocrypha,* edited by W. Schneemelcher; English trans. edited by R. McL. Wilson (SCM Press 1965). It should also be noted that some other, more orthodox literature from the early church can be found conveniently in a collection of writings referred to as the 'Apostolic Fathers'. A good translation is found in Kirsopp Lake, translator, *The Apostolic Fathers,* Loeb Classical Library (Harvard University Press 1912, 1913), but other useful translations are also available.

141. This is not meant to imply that subjective impressions of God's will are useless, or that they should be ignored. That would suggest almost a deistic view of God's (non-)involvement in the lives of his children, and a rather mechanical, impersonal view of guidance. God can and indeed does use subjective impressions of his will to remind and encourage us, and often to prompt our thoughts in the right direction in many rapid decisions that we make throughout the day. Yet these verses on the sufficiency of Scripture teach us that such subjective impressions can only *remind* us of what is in Scripture, they can never *add to* the commands of Scripture, or *replace* Scripture in defining what God's will is, or *equal Scripture in authority* in our lives.

142. The primary reference of this verse is of course to the book of

Revelation itself, but its placement here at the very end of the only book which could come last in the New Testament canon can hardly be accidental. Thus, a secondary application of this verse to the entire canon does not seem inappropriate. (See Appendix B, above, on the canon, especially p. 290.)

143. I do not wish to imply at this point that I am adopting a 'cessationist' view of spiritual gifts (that is, a view which holds that certain gifts, such as prophecy and speaking in tongues, ceased when the early apostles died). I only wish at this point to state that there is a danger in explicitly or even implicitly giving these gifts a status that effectively challenges the authority or the sufficiency of Scripture in Christians' lives.

144. Of course, human societies such as nations, churches and families can make rules for the conduct of their own affairs (such as, 'Children in this family may not watch TV on week nights'). No such rule can be found in Scripture, nor is it likely that such a rule could be demonstrated by implication from the principles of Scripture. Yet obedience to these rules is required by God because Scripture tells us to be subject to governing authorities (Rom 13:1–7; Eph 6:1–3; 1 Pet 2:13—3:6, *et al*). A denial of the sufficiency of Scripture would occur only if someone attempted to give the rule a generalized application outside of the situation in which it should appropriately function ('No member of our church should watch TV on week nights,' or, 'No Christian should watch TV on week nights'). Then it has become not a rule for conduct in one specific situation but a moral command which apparently is intended to apply to all Christians no matter what their situation. We are not free to add such rules to Scripture and to attempt to impose them on all the believers over whom we have influence, nor can the church as a whole attempt to do this. (Here again, Roman Catholics would differ and would say that God gives *to the church* the authority to impose moral rules in addition to Scripture on all the members of the church.)

Abbreviations

Editions are indicated by small superior figures: 1975^3

I. Books and Journals

ASV	*American Standard Version*
AV	*Authorized Version (King James'),* 1611.
BAGD	W. Bauer, W. F. Arndt, F. W. Gingrich, and F. W. Danker, *A Greek-English Lexicon of the New Testament and other Early Christian Literature.* Chicago: University of Chicago Press, 1979^2
BibSac	*Bibliotheca Sacra*
ICC	*International Critical Commentary* series, T. & T. Clark
KJV	*King James' Version* (=AV)
LSJ	H. G. Liddell, R. Scott, and H. S. Jones, *Greek-English Lexicon.* Oxford: University Press, 1940^9
NASB	*New American Standard Bible,* 1963
NEB	*New English Bible*: NT, 1961; OT, Apocrypha, 1970
NIC	*New International Commentary* series (Paternoster/Eerdmans)
NIV	*New International Version*
NovTSup	*Novum Testamentum,* Supplements
NTS	*New Testament Studies*

RSV   *Revised Standard Version*: NT, 1946; OT, 1952; *Common Bible*, 1973

TDNT   G. Kittel and G. Friedrich, editors. *Theological Dictionary of the New Testament*. Translated by G. W. Bromiley, 10 vols. Grand Rapids: Eerdmans, 1964–76

TNTC   *Tyndale New Testament Commentary* series (Inter-Varsity/Eerdmans)

UBS   United Bible Societies, *The Greek New Testament*. Edited by K. Aland, *et al.*, 1975[3]

WTJ   *Westminster Theological Journal*

II. Ancient Extra-Biblical Literature

1QS   Dead Sea Scrolls, *Manual of Discipline*
Ant.   Josephus, *Antiquities of the Jews*
b.Ber.   Babylonian Talmud, *Berakoth*
b.Meg.   Babylonian Talmud, *Megillah*
b.Sanh.   Babylonian Talmud, *Sanhedrin*
b.Sot.   Babylonian Talmud, *Sotah*
b.Yom.   Babylonian Talmud, *Yoma*
Bar.   Baruch (Apocrypha)
Det.   Philo, *the Worse Attacks the Better*
Jos.   Philo, *on Joseph*
Mig.   Philo, *On the Migration of Abraham*
Mut.   Philo, *On the Change of Names*
Quod Deus Philo, *On the Unchangeableness of God*
Sir.   Sirach (Apocrypha) (=Ecclesiasticus)
Spec Leg. Philo, *Special Laws*
Wars   Josephus, *Jewish Wars*
Wisd.   Wisdom of Solomon (Apocrypha)

Bibliography

Aune, David. *Prophecy in Early Christianity and the Ancient Mediterranean World* (Eerdmans 1983).

Basham, Don. *A Handbook on Tongues, Interpretation and Prophecy* (Whitaker Books 1971).

Bennett, Dennis and Rita. *The Holy Spirit and You* (Kingsway Publications 1971).

Bridge, Donald. *Signs and Wonders Today* (IVP 1985).

Bridge, Donald and David Phypers. *Spiritual Gifts and the Church* (IVP 1973).

Budgen, Victor. *The Charismatics and the Word of God* (Evangelical Press 1985).

Carson, D. A. *Showing the Spirit: A Theological Exposition of 1 Corinthians 12–14* (Baker 1987).

Chantry, Walter J. *Signs of the Apostles: Observations on Pentecostalism Old and New* (Banner of Truth, 1976).

Clements, Roy. *Word and Spirit: The Bible and the Gift of Prophecy Today* (UCCF Booklets 1986).

Gaffin, Richard B. *Perspectives on Pentecost* (Presbyterian and Reformed 1979).

Gee, Donald *Spiritual Gifts in the Work of Ministry Today* (Gospel Publishing House 1963).

Gentry, Kenneth L., Jr. *The Charismatic Gift of Prophecy: A Reformed Analysis* (Whitefield Seminary Press 1986).

Green, Michael. *I Believe in the Holy Spirit* (Hodder and Stoughton 1975).

Grudem, Wayne. '1 Cor. 14:20–25: Prophecy and Tongues as Signs of God's Attitude,' *Westminster Theological Journal* 41:2 (Spring 1979), pp. 381–396.

Grudem, Wayne. *The Gift of Prophecy in 1 Corinthians* (University Press of America, 1982).

Grudem, Wayne. 'Prophecy—Yes, but Teaching—No: Paul's Consistent Advocacy of Women's Participation Without Governing Authority,' *JETS* 30:1 (Mar. 1987), pp. 11–23.

Grudem, Wayne. 'A Response to Gerhard Dautzenberg on 1 Cor. 12:10,' *Biblische Zeitschrift*, N.F., 22:2 (1978), pp. 253–270.

Grudem, Wayne. 'Review of David Aune, Prophecy in Early Christianity and the Ancient Mediterranean World (Grand Rapids: Eerdmans, 1983),' *Evangelical Quarterly* 59:4 (Oct. 1987), pp 351–355.

Grudem, Wayne. 'Review of David Hill, *New Testament Prophecy,*' in *Themelios* 7:2 (Jan. 1982), pp. 25–26.

Hagin, Kenneth E. *Seven Steps for Judging Prophecy* (Kenneth Hagin Ministries 1982).

Harper, Michael. *Prophecy: A Gift for the Body of Christ* (Logos 1964).

Hill, David. *New Testament Prophecy,* New Foundations Theological Library (Marshall, Morgan and Scott 1979).

Hummel, Charles E. *Fire in the Fireplace: Contemporary Charismatic Renewal* (Inter-Varsity 1978).

Kydd, Ronald A. *Charismatic Gifts in the Early Church* (Hendriksen 1984).

Macarthur, John F., Jr. *The Charismatics: A Doctrinal Perspective* (Zondervan 1978).

Mallone, George, ed. *Those Controversial Gifts* (IVP 1983).

New Wine 9:1 (Jan. 1977). [This entire issue of a popular charismatic journal is devoted to articles on the gift of prophecy.]

Pain, Timothy. *Prophecy* Ashburnham Insights series (Kingsway Publications 1986).

Packer, J. I. *Keep in Step with the Spirit* (IVP 1984).

Reymond, Robert L. *What About Continuing Revelations and*

Miracles in the Presbyterian Church Today? (Presbyterian and Reformed 1977).

Robertson, O. Palmer. 'Tongues: Sign of Covenantal Curse and Blessing', *WTJ* 38 (1975–76), pp. 43–53.

Schatzmann, Siegfried. *A Pauline Theology of Charismata* (Hendrickson, 1987).

Turner, Max. 'Spiritual Gifts Then and Now', *Vox Evangelica* 15 (1985), pp. 7–64.

Warfield, Benjamin B. *Miracles: Yesterday and Today, True and False* (formerly published as *Counterfeit Miracles*, 1918) (Eerdmans 1953).

Yocum, Bruce. *Prophecy* (Word of Life 1976).

Index of Scripture Passages

Index of Citations from Extra-biblical Literature

Index of Subjects

Signs
    may be positive or negative, or both, 174–176
    prophecy and tongues as 'signs', 173–174
Silas and Judas (as prophets), 156
Silence of woman while judging prophets, 220–224
Speaking in tongues,
    interpretation of, 178–179
    purpose of, 172–177
Sufficiency of Scripture, 299–312
Teaching (NT),
    definition of, 140–142
    difference between teaching and prophecy, 142–143,
        153–154
    why women could prophesy but not teach, 144–146
Timothy and prophecies, 157–160
Tongues, speaking in *see* speaking in tongues
Women as prophets, 86–87; 95–96; 215–225

Index of Authors